Library of
Davidson College

Passive Revolution

Passive Revolution

Politics and the Czechoslovak Working Class

1945 - 1948

Jon Bloomfield

St. Martin's Press
New York

Copyright © Jon Bloomfield 1979
All rights reserved. For information, write:
St. Martin's Press, Inc., 175 5th Avenue, New York, NY 10010
First published in the United States in 1979
Printed in Great Britain

ISBN 0-312-597886

Library of Congress Cataloging in Publication Data

Bloomfield, Jon.
  The passive revolution.

  Bibliography: p.
  1. Czechoslovakia—Politics and government—1945-
I. Title.
DB2218.7.B55 1979   320.9'437'04   78-25922
ISBN 0-312-59788-6

To Irena, Marian, Marie, and Víta
who all contributed to the revolution
and continue to live by its ideals

Acknowledgements

This book is based on a thesis which I wrote at Cambridge University from 1971 to 1974. Several of its arguments have been refined in the light of subsequent criticism.

Research for the thesis was primarily carried out at the University Library in Cambridge, the British Museum and its Newspaper Library in London, the Charles University Library in Prague, and the All-Trade-Union Archives in Prague. The library staff at all these institutions helped my work and smoothed my path, enabling the research to be based on an extensive study of contemporary documentary material, full details of which are contained in the bibliography.

For the stimulation and encouragement they have variously given me I am especially grateful to John Barber, Judy Bloomfield, Maurice Dobb, Hedi Frominge, Martin Jacques, Monty Johnstone, Martin Myant, Jill Sheppard, Jan Šling, Marian Šlingová, Mutyo Teich, Naomi Wayne, and Jane Woddis. I owe a special debt of gratitude to the many people who helped me in Czechoslovakia. My greatest debt remains to my supervisor, Alice Teichová, whose guidance and criticism were invaluable in shaping this work in the spirit of Czechoslovakia's national motto.

Contents

List of tables / 8
Preface / 9
Abbreviations / 15
Chronology / 17

I
The Setting
1 The First Republic / 23
2 War at Home / 29
3 War Abroad / 39
4 Final Conflagration / 49

II
The National and Democratic Revolution
5 The Košice Programme / 59
6 Unity and Diversity: The Politics of Nationalisation / 68
7 Works Councils and Trade Unions / 91

III
The Calm
8 The Determinant Force / 109
9 The Main Transmission Belt / 124
10 A Period of Consolidation / 143

IV
The Storm
11 "Who is Master of Bohemia is Master of Europe" / 177
12 Approaching the Climax / 189
13 The February Events / 207
14 The Passive Revolution / 231

Notes / 241
Glossary / 272
Bibliography / 275
Index / 285

List of Tables

		page
Map	The Czech Lands, illustrating the location of the District Trade-Union Councils	16
Table 1	Nationalised Industries in 1945	84
Table 2	Nationalised Enterprises in the Foodstuffs Industry	84
Graph	The Pattern of Growth of KSČ Membership from May 1945 to May 1947	114
Diagram	The Internal Structure of ROH	126
Table 3	The State of Trade Unionism in the Czech Lands on 31 December 1945	129
Table 4	The Results of the General Election in Czechoslovakia on 26 May 1946	150
Table 5	Delegates from Bohemia and Moravia at the Works Councils Congress, 22 February 1948. Breakdown by Union and District	220

Preface

Pravda zvítězí — "Truth Will Prevail" — is the national motto of the Czech and Slovak people. It is appropriate to recall the motto in this anniversary year. It is sixty years ago that the independent Czechoslovak republic was founded. Twenty years later that republic was broken up by Nazi aggression officially endorsed by the British and French governments at Munich. It is thirty years since the revolution that forms the subject of this book, while it is a decade since the Prague Spring, a period of renewal within Czechoslovak socialism which was crushed by the troops of the Soviet Union and other Warsaw Pact countries. In many ways the events of 1945-48 are linked to all these events, and yet today the truth of those events still remains hidden or only partially revealed.

What happened then in Czechoslovakia, just as with Munich and the Prague Spring, was important not only for the Czech and Slovak people. These events and their consequences had enormous political and ideological significance for all the peoples of Europe. Neville Chamberlain could contemptuously describe Czechoslovakia as "a faraway country of which we know nothing" — and cared even less, if we can judge by his eagerness to accept Hitler's schemes at Munich. Yet both then and later the ramifications of developments in Czechoslovakia were enormous. Indeed, in all the anniversaries that the country celebrates (or commemorates) this year, international politics and major foreign powers had a decisive influence.

This is certainly true of the period under scrutiny in this book. It is also fair to say that the escalation of the cold war, which the events in Czechoslovakia partly expressed, had ideological and intellectual as well as political and military repercussions. It seriously stifled any thorough analysis of the period. The overwhelming majority of what was subsequently published on the subject was designed to serve the political or propaganda requirements of either Czechoslovakia or Western orthodoxy. Only for a brief period in the mid-1960s were Czech and Slovak historians able to break from these constraints and begin to analyse the period thoroughly. Their work was one of the minor casualties of the "normalisation" process after the Soviet occupation in August 1968. It is my hope that I have carried on and developed from where they left off.

In this book I concentrate on four, interrelated questions that are crucial if the rather elusive character of the 1945-8 period is to become clear. First, the period is located in its international context, and the ways by which the altered international balance of power in Eastern Europe at the end of the Second World War affected internal developments are investigated. Secondly, close attention is given to the relationship between the KSČ (Czechoslovak Communist Party) and the Soviet government. This was a factor of the utmost significance, given the degree of Soviet influence on the country after the war. Thirdly, the specific position of the KSČ in Czechoslovak society and especially its relationship with the trade-union movement is studied. Finally, the role and actions of the working class itself in the determination of events are assessed. Here I have paid much attention to the exact nature of the relationship of the working class to its own mass organisations — trade unions and works councils — and to working-class political parties, primarily the KSČ.

A thorough survey of the available material and careful analysis of it leads me to a decisive rejection of the two prevalent orthodoxies: that February was the culmination of a masterful KSČ strategy clearly worked out and fully and enthusiastically backed by the mass of the people; or the Western version that it was a "coup", a sleight-of-hand pulled by the communists to seize power against the wishes of the masses and forcibly imposed on them.

Instead I argue that the period is best viewed as a "passive revolution". The working class was a largely willing accomplice of the revolution, but not its driving force. The determining factors were Czechoslovakia's position within the Soviet sphere of influence and the KSČ leadership's belief that the interests of the Czechoslovak working class were best served by a policy in harmony with the Soviet Union's strategic requirements. The role of party organisations and members, along with the trade unions, works councils and other mass organisations, was to implement a policy agreed elsewhere. At no time were they involved in any formulation of strategy, any decisions about the "road to socialism" or what kind of socialism it would be. The impetus to the revolution came from above and from abroad, and this had enormous implications for democracy in the future socialist state. Thus while this period saw the decisive removal of capitalist property relations in the economy, the political power that shifted into the hands of the working class was limited. Hence the phrase "passive revolution", expressing the paradox of the period and its complexity.

Why should all these events in that "faraway country" interest the reader?

The amount of serious analytical material available on this topic is extremely small. This is an attempt to write a clear account and analysis of the revolution which would both stand up as a piece of historical research and help to eradicate the ignorance that Chamberlain showed and which is still pervasive today.

The topic also has broader, political significance, with a scope of interest extending well beyond the academic reader. Czechoslovakia is the only advanced capitalist country with a traditional bourgeois democratic political system which has undergone a socialist revolution. The manner in which this was achieved and the question of whether this represents a model which can (or should) be applied elsewhere are issues of interest to everyone involved in politics. Furthermore, one of the key factors holding back the socialist movement in the advanced capitalist world has been the experience of stalinism and the neglect of democratic rights and activity in those already existing socialist countries. In the Soviet Union it was once possible to explain how such deformations arose after the catastrophic civil war and the isolation of the world's first socialist state, though such reasons have long ago lost their validity. Yet in Czechoslovakia, within a couple of years of communists taking power, there came the persecution, harassment and imprisonment of thousands of innocent communists and other citizens, along with the execution of eleven communist leaders. These events and similar ones in other parts of Eastern Europe gave credence to the thesis that socialism was inevitably totalitarian. This book does not tackle the post-February period but it does analyse the stalinist ideas and practices that bred the conditions for such developments. These features were departures from the outlook and principles of the founders of socialism from whom the KSČ drew their inspiration. Yet it was precisely these features that were canonised as marxist orthodoxy, that have been popularly seen as what socialism is, and that have scarred the socialist movement so deeply. In this book I have examined the specific application of these stalinist practices to Czechoslovakia and attempted to show how the departure from fundamental socialist principles determined the character of the revolution and its subsequent development. As such the book is an antidote to all those who equate stalinism with socialism.

A rather more powerful antidote came from the Czech and Slovak people themselves in 1968. In revulsion against their experiences under Novotný, and drawing on the best traditions of their working class and revolutionary movement, the "Prague Spring" and the KSČ's Action Programme represented a renewal of Czechoslovak socialism. The Action Programme recognised that the KSČ had to win its support among the people. No longer could it just impose its policies. Mass popular organisations had to play their full part in economic, social and political life. They could not continue as transmission belts for party directives. These bodies had to have their own autonomy and scope for activity. Furthermore, if working people were to take a more active role in politics and decision-making, then there had to be genuine discussion and debate in the press and media. The Programme's strategic perspective and immediate policies represented a major attempt to overcome the legacy of Novotný.

The Action Programme was the most important political initiative of the Prague Spring. It gave direction to the many movements emerging among wide strata of Czechoslovak society. The trade unions began to reassert themselves and play a significant part in economic and industrial issues, while a works councils movement re-emerged after two decades, involving workers in the issues of investment, production and managerial appointment. Within the popular movement there were certain anti-socialist trends, while some elements in the party and state apparatus resisted any fundamental changes. Yet the general impulse of developments was clear. The emerging popular movement under the KSČ's leadership wanted a different kind of socialism, where there would be genuine, democratic involvement of the people.

They wanted "socialism with a human face".

That movement was crushed by the military occupation of Soviet and other Warsaw Pact troops on 20-21 August 1968. However, the ideas and inspiration of that movement live on. It has been one of the elements spurring the evolution of the Euro-Communist policy and theory of several Communist Parties in Western Europe, with their resolute affirmation that socialism and democracy are complementary and inseparable. It is in this spirit, and in the spirit of the country's national motto, that I have written this book. I hope it illuminates the paths and pitfalls of the Czechoslovak experience, and that everyone in Czechoslovakia and elsewhere who seeks the development of socialism in liberty and democracy will be able to draw lessons from the passive revolution.

Abbreviations in Text

DS—*Demokratická strana* (Democratic Party).
KOR—*Krajská odborová rada* (District Trades Council).
KSČ—*Komunistická strana Československa* (Communist Party of Czechoslovakia).
ÚV KSČ—*Ústřední výbor KSČ* (Central Committee of the KSČ).
KSS—*Komunistická strana Slovenska* (Communist Party of Slovakia).
LS—*Lidová strana* (People's Party).
NSS—*Národně-socialistická strana* (National Socialist Party).
ROH—*Revoluční odborové hnutí* (Revolutionary Trade Union Movement).
SDS—*Socialně-demokratická strana* (Social Democratic Party).
ÚRO—*Ústřední rada odborů* (Central Trades Union Council).

Abbreviations in Notes

ČsČH—*Československý časopis historický* (The Czechoslovak Historical Journal).
FRUS—*Foreign Relations of the United States.*
Pkd KSČ—*Příspěvky k dějinám KSČ* (Contributions to the History of the KSČ).
VZR—*Věstník závodních rad* (Bulletin of Works Council).
ZTK ÚRO—*Zprávy tiskové komise ÚRO* (Reports of the ÚRO Press Commission).

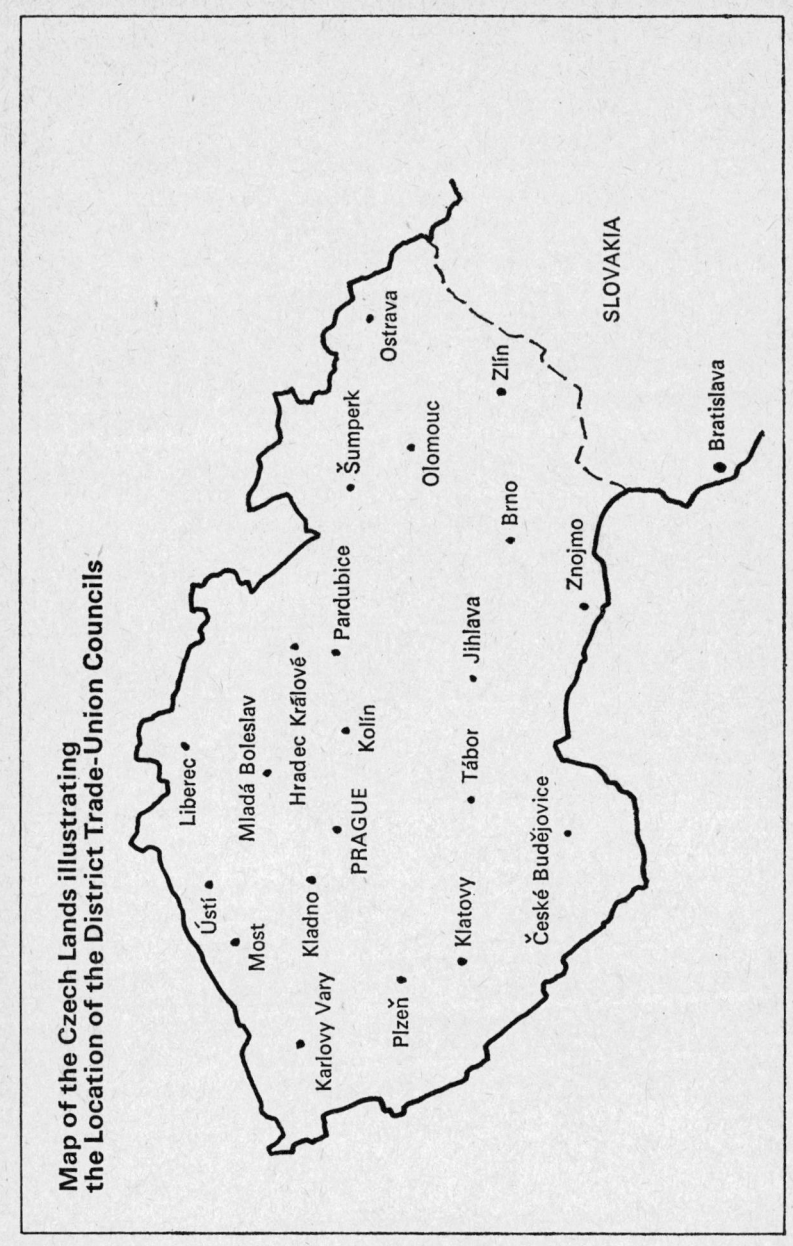

Map of the Czech Lands illustrating the Location of the District Trade-Union Councils

Chronology

1918 *28 October:* Independent Czechoslovak republic established.
1920 *December:* General strike and strong socialist movement suppressed by police and army intervention.
1921 Communist Party formed.
1929 At the Fifth Congress of the KSČ, a new leadership elected, headed by Klement Gottwald.
1933 Hitler comes to power in Germany.
1935 The Communist International at its Seventh Congress reverses its strategy, ends the characterisation of social-democracy as social fascism and calls for the development of Popular Fronts to oppose the fascist threat.
Beneš becomes president of the republic.
1936 *April:* Seventh Congress of the KSČ follows suit.
1938 *29 September:* At Munich the four main European powers — Britain, France, Italy and Germany — decide on the surrender of Czechoslovak territory. By the agreement Czechoslovakia is forced to give up large sections of its border regions. The conference, to which the Czechoslovak government is not invited, effectively ends the existence of the republic.
1939 *14 March:* Fascists in Slovakia declare an independent state.
15 March: Nazi Germans invade Prague.
1941 *22 June:* Soviet Union invaded by Germany. Immediately USSR joins the anti-fascist coalition with British and American governments.
1943 *12 December:* Soviet-Czechoslovak treaty signed by President Beneš.
1944 Resistance activity escalates.
29 August: Slovak National Rising: 80,000 anti-fascists gain control of large parts of Central Slovakia and stave off Nazi counter-attacks until the autumn.
1945 *January:* Partisan actions occurring throughout the country.
22 March: Representatives of the four anti-fascist parties

in emigration meet at the Czechoslovak embassy in Moscow to decide on the republic's post-war policy.
5 April: The policy agreed at Moscow, for a National Front government of Czechs and Slovaks, announced at the liberated town of Košice, Eastern Slovakia.
April: Red Army liberates Brno and Eastern Moravia.
5-9 May: The Prague Rising sees fierce fighting, the construction of 1,600 barricades and the final defeat of the Nazis with the entry of the Red Army. Smrkovský, the vice-president of the Czech National Council, plays a major role in the rising.
10 May: The government returns to Prague.
May-June: National committees set up to run local administration.
June-July: Presidential decrees on Land Reform issued.
Summer: Enormous advances made in the organisation and membership of works councils and trade unions. By the end of the year there are over 11,000 councils, 8,000 trade-union branches, and ROH has a membership of almost $1\frac{1}{2}$ million.
24 October: Decrees on nationalisation passed affecting major industry and three-fifths of the industrial labour force.

1946 *28-31 March:* KSČ Congress, where Gottwald gives the main report outlining his party's perspectives. KSČ already has over one million members.
19-22 April: 1,200 delegates attend the ROH Congress.
26 May: Elections held to the National Assembly. KSČ emerges as the strongest party with 38 per cent of the vote.
2 July: New coalition government announced involving all the parties, with Gottwald as prime minister.
September: US government withdraws 50 million dollar credit from Czechoslovakia intended to buy army surplus property. Discussions for a loan simultaneously suspended.
25 October: National Assembly approves Two-Year Economic Plan to begin in January 1947.
By the end of the year $2\frac{1}{4}$ million German-speaking inhabitants of the border regions have been transferred to

Germany, as agreed by the major powers.

1947 *Winter months:* Controversy over the destination of confiscated enterprises; climax is the dispute and strike at Varnsdorf, Northern Bohemia, on 5 March.
Spring: Protracted set of works council elections.
12 March: Launching of the Truman Doctrine, signalling a major ideological and economic crusade against communism. Marshall Aid announced. Communists removed from government in Italy and France.
July: Czechoslovak government accepts invitation to go to Paris to attend conference on Marshall Aid. Then, after discussions in Moscow, it reverses its position and rejects the invitation.
September: Dispute over KSČ's proposal for a millionaires' tax.
Late September: Cominform set up, with Slánský as the main KSČ representative.
October-November: Serious political crisis in Slovakia.
Autumn: Growing food shortages result in an escalating black market and speculation.
November: SDS Congress sees a defeat of the left as Fierlinger is removed from office.

1948 *January:* Dispute over public employees' pay reaches a head. With all the signs of a growing crisis KSČ begins to take steps to draw in mass organisations. In early February preparations for a Works Council Congress and a Peasants' Congress are announced.
13 February: The removal of non-communist security and police chiefs and their replacement by communists raised in the Cabinet. NSS ministers demand their reinstatement.
20 February: Twelve ministers resign over the security issue. SDS and the two non-party ministers stay in the government, which can still legally continue functioning.
21 February: KSČ argues that resignations should be accepted and that new ministers should be appointed who will be loyal to the government programme. Demonstrations are held in all large cities in support of the KSČ policy.
22 February: 8,000 delegates at the Works Council Congress back Gottwald and call for more nationalisation. A

one-hour strike is called for 24 February to back up their demands.

23 February: SDS sways towards the left.

24 February: Strike call almost universally followed.

25 February: KSČ organises People's Militia in Prague and other main cities. President Beneš sees he has no alternative other than to accept the resignations of the ministers and the proposals of the KSČ.

10 March: A new government formed under clear KSČ domination.

1 May: After further nationalisation laws only 5 per cent of the labour force remain employed in the private sector. KSČ becomes the sole effective political force in the country.

1950-3 Thousands of communists and ordinary citizens harassed and persecuted. In the most notorious rigged trial eleven leading communists are sentenced to death.

1956 Khrushchev's speech at the Twentieth Congress of the CPSU reveals some of the crimes of the Stalin era.

1963 Partial rehabilitation of those sentenced in early 1950s.

1968 KSČ attempts to renew Czechoslovak society in a democratic direction expressed by the slogan "socialism with a human face". Occupation of the country on 21 August by Soviet and other troops seeks to reverse the movement of the "Prague Spring".

I
The Setting

1
The First Republic

As the representatives of the four Czech political parties in emigration met in the Czechoslovak Embassy in Moscow on 22 March 1945 to discuss forming a new government and programme, the Red Army was already liberating eastern parts of the country. From the summer of 1944 the Red Army had been rolling back the Nazi forces throughout Eastern Europe from Poland to Bulgaria. In the autumn it had encountered fierce resistance, but by spring 1945 the overall ascendancy of the Soviet Army was no longer in question. The length of time to liberation was unknown. Yet it was clear that the dynamic of the Stalingrad victory was going to take the Red Army "to the beast in his lair".

At the Moscow meetings the LS (People's Party) was represented by Šrámek and Hála; the NSS (National Socialist Party) by Stránský, J. David, dr. Drtina and F. Uhlíř; the SDS (Social Democratic Party) by Z. Fierlinger, B. Laušman, V. Majer and V. Pacák; and the KSČ (Communist Party of Czechoslovakia) by Klement Gottwald, R. Slánský, V. Kopecký, V. Nosek and B. Laštovička.[1] All present knew that the Czechoslovak Republic which had been mutilated at Munich and completely destroyed in March 1939 was shortly to be reborn. The experiences of the twenty-year history of the First Republic and the lessons to be drawn from them figured prominently in the thoughts of those meeting in Moscow, just as they did among those fighting inside Czechoslovakia.

An independent Czecholslovak state had emerged on 28 October 1918 from the debris of the Austro-Hungarian Empire. The Czech national leadership, notably Masaryk and Beneš, wanted British and French diplomatic support for an independent Czechoslovakia. This they received at Versailles as the Allied powers sought to build Czechoslovakia into a strong island of "peace and order" amidst the turmoil of Central and Eastern Europe.[2] In return the Czechoslovak government moulded the new republic on Western lines, having broken the strong revolutionary movement by military suppression in December 1920.[3] The constitution was based on a Western, liberal democratic model with a national assembly, a guarantee of fundamental civil liberties and security for the private ownership of industries and banks, thereby ensuring the support of the domestic bourgeoisie and prospective Western investors. The 1920s saw massive Western investment as the most economically developed country in Central and Eastern Europe, containing over 70 per cent of the former empire's industrial capacity, underwent a rapid process of concentration and cartelisation.[4]

The class and social structure of the country grew more similar to that of other industrialised capitalist countries. By 1930 the working class, increasingly concentrated in large factories and enterprises, constituted the major component of the labour force (37.5 per cent) while the tertiary sector accounted for another sixth, although these trends were not repeated in Slovakia, where agriculture retained its predominance.[5]

Parallel with these developments came a swift growth in the trade-union movement. By 1935 there were 1,170,470 manual workers and 937,250 clerical workers in trade unions, a sixfold increase over the membership figures in 1918. However, since the 1890s, in accord with the nationality policy of the Austro-Hungarian Social Democratic Party, the trade-union movement had been split on a national basis. This division was augmented by fragmentation on a craft and party political basis. Unions were almost wholly organised by crafts, and within the same crafts different and antagonistic unions were formed under the sponsorship of nationalities or political parties. On 31 December 1937 there existed 18 separate trade-union centres in which 485 union organisations were grouped, while there were another 224 trade unions which maintained no connection with any central organisation.[6]

This fragmentation of the trade-union movement severely weakened the development of unified working-class action over economic issues and broader political questions. Little collective response came from the trade-union leaderships to the economic problems created by the Great Depression. Similarly they were unable to counter the threat posed by the resurgence of a pan-Germanic nationalist movement amongst the "Sudeten" Germans in the border regions of Northern Bohemia. Working-class political parties also failed to engage in united action against this movement, which sought to destroy the Czechoslovak state. The right-wing leadership which dominated the SDS after 1920 opposed joint action with the Communists, while the chequered history of the KSČ hampered its ability to project successful unity initiatives.

As with the great majority of communist parties established at the end of the first world war, the KSČ was formed after a split within the ranks of Czech social democracy. Adhering to the 21 points of the Communist International, the KSČ set itself the dual task of overcoming reformism in the workers' movement and leading the working class and its allies to socialist revolution. In attempting to accomplish these tasks the KSČ, along with the other sections of the Comintern, was profoundly affected by the course of the revolution in the Soviet Union.

The whole of Bolshevik strategy in 1917 had been underpinned by the belief that theirs was to be the first in a series of revolutionary conflagrations that would bring socialism to most of Europe. The Comintern was seen as the General Staff of the revolutionary forces. No sooner had it been established than the post-war revolutionary tide began to ebb. Isolated in a hostile world, the Bolsheviks faced the task of building socialism in one country. This situation, and the political approach adopted under Stalin to resolve it, deeply affected the character of the Comintern and all of its sections. From its original perspective as a unifying revolutionary organisation, the priorities of the Comintern slowly shifted to the defence of Soviet national interests abroad. Enjoying the enormous prestige of being the only socialist country, and with the General Secretariat based in Moscow, the Soviet leadership was able to turn the Comintern into one of its policy instruments. By various administrative measures those elements in other parties which disagreed with current Soviet policy were removed, and where necessary the policy line altered. Thus the impetus for the changes in communist leadership, policy and organisation that occurred originated primarily in Moscow rather than as a result of the social struggles in the countries concerned. Most significantly, the extreme shift in Comintern strategy to the "class against class" position of 1928-1935 occurred as a complement to internal Soviet developments rather than as a result of any change in the balance of class forces within the capitalist countries. The new leaderships that had been installed at the behest of the General Secretariat and the reforms in party organisational structure that had been undertaken ensured that the new line was followed. The general trend of development outlined here was reflected in the history of the KSČ.

On its formation in 1921 the KSČ was the largest workers' party in Czechoslovakia. There were differing tendencies within this mass party, and friction between the leadership and the Comintern. As the nature of the Comintern changed, so the main aim of the General Secretariat became to secure a KSČ leadership amenable to Comintern and Soviet directives. This was achieved at the Fifth Congress of the KSČ in February 1929, when with the direct intervention of the Comintern the leadership was overthrown and replaced by a new grouping headed by Klement Gottwald. This congress is described officially as the "congress of Bolshevisation", but it was chiefly significant for the subordination of the KSČ to Soviet leadership policy. In the coming decades the group around Gottwald was to form the leading nucleus of the Party, Rudolf Slánský, Václav Kopecký, Jan Šverma, Václav Nosek, Bruno Kohler, Josef Krosnář, Viliam Široký and Marie Švermová being among their number.[7]

Their elevation to the leadership was a result of the decisive action taken by the Comintern: that this did not have the support of the rank and file was illustrated most dramatically by the drop in party membership from around 100,000 in 1928 to 24,000 by April 1929.[8] Their installation from outside sharply illustrated the undemocratic internal nature of the party. The distortions of inner-party democracy that developed in the Bolshevik party in the 1920s and came to be accepted as "leninist" norms were transmitted through Comintern mechanisms to all of its sections. Although the KSČ was to survive the losses that resulted from the Fifth Congress and slowly rebuild its base, it was not to be able to overcome the destruction that had been wrought on its functioning as a democratic centralist organisation.

The crucial questions of policy and personnel affecting the party had been decided upon from above and from abroad, and against the wishes of the majority of the membership. As Gottwald proudly stated, "Our highest revolutionary staff is really Moscow,"[9] and as the resolution the General Secretariat sent on 15 April 1929 reminded the KSČ, relations between the Comintern and its sections were not "relations of partners who are negotiating with each other" but were "based on the principles of proletarian discipline."[10] Henceforth all the key policy decisions were to be taken by the top leadership, applying the existing Soviet strategy to Czechoslovak conditions. Centralism was the keynote of the party's internal operations, with the membership's task being to fulfil the leadership's directives. The locus of power within the party was centred firmly in the Politburo, while the administrative machine and apparatus of the party acquired greater importance with this centralist emphasis. Inner-party discussion was limited to enactment of "the line" rather than its actual direction. Having been placed in the leadership as a consequence of Comintern intervention, the Gottwald grouping loyally followed the shifts in Comintern and Soviet policy. From 1929 to 1935 a "class against class" policy viewing social democracy as social fascism was followed, a sectarian policy which hindered the development of united action in Czechoslovakia as well as the rest of Europe.

The policy had disastrous consequences, above all in Germany. At the Seventh Congress of the Communist International in 1935 the communist movement, facing a calamitous situation throughout Europe, shed its sectarianism. The speech of the general secretary, Dimitrov, and the congress resolution located the main enemy as fascism, and not social democracy, as had previously been the case. The key task was to unite the maximum forces around the working class in order to isolate the fascists. The resolution emphasised that "it is imperative that unity of action be established between all sections of the working class, irrespective of what organisation they belong to,"[11] and that links be forged between the working class, peasantry, petty bourgeoisie and middle strata. Communist parties were encouraged to develop this popular front strategy in accordance with their own specific, national conditions.[12]

This is what the KSČ began to do at its Seventh Congress in April 1936. Gottwald's keynote speech called for a broad, united Popular Front to defend the republic. His main themes were the fulfilment of the economic and social needs of the people; the granting of national rights to all the nationalities of Czechoslovakia; and the democratisation of the state machinery, above all the purging of fascist supporters in the army.[13] This represented a programme on which broad unity could be won. Yet the legacy of previous sectarianism proved too severe a handicap to overcome quickly. The formation of an effective Popular Front was not achieved before the war. Within the country, opposition to the pan-Germanic nationalist movement and its Nazi backers remained divided, while a considerable section of the Agrarian Party — the major conservative party — took up semi-fascist positions.

As the expansionist designs of Nazi Germany became more obvious, the Entente framework within which the First Republic had been created became redundant. The dominant trend of the foreign policy of the Chamberlain government was the appeasement of Germany's demands.[14] By mid-1938 Czechoslovakia represented the last major obstacle in the path of appeasement, and throughout the summer Britain attempted to resolve the question in collaboration with Germany. The entire weight of British diplomacy, which France followed, was concentrated on gaining the Prague government's acceptance of the German demands. The matter was settled at Munich on 29 September when the four main European powers — Britain, Germany, France and Italy — decided on the surrender of Czechoslovak territory at a conference to which the Czechoslovak government was not invited. By the agreement Czechoslovakia was forced to cede large sections of its border regions and one-third of its industrial capacity.[15] The First Czechoslovak Republic ceased effectively to exist as an independent state.

The tragedy which Munich represented for the overwhelming majority of the Czechoslovak people made necessary a fundamental re-examination of the decisive political features of the First Republic. Reliance on the Western powers had proved fatal at the crucial moment of the nation's history; the German minority had not been successfully integrated into the republic; disunity and divisions within the trade unions and amongst the socialist parties had hindered firm resistance to the dismemberment of the republic; the right-wing parties had aided that dismemberment and after Munich were actively to collaborate in it. These were the experiences which must have been prominent in the minds of the politicians meeting in Moscow in March 1945 as they proceeded to discuss the government programme which was to shape the new republic.

2
War at Home

The Munich "diktat" and its aftermath left three fundamental possibilities open to Czechoslovakia: a return to the social and political system of the First Republic; the annihilation of an independent Czechoslovak state; or a renewed republic built on changed social and political foundations. By the time the representatives of the four parties sat down in Moscow they were only concerned with the latter. Their discussions on the character of the renewed republic were influenced, and in many ways determined, by the manner in which the first two possibilities had been ruled out.

The major focus of Nazi German expansionist activity centred on countries contiguous to it on the continent of Europe, especially those to the east and south-east. The aim was for these countries to become satellite dependencies of Germany within Hitler's "New Order". During the war Nazi political control of occupied countries was manifested in one of three ways: either direct incorporation into the Reich, as with the border regions of Czechoslovakia; close attachment with a view to later assimilation or "colonisation", as with the rest of the Czech Lands; or military, semi-military or civilian administration where countries retained a nominal independence, as in Slovakia.

During its seven years of occupation Czechoslovakia was to experience the gamut of Nazi methods. After an initial post-Munich hesitation the logic of Nazi expansion resulted in the complete demolition of an independent Czechoslovak state. Preparations were made jointly with the Slovak separatists, who declared an independent Slovak state on 14 March 1939. A day later German troops entered Prague.

On 16 March on Prague Radio Ribbentrop announced a new decree which established the Protectorate of Bohemia and Moravia under German government control. This decree granted huge powers to the Nazi occupation forces. During the occupation they pursued extensive "Germanisation" policies in the economic, administrative, security and cultural fields, utilising their control of the machinery of state and government. In fulfilment of their goals of complete domination of the Czech Lands via a policy of "Germanisation" the Nazis were significantly aided by Czech collaborators. Shortly after the German occupation the Beran government resigned, yet the new government differed little in personnel, the majority of them having been active politicians in the First Republic. The position of any Czech government had been clearly outlined in the decree, its complete subordination to the demands of the Reich being unquestionable. Such a government could only aid the Nazis and damp down internal opposition to them. A similar function was served by *Národní Souručenství* ("National Solidarity"), the only Czech political organisation permitted after the occupation. Most of its leaders were former Agrarians, and its stated aims were national self-preservation and national unity.

These were merely empty phrases attempting to hide blatant collaboration with the occupation forces. These collaborators were discredited in the eyes of the Czech people and their role became more exposed as the Nazi terror increased from the winter of 1941-2 onwards. By their actions during the occupation, Czech right-wing political parties forfeited their participation in the post-war republic, as did the Hlinka Party in Slovakia.

The economic position of the Czech bourgeoisie was seriously undermined by Nazi policy as German capital penetrated and increasingly dominated the economy. The major Czech banks had their vast assets taken over by German banks, primarily the "Deutsche" and "Dresdner", in 1938 and 1939; this control was crucial to Reich economic policy. Many leading Czech enterprises, including the Škoda Works, Vitkovice and Poldina Iron Works and Brno Zbrojovka Small Arms, came under the control of the Göring concern,[1] while the overall level of German investment in the Czech economy rose phenomenally. During the war the investments of Reich German and Austrian capital in the Czech economy increased by 571 per cent.[2]

"Germanisation" of the economy was furthered by the accelerating trend of the concentration and centralisation of capital. In the course of the war 3,200 industrial enterprises, 3,500 businesses and 8,500 workshops and trades were closed down, with

99 per cent of the closures being of Czech firms.³ This process had the dual effect of undermining the position of the Czech petty and middle bourgeoisie while strengthening the grip of large-scale German capital concentrated in monopoly concerns.⁴

This German penetration of the economy severely undermined the position of the large Czech bourgeoisie. Yet the majority of them preferred a subordinate place as the junior partner to German capital, rather than engaging in opposition to it. Indeed there were numerous examples of their active collaboration with the Protectorate régime.⁵ The actions of the Czech upper bourgeoisie both during the Munich crisis and the occupation left them totally discredited in the eyes of the great majority of people. Nazi rule undermined the economic strength of all sections of the Czech bourgeoisie, while by their co-operation with it the major Czech financial and industrial magnates, along with their political allies, lost all significant popular support. Both the vitality and the credibility of the Czech bourgeoisie had drained away and with it the hopes of those who sought an immediate restoration of the political and economic system of the First Republic.

That an independent, Czechoslovak state emerged from the war was due primarily to the three-power anti-fascist coalition that was formed in 1941. On 22 June Germany renewed its *Drang nach Osten* and invaded the Soviet Union. Immediately the Soviet government joined in an anti-fascist coalition along with the British and American governments. This somewhat improbable coalition was bound together by a joint need to defeat a common enemy. While the war still held the coalition together, the contradictions within it were resolved by compromise. This being so, it can be seen that the winter of 1942/3 was decisive in the course of the war as far as Eastern and Central Europe were concerned. With their victory at Stalingrad the Red Army took the initiative. The westward advance of the Soviet armies into Eastern Europe was the decisive factor determining Allied diplomacy in the region. Beneš, the main representative of the London centre of the Czechoslovak emigration, understood this. A supremely realistic bourgeois politician, he recognised the political role the USSR was to play in Central Europe after the war and the necessity of coming to terms with it if his social-democratic conception of post-war Czechoslovakia was to have any chance of success. His policy was an attempt to channel the revolutionary forces within the country in a non-revolutionary direction. A crucial component of this policy was to reach agreement with the state with which the revolutionary forces identified. Although this posed enormous political dilemmas, it was undoubtedly a more realistic policy than that of the Polish government in exile.

On 12 December 1943 the Soviet-Czechoslovak treaty was signed. British opposition and the Foreign Office's preference of a federalised Eastern Europe had been overcome at the foreign ministers' meeting at Moscow in October. The treaty was to last twenty years and spoke of the two countries uniting in a policy of permanent friendship and friendly post-war co-operation, as well as of mutual aid of all kinds during the war against Germany.[6] The treaty represented a fundamental shift in Czechoslovak foreign policy, a realignment away from the Western powers and a recognition of the new international power balance in Central Europe. As such it strengthened the revolutionary forces and narrowed the area of manoeuvre open to the supporters of Beneš. The manner of the republic's survival firmly placed the political initative in the hands of the left at Moscow.

Growth and unity of the domestic resistance

This grip was strengthened by the dominance of the left within the domestic resistance. As the liberation of Europe from Nazi dictatorship came nearer, so the political struggle over the character of post-war Europe intensified, not only among the great powers but also within the resistance movements. By March 1945 it was clear that the revolutionary forces under the leadership of the KSČ and KSS were in the ascendant within Czechoslovakia. The two communist parties had been able to surmount the difficulties caused by their sectarian "imperialist war" position of 1939-41 and the havoc wreaked in their ranks by the Gestapo.[7] Since they were the only political parties who retained an organised existence within the resistance, it was they who gave political leadership to the growing movement in the latter stages of the war.[8]

Resistance activity began to develop significantly from autumn 1943, and the most influential groups were those with socialist and communist politics, the largest of such groups being the Communist organisation *Předvoj*.[9] The role of the "Communist

Party, which has led the illegal struggles against the occupiers . . . in spite of the most heavy losses it has suffered"[10] was recognised by all sections of the resistance. In December 1944 the KSČ was able to set up its fourth illegal central committee, the third having been eliminated by the Gestapo in the summer.[11] The whole emphasis of the policy of the fourth ÚV KSČ was that the Czechoslovak people must liberate themselves and not await passively the arrival of the Red Army. Obviously co-ordination with the advancing Red Army was essential. Yet the internal leadership laid great stress on the need to arouse mass actions in opposition to the Nazi occupation which would culminate in an armed rising. By contrast the external KSČ leadership viewed resistance activity as complementary to the requirements of the advancing Red Army and subordinate to it. The Gottwald leadership, following the position of the Soviet government, was wary not only of independent resistance actions undertaken with anti-Soviet motives, as at Warsaw, but also of independent initiatives made by communist-led movements, as in Yugoslavia, Slovakia and Prague. These differences between the domestic and external communist leaderships were to become more apparent in their plans for the post-war republic.

These differences, however, did not seriously undermine communist leadership of the resistance. No consistent challenge to their hegemony came from the domestic, bourgeois-democratic opposition. These sections preferred orthodox military rather than mass resistance actions. The Council of Three, the main Beneš group operating in the Czech resistance, viewed matters similarly and wanted to be the leading organ of the liberation movement.[12] Such a move would have placed a military grouping at the head of the resistance struggle and would have undoubtedly resulted in narrowing the boundaries of resistance activity, cramping its mass character and weakening its revolutionary content. These designs were easily thwarted, mainly because the London emigration, while securing Czechoslovakia's national sovereignty, had done very little to develop concrete actions within the country. The dilemma the Beneš supporters had faced over the Soviet Union was repeated: the necessity of working with the revolutionary forces but against the revolution. The London emigration government's wariness of encouraging mass resistance activity because of its revolutionising effects led them to emphasise the foreign rather than the domestic aspects of the liberation struggle. They attempted to resolve the dilemma by ignoring it, so that during the last winter of the war they were unable to produce illegal journals and leaflets or initiate widescale partisan actions. As resistance activity increased, it was the left which gained in influence within the country.

The emergence of an effective resistance movement had been an exceptionally hazardous process. It was only in late 1943 that organised guerrilla activity, as against sporadic sabotage, began to take place.[13] The movement in the Czech Lands was inspired by the example of the Slovak National Rising. Beginning on 29 August 1944 this mass rising of 80,000 armed anti-fascists gained control of large areas of Central Slovakia. Although they were unable to defeat the Nazi counter-attack in October, partisan activity continued in the mountains while the position of the Nazis and their collaborators in the country was severely weakened. The rising widened the anti-fascist front among the mass of the people and deepened its revolutionary character.[14] It also gave a boost to the movement in the Czech Lands. By the end of 1944 partisan units were carrying out forty actions daily.[15]

Of tremendous significance for the future development of the republic was the way that pre-war divisions among the left were dispelled. There was an unparalleled unity of forces within the anti-fascist front. The communists were especially keen to develop organs of the resistance which could draw the broadest mass of people into action against the occupying forces. The Slovak communists helped set up the Slovak National Council in December 1943, the body that was to lead the uprising. In the Czech Lands it was the KSČ along with the illegal trade unions that were the major forces in the establishment of a Czech National Council. In the early months of 1945 this body became the major directive force of the Czech resistance and was to lead the Prague rising in May.

One of the major unifying forces of the resistance was the illegal trade-union movement. In 1943 a group of trade unionists including Evžen Erban, Josef Kubát, František Jungmann and Václav Cipro formed a resistance group within the National Federation of Employees.[16] This was a central trade-union organisation under direct Nazi control which had been set up in 1941. The Protectorate régime had amalgamated all existing trade-union organisations into two major organisations of manual workers and public employees. These measures were of historic significance since they broke the particularist structure of Czech trade unionism. Although the national federations were nothing more than tame syndicates with the function of smoothing the regimentation of labour in the Protectorate, the Czech trade unionists who joined the resistance movement had no wish to return to their pre-Munich forms of organisation. As one postwar ÚRO functionary explained, "the organic unity which we did not achieve pre-war was done for us by administrative means by the Germans."[17]

In 1943 ÚRO, as the organ of the revolutionary trade unions, was created.[18] By the start of 1945 it had a widespread illegal network.[19] ÚRO policy was similar to that of the other left forces. It recognised the necessity of a unified organ of national resistance and was prominent in the establishment of the Czech National Council. It also supported the strategy of large-scale resistance culminating in a rising, and it established organisation in large factories throughout the Protectorate, wherever possible forming groups of workers' militia as well as producing leaflets and general political propaganda.[20] In this way the revolutionary trade-union movement was to play a central part in the Prague rising and was in a position to create a unified trade-union movement on liberation.

Fighting for a new social order

The activities of the domestic resistance movement helped to bring about the downfall of the Protectorate régime; the political unity and consequent organisational forms created by the left leadership of the resistance also strengthened those forces desiring radical social changes at the end of the war. The resistance movement was not just concerned with the defeat of the Nazis. They were also fighting for a new social order after the war had been won.

In many respects their policy followed on logically from their analysis of the war. For example, while recognising that the primary task was the complete defeat of Nazi Germany, nevertheless, the resolution of January 1945 of the illegal fourth ÚV KSČ also considered the imperialist aims of Britain and the United States and how, as in Greece, Belgium and Poland, they were attempting to rearrange Europe in accord with their own designs rather than in accord with the people of those nations.[21] Resolute opposition was stated to "all attempts by treacherous bourgeois elements" to re-establish "an anti-popular, exploitative order"[22] in Czechoslovakia. The ROH Action Programme of March 1945 made a similar international analysis[23] and then related this much more clearly to the domestic political situation. They considered there were two basic camps, one of reaction and the other of progressive forces. Within the latter, two trends could be discerned: that of the Czech democratic bourgeoisie, which orientated itself more towards the Western powers; and that of the working class, which saw political alliance with the USSR as the most reliable guarantee of national freedom and socialist advance. The working class trend considered that the liberation of the country from the occupying forces was the first and major task, but that this was a prelude to the second task of initiating a socialist order.[24] The two tasks were intimately linked in the left's strategy, and the widest possible mobilisation of the people was essential to both. By contrast, bourgeois democratic resistance sections preferred orthodox military actions and were extremely wary of encouraging partisan warfare and mass armed risings.

The post-war demands of the left leadership of the resistance reflected this concern for a new social order. In January 1945 the resolution of the fourth ÚV KSČ stated that "the nationalisation of all kinds of large industry and banks and the handing-over of estate-owners' land to small peasants must be among the first laws of the republic."[25] The Slovak National Council in session on 2 March formulated their view on the position of Slovakia in the post-war republic and also stated that they wanted the country built on new foundations with important enterprises nationalised. Industrial, financial and trading concerns were to contribute their wealth to the state and not to individuals.[26] On 19 March ÚRO sent a despatch to the delegations assembling in Moscow, and this contained the most precise and extensive economic proposals of any domestic resistance organisation. The despatch stated:

> The main demands of the working people at home (are) the nationalisation of the mines, of all large industrial, metal, chemical and foodstuffs factories, of banks and insurance,

of forests, as well as the public ownership of agricultural property over thirty hectares in area; this we consider the minimum economic programme of the first domestic government.[27]

Similar demands came from many other sections of the resistance, including partisans in Western Moravia and factory delegates in Podbrezová, Slovakia.[28]

An evaluation of the breadth of popular support for these demands is difficult, as they originated from organisations that were illegal. Yet such demands were no isolated Czech phenomenon. A strong revolutionary trend appeared in resistance movements throughout Europe.[29] In Czechoslovakia the demands for widespread anti-capitalist measures came from a considerable number of organisations, and not just from the national leaderships but also from the rank-and-file. Thus the evidence available and comparative experience support the contention that these demands articulated the aspirations of wide sections of Czechoslovak working people.

The demands were based on an understanding that the overthrow of Nazi rule would result in a severe social and political crisis in the Czech Lands. The old ruling order was in no position to re-establish itself, and a political vacuum existed. The policies of the resistance were designed to resolve such a situation in a socialist manner. During the 1960s Czech historians began to recognise that in their analyses and policies domestic resistance organisations had differed significantly from their counterparts in emigration. However, no serious consideration was given to these alternative policies, and they were either disregarded or seen as sectarian.[30] While undoubtedly there were among some communists sectarian survivals of earlier policies such as "class against class", the Czech historians failed to do justice to the domestic resistance.

The ROH Action Programme considered that their policies would gain the support not only of the industrial working class but also of "wide strata of the working people and of the progressive intelligentsia".[31] It was this understanding of class alliances that underpinned the KSČ's twin strategy of "struggle against the occupiers and for a new, free socialist republic."[32] It represented an attempt to grapple with the problems of socialist strategy in a situation where fascism was on the brink of defeat and where the strategy and tactics of the Popular Front needed new application to the more positive objective circumstances. The left was now in a position to move on to the offensive, and the domestic resistance organisations were prepared to take the initiative. The differences between the left within Czechoslovakia and the KSČ leadership in Moscow resulted from differing analyses of the anti-fascist coalition and the character of the domestic resistance. Indeed, the major analytical weakness of the domestic left was its failure to recognise the existence of just these differences within its ranks. This disarmed it. When conflicts arose with the KSČ leadership in Moscow, it was unable to put forward a politically coherent alternative strategy. It did not see the need for one.

Its fundamental weakness, however, lay not in its analysis but rather in its "lack of battalions". In Czechoslovakia, as in the rest of Europe, the resistance movement was only an adjunct to the Allied armies in the overthrow of fascist rule. The only exception was in Yugoslavia, where Tito's communist partisans were instrumental in the downfall of the German occupation. In the Europe emerging from the chaos of the war the primary fact was the Great Power element in the determination of the internal affairs of the various states. It was no longer a question of which indigenous political force had majority support. Throughout Western Europe the swiftly growing strength of the left was cramped and hindered by the presence of the Anglo-American armies. In Czechoslovakia the revolutionary enthusiasm of the domestic resistance was to be harnessed to the more restrictive, cautious policies of the KSČ leadership in Moscow. Only the Yugoslavs had secured a base from which to pursue an independent path. At the Moscow discussions the initiative lay with the left, but in a situation primarily created by the Soviet Army. Thus it was the political strategy reflecting the wishes of the Soviet government that was to carry most weight in the discussions. Such a strategy had been formulated by the KSČ leadership in emigration.

3
War Abroad

With the victory at Stalingrad, the military initiative had passed to the Red Army. It consolidated its position in the following months and then launched a devastating offensive in the summer of 1944. The political significance of these developments was recognised by the Soviet government, which during this period formulated its post-war strategy. The fundamental political dilemma, as Roy Medvedev has expressed it, was:

> It had to define its relationship as the centre of the world revolutionary movement to revolutionary movements on the rise in many countries. At the same time the Soviet Union had to define its relationship to its allies in the anti-Nazi coalition, especially to the ruling circles of the United States and Great Britain. . . . These relationships were often at odds.[1]

In addition, the Soviet government faced the paradox of emerging from the war with tremendous prestige and military power yet severely weakened by the immense human and physical losses the war had wrought.[2]

The strategy that the Soviet leadership adopted in the face of these dilemmas was essentially a cautious, nationalist one. It was hoped that the anti-fascist coalition would continue after the war;[3] that as a consequence of Red Army liberation of the countries of Eastern Europe their post-war governments would be friendly to the Soviet Union; and that on this basis of security and stability the vital post-war reconstruction of the USSR could be undertaken, aided by reparations from Germany and possibly a loan from the US government.[4]

The mainspring of the strategy was that the anti-fascist coalition would continue. It was on this basis that the Soviet government negotiated at Teheran, Yalta and Potsdam. Considerations of their own security dominated their thinking, as the stance adopted on the issues of Greece and Poland showed most clearly.[5] The tension evident in the negotiations over the post-war Polish government underlined the fragility of the grand coalition. The cohesion provided by the need to overcome a common enemy began to fragment as soon as fascism was on the verge of defeat. The Soviet government seemed not to recognise the conjunctural character of the war-time alliance and that it would be overridden by more basic class antagonisms once the war had been won, especially given the immense material superiority of the United States.[6] Until spring 1947 Soviet policy was to remain based on the premise of the possibility of inter-allied co-operation.

Unable to disentangle their own state strategy from that of the working class in each country, the Soviet Union also encouraged foreign communist parties to follow this policy. National fronts uniting all anti-fascist forces were the logical complement to the international anti-fascist coalition. These were not necessarily wrong, but their character and orientation was dictated by these diplomatic requirements rather than by the social conditions existing in each country. The national and patriotic aspects of the anti-fascist struggle were stressed at the expense of the social. The political strategy communist parties were urged to adopt was the same as that employed for defence against fascism — even though fascism and with it most of the old order lay in ruins. The policies of the Gottwald leadership fell neatly into this pattern, though they enjoyed considerably more freedom of manoeuvre than their Western counterparts.

The changed balance of power internationally and the altering political attitudes and outlook of the Czechoslovak people meant that the KSČ was the decisive force in post-war Czech politics. President Beneš recognised this clearly. When he had discussions with the KSČ leadership in Moscow, he told them, "You will be the strongest element of the new régime."[7] The formulation and orientation of KSČ policy in response to this situation was in many ways determined by stamp which the international communist movement had imprinted on the party. The entire political and ideological outlook, training and experience of this communist leadership led them to consider that the fulfilment of Soviet strategy was the correct and indeed the only way to promote the interests of the Czechoslovak working class. With the Czechoslovak-Soviet treaty having laid the basis, the KSČ aim in their discussions with Beneš was to implement the strategy of antifascist coalition, a position at variance with that being followed by their colleagues inside Czechoslovakia.

Gottwald submitted the proposals of the Moscow leadership to Beneš on 16 December 1943.[8] In order to develop domestic resistance, all sectors of the resistance movement were urged to form national committees, to oppose clearly the Hacha collaborators and to initiate armed partisan warfare. The proposals envisaged that the political unity welded in the struggle for national independence would be continued post-war with a National Front government. This government was to be based on the three socialist parties, as well as representatives of other groups such as catholics and farmers. It would ensure that friendship with the Soviet Union was a major pillar of state policy and that large properties of Germans and traitors would be taken into national management until a properly constituted National Assembly met. Considerable emphasis was laid on the role national committees would play as organs of popular, democratic power, while it was clearly said that the state apparatus was to be purged of anti-democratic elements and the army built on a democratic basis, with its officers being drawn from those who were fighting in the struggle for liberation. These proposals were similar in many respects to those which Gottwald had outlined at the Seventh KSČ Congress, although in some areas, notably in measures to democratise the state apparatus and army, they were more far-reaching. Nevertheless, as victory over fascism loomed nearer, these proposals, especially in the economic arena, lagged behind the objective possibilities existing for the left in Czechoslovakia.

The imminent defeat of fascism meant that the left-wing forces throughout Europe were in a significantly stronger position than at any time since the end of the First World War. In Czechoslovakia the former ruling circles were discredited in the eyes of the vast majority of the population. The working class, in particular, no longer retained its former passive affiliation to the dominant political formation. A return to the *status quo ante bellum* was impossible.

The political attachment of the working class had also changed. As Gramsci has expressed it, "Among the subaltern groups, one will exercise or tend to exercise a certain hegemony through the mediation of a party."[9] Pre-war the KSČ was not in this position, as its inability to bring about a Popular Front illustrates. However, by the end of the war the KSČ and KSS were the dominant forces in the resistance movement and on liberation occupied a hegemonic position among the Czechoslovak working class.

From the pre-war period there had been a marked shift in the political terrain. The old order had been undermined; the working people were seeking alternatives; and the KSČ was the dominant political force among the Czechoslovak working class. Recognising these developments, communists and socialists inside Czechoslovakia evolved a new, twin strategy linking the battle for national independence with the creation of a socialist republic. However, the KSČ leadership in Moscow refused to shift to such a strategic *offensive*. Particular policies could be made more radical and extensive, yet they were to remain bound within a restrictive interpretation of the Popular Front framework. The strategic *defensive* was to remain the pole of the KSČ position.

The Gottwald leadership was exceedingly cautious in its handling of issues that threatened to go beyond this framework. This was most obvious over the question of nationalisation, which figured prominently in the demands of the domestic resistance. Limited to its perspective of a strategic defensive, the Gottwald leadership made no explicit reference to nationalisation in the proposals it submitted to Beneš in December 1943. Their caution on the matter was displayed again when Gottwald, Šverma, Kopecký and Šmidke met a Czechoslovak government delegation composed of Uhlíř, Hála, Laušman and Valo in Moscow on 29 August 1944.[10] When economic matters were discussed, all present agreed with the propositions Hála submitted. Economic problems would be dealt with in two stages. The first measures would ensure that all enterprises became operative as rapidly as possible. The issues of expropriation, agrarian reform, of industry and questions of ownership would be raised once a National Assembly had been elected.[11] To the Gottwald leadership the issue of nationalisation was not fundamental at this stage. Slánský had written:

> We have deliberately limited ourselves just to some of those urgent problems. We have not concerned ourselves for

example with the questions of the nationalisation of the big enterprises, state control of the economy, economic planning, etc. The most pressing question in the economic field shall be the securing of a real government of the people.[12]

When the KSČ put its proposals to the meeting in Moscow in March 1945, again no explicit mention was made of nationalisation. Thus a contradiction remained between this programme and the demands of those left forces within Czechoslovakia which spontaneously desired to move on to the strategic offensive. The May to October 1945 period was to see tension on the questions of nationalisation and factory councils, yet throughout the Gottwald leadership was easily to contain these "left" elements. The huge prestige which the Soviet Union gained by its liberation of Czechoslovakia immensely strengthened the political position of the KSČ and its leadership, which was able to direct the strong revolutionary and radical currents among the population along the mainstream of its own perspective.

The considerable shift to the left within Czechoslovakia affected the policies and attitudes of the other Czech anti-fascist parties and of President Beneš. It was recognition of this shift that had led Beneš to sign the treaty with the USSR in December 1943, and had brought general agreement in his discussions that month with the Gottwald leadership "about the procedure for establishing a single national front at home immediately after the revolution." The government parties were to "form a united national front after liberation . . . jointly prepare a single post-revolution programme and . . . jointly undertake to fulfil it."[13] For a considerable time Beneš had realised that wide-ranging economic and social reforms would be part of any such programme. In conversation with Feierabend he had said:

> In economic and social conditions the principle of revolution applies. If after the war there are radical changes in economic and social relations in Europe, we shall join this revolutionary movement, just as it would be a mistake to lag behind it. For the present we do not see its outlines, but we can assume that it will mean supplementing political democracy by economic and social democracy. . . . We must, however, take care to keep this revolution within reasonable

bounds and prevent the communisation of the government and the country.¹⁴

This position could be maintained within the proposed National Front framework, and in this way Beneš hoped to contain the revolutionary forces within a revitalised social-democratic republic.

As the date for the Moscow discussions approached, so the two other socialist parties clarified their position on the post-war government and its programme. On 31 January 1945 representatives of the Czech National Socialist Party in London agreed on a policy.¹⁵ Their resolution supported the formation of a National Front government. Foreign policy was to be based first on the treaty with the USSR, while the army and organs of public life were to be democratised, though the proposals here remained vague. The resolution declared itself in favour of "the immediate nationalisation of mines, the coal trade, iron works, heavy industry . . . and relevant areas of public finance".

More marked was the shift to the left within the Czechoslovak Social Democratic Party. The action programme which they agreed to in London on 18 February 1945 committed them to a firm, socialist position.¹⁶ They supported a National Front government and the alliance with the USSR, and made specific proposals on how to democratise the state apparatus and army, in addition to purging all those elements which had collaborated. Above all their programme dealt with the creation of a new economic and social order. Public ownership was central to the foundation of a new social order and had to include all "natural mineral resources, banking, finance and credit, all heavy industrial enterprises and other large industrial enterprises, all transport and large distribution concerns." All agricultural land not owned by the state was to go to those who worked the land, to be run either individually or co-operatively. Guarantees of full employment, universal social security, adequate wages, a minimum fortnight's holiday and a maximum forty-hour working week were other aspects of this radical economic and social programme. The SDS programme was clear in its intention that the new republic be a socialist one.

The Moscow discussions

Representatives of the four anti-fascist parties in emigration met at the Czechoslovak Embassy in Moscow on 22 March. These negotiations were decisive in determining the character of the post-war Czechoslovak republic, and from their previous discussions and statements it was apparent that there existed considerable areas of agreement amongst the parties in emigration. Kopecký introduced the proposals of the Moscow Communist Party leadership for the government programme and spokesmen for the three other parties, Laušman, Hála and Stránský accepted the 16-point programme as a basis for discussion.[17]

Several major aspects of the post-war government and its programme were accepted by all the parties at the negotiations. They agreed that the government would be composed of a single, national front of the four Czech anti-fascist parties, along with the two Slovak anti-fascist parties, the Slovak Democratic Party and the KSS. Already it had been unanimously agreed in London that the Agrarian Party and its representatives could not enter the National Front government.[18] Only anti-fascist parties were to be permitted in the new republic. On the matter of foreign policy there was agreement that Czechoslovakia was to forge the closest alliance with the USSR in accordance with the treaty of 1943.[19] Furthermore the representatives were unanimously of the view that all Germans and Hungarians of Czechoslovak citizenship who had not been active anti-fascists during the war would be transferred out of the country. These three major areas of agreement were a solid framework for the establishment of a common programme.

The main conflicts in the negotiations arose on the questions of the army, the state administration and the relations between Czechs and Slovaks. The KSČ proposed radical revisions in the structure of the army and the creation of new organs of state and public administration: national committees, chosen and directly responsive to the people. These proposals aroused strong opposition from NSS and LS representatives,[20] yet it was on the issue of Czech-Slovak relations that the sharpest differences arose.[21] The Gottwald leadership disagreed with the policy of the KSS and the Slovak National Council (SNC), which sought a common, united, *federative* state with the SNC the supreme representative, legislative and executive organ in Slovakia. The Gottwald leadership considered this a "dualist" approach which would undermine the unity of the republic.[22] Their proposals broadly accepted the rights of the Slovak nation, but avoided the term "federation". The central government of the republic was to exercise common state functions in closest co-operation with the SNC. Fierce opposition to these policies came from the NSS, supported by Hála and Majer. However, after heated argument the essence of the KSČ proposals was accepted.

In tune with their overall policy, questions concerning the economic and social order of the new republic, as against its political aspects, did not figure prominently in the KSČ proposals. The resolutions and demands of the domestic resistance were ignored. Even the fate of properties owned by Germans, Hungarians and Czechoslovak collaborators was not settled. They would be placed under national management, but as Gottwald stated, the question "which we deliberately have not resolved is how to deal with these properties. Whether to return them and to whom or whether to nationalise them or make them co-operative — *that remains open.*"[23] The KSČ leaders in Moscow refused to commit themselves on the issue. Hence the programme of the National Front government of Czechs and Slovaks, which was announced in the liberated town of Košice in Eastern Slovakia on 5 April 1945, contained no explicit mention of nationalisation.

The Košice programme was the outcome of the Moscow discussions, and it was on this foundation that the reborn republic was to function. To President Beneš, the NSS and LS the programme represented a framework within which they hoped to contain the popular revolutionary tide. Once this began to ebb they hoped to effect certain changes, notably in the national committees and army, to bring the republic into accord with their own political outlook. For the moment they accepted the Košice programme, hoping this would give them the necessary breathing space to reorganise their forces and regain popular support.

To the Gottwald leadership the Košice programme was an undoubted success. Gottwald proudly stated:

> All the main, fundamental and principal points that comprise the government programme were formulated and suggested already at those meetings with the president in autumn 1943. . . . Our party . . . already while abroad . . .

formulated the fundamental line of our development, the development of our republic.²⁴

The alternative line of development contained within the proposals of the domestic resistance had been ignored, their suggestions not even being mentioned at the Moscow talks. This was despite Gottwald's recognition that in Czechoslovakia,

> Reaction, the bourgeoisie as the governing class, is discredited. With the defeat of Germany so also is their power, chiefly with regard to the state apparatus, severely shaken. For the working people in Slovakia and in the Czech Lands the situation is much better and more favourable than in other liberated countries.²⁵

Despite this there was to be no steady advance to socialism but rather support for a national, democratic republic based on "a bloc of the working class, peasants and farmers, small urban bourgeoisie, the intelligentsia and that part of the democratic bourgeoisie which wants to carry out the National Front programme together with us."²⁶

The last grouping in this bloc was not allied on a social basis but a political one, and the composition of this entire alliance was in accord with the requirements of the left in the pre-war republic rather than the post-war one. Political and social demands were consequently expressed in national rather than class terms. Gottwald spoke of power having passed "into the hands of the Czech and Slovak nation,"²⁷ while the policy of transferring all Germans and Hungarians except active anti-fascists encouraged nationalist and chauvinist sentiments among the Czech people. Social demands, calls for redistribution of land and public ownership were couched in nationalist terms, with Gottwald stating that "the government wants this time to do away completely and definitively with the consequences of Bílá Horá."²⁸* Such statements encouraged nationalist tendencies in the Czech working class and aided the nationalist ideology of the NSS and other parties. Yet the KSČ saw this all as a part of the national and democratic revolution, with Czechoslovakia being a Slav state

---

*At the battle of Bílá Horá in 1620 the Czechs were defeated by the Habsburgs, who were to rule Bohemia for almost the next three centuries.

bound in solidarity with the other Slav nations, above all the Soviet Union.

The Košice programme expressed the Gottwald leadership's political strategy. Based squarely on the approach of the Seventh Comintern Congress, the programme was seen as being able to galvanise the democratic and progressive forces in the nation around the leadership of the working class to build "a new, really democratic, truly popular republic."[29] In the immediate post-liberation period the major problems they were to face in enacting this strategy were to come not from disorganised and discredited bourgeois sections but rather from spontaneous attempts by sections of the working class to give the strategy a more offensive character, especially on the issues of nationalisation and factory councils.

4
Final Conflagration

The revolutionary temper and activity of the Czechoslovak people flared dramatically as the final defeat of Nazism came closer. With the Allied armies boring into the heart of the Reich, the disintegration of the Nazi state machine accelerated. The Czechoslovak resistance, permitted greater manoeuvrability and spurred by the proximity of the Allied armies, stepped up its activities, which were climaxed by uprisings in Prague and other towns during the last days of the war.

Within the resistance political divisions remained. As the war drew to its conclusion right-wing elements, based within the administrative apparatus and middle bourgeoisie, attempted a variety of manoeuvres aimed at transferring power into Czech hands without mass involvement. Generally, these attempts were thwarted by the left, which continued to dominate the resistance. This was despite suffering periodic setbacks at the hands of Nazi security and military forces; the KSČ experienced one such setback in March 1945, when its entire Prague leadership was captured.[1] In the last months of the war the KSČ's aim of mobilising the largest number of people in a wide variety of resistance activities was increasingly realised.

In Slovakia the primary force in the resistance movement was the partisans under communist hegemony. Having weathered the Nazi onslaughts of autumn 1944, the partisans claimed a strength of 13,000 by the turn of the year.[2] They played a valuable supportive role as the Red Army liberated the country in the following months. Partisan activity was also heavy in Moravia, where between August 1944 and April 1945 partisan groups carried out over three hundred attacks.[3] By mid-December partisan groups had begun to operate in the highland areas of Eastern Bohemia.[4]

During the last months of the war partisan warfare was widespread, with sabotage of trains, railway wagons, tracks and bridges being especially common.[5] In addition partisan groups created illegal national committees. To the KSČ these national committees were of crucial importance, since they represented a new element in the state apparatus: popular democratic institutions which replaced the pre-war bureaucratic machinery inherited from the Austro-Hungarian monarchy. As such they were an essential component of the national democratic revolution and were constantly stressed in communist propaganda.[6] A notable example was the underground resistance in Brno which created national committees during the occupation, so that when the troops of the Second Ukrainian Front liberated the town on 26 April, these committees were able to assert popular control.

With Brno liberated and the Allied armies triumphant throughout Europe the last days of the war were to see armed uprisings throughout the Czech Lands, most significantly in Prague on 5 May.

The Prague Rising

The KSČ had undertaken considerable preparations for an armed uprising, as had ÚRO, which sent out cyclostyled directives to factory organisers on how to form works militias and prepare for a general strike.[7] On 5 May the trade unions, along with the Czech National Council, held a meeting of seventy factory delegates in Prague, many of whom demanded an immediate armed rising.[8] The line of the KSČ leadership, especially fearful of a repeat of the tragedy at Warsaw, was that it was not the correct time to rise, given the limited weapons at their disposal. Yet events were already overtaking the meeting as the working people of Prague spontaneously took to battle.

The Prague Rising, spearheaded by the working class, was the culmination of Czech resistance activity. On 5 May crucial strategic and military targets were attacked, with fierce battles at the two central railway stations, barracks, factories and the radio station, which was captured by nightfall. The Czech National Council immediately placed itself at the head of the rising. ÚRO broadcasts called for a full-scale mobilisation of workers in the factories and urged that street barricades be built. Specific instructions were given on building roadblocks with heavy materials to a height of at least one metre, at the narrowest part of the street. During the night of 5-6 May barricades made from cobblestones, trams, earth, wood and lorries were constructed. In all perhaps

80,000 people took part in building the 1,600 barricades that appeared during the rising, using up 300,000 metres of Prague paving stone.[9] Nowhere was the mass involvement of the working people more clearly demonstrated.

The barricades enabled the insurgents to maintain their positions on 6 May, but they came under heavy pressure and sustained serious losses on the 7th. While the rising was assuming its mass character, various bourgeois groupings continued to work for a compromise solution. The differences within the Czech National Council and with various other military elements expressed themselves over the questions of Vlasov's army[10] and whether to negotiate with the Nazis. As the Nazi General Pückler put it, "Czech bourgeois circles would like to stop the struggle. The communists lead and fight."[11] Overall it was the left which won out.

The spirit of the rising, its political aims and the revolutionary enthusiasm it generated were expressed in Smrkovský's statement, broadcast on the night of 7-8 May as the tired rebels withstood the last desperate Nazi assault:

> We have just one condition: the unconditional surrender of German troops into the hands of the Czech National Council and Czech armed units. . . . Comrades, workers, working people and you, working women, to the barricades. Our rising, our revolution is above all the affair of our workers. We know what we're fighting for . . . not only for the freedom of the nation but also our social freedom. The new free republic . . . shall be our republic, the republic of the working people. We shall be supreme in it. We shall manage it. There shall be no capitalist leeches. There shall be no poverty or exploitation. The people shall march forward to wealth, the people shall march forward to happiness.[12]

Nothing better captures the revolutionary message and essence of the rising.

Despite the surrender of the Nazis at Rheims on 7 May, the fighting continued. Desperately short of arms and uncertain of the proximity of Allied help, representatives of the Czech National Council met General Toussaint on 8 May and agreed to an armistice which permitted the free exit of German troops and arms from Prague to the American Allied lines. The right-wing political groupings involved in the rising had used the situation to pressurise the Czech National Council into agreeing to an armistice that was not unconditional Nazi surrender. Indeed, the armistice gave the Nazi forces the crucial condition they desired — an opportunity to flee westwards away from the advancing Soviet armies. These armies arrived in Prague on 9 May, rapidly cleaning out the last pockets of Nazi resistance, and they received an ecstatic welcome from the people of Europe's longest-occupied capital.

The Czech National Council pledged its allegiance to the Košice government and helped the national committees and works militias to take over control in the localities and factories, as well as to ensure that weapons remained in the hands of the barricade fighters and armed units. These final resistance actions heightened the revolutionary character of the struggle for national freedom and the revolutionary mood among the industrial working class and other sections of working people.

The international dimension

What the rising also illustrated was Czechoslovakia's delicate international position. As the war drew to its close, the military divisions of the continent that had been agreed upon at Teheran and Yalta by the Big Three assumed a more obvious political character. Despite the obligatory reference to "non-interference in the internal affairs" of other countries which accompanied almost every Allied declaration, each of the three powers recognised the political and ideological implications of military occupation. It was not usually a question of an Allied army directly foisting their kind of government on the liberated country, although this did occur (as in Greece). The question was whether the country as liberated by the Red Army or Western armies determined the political terrain on which the different domestic political forces were to operate, and correspondingly whether left-wing or right-wing elements were to hold the upper hand in the anti-fascist coalition governments that emerged in all these countries. With the military defeat of Nazi Germany at hand it was these political considerations that were uppermost in the minds of the Anglo-American politicians and chiefs of staff. The Soviet government was similiarly aware of the political significance of the military moves.

During April 1945 General Eisenhower came under strong pressure from Churchill and British chiefs of staff to advance his armies as far eastwards as possible, irrespective of the occupational boundaries already agreed upon by the three governments with regard to Germany. When General Alexei Antonov, Red Army Acting Chief of Staff, queried this, Eisenhower hastened to assure him that no alteration of these plans was envisaged.[13]

British pressure for a further eastward advance increased towards the end of April. Shortly before leaving for Washington Sir Alexander Cadogan wrote to the US Ambassador in London. Quoting from Eden's memorandum, he stressed:

> Great political advantages . . . would result if United States troops could press forward into Czechoslovakia and liberate Prague. In our view the liberation of Prague and as much as possible of the territory of Western Czechoslovakia by United States troops might make the whole difference to the post-war situation in Czechoslovakia, and might well influence that in nearby countries. On the other hand, if the Western Allies play no significant part in Czechoslovakia's liberation that country may go the way of Yugoslavia.[14]

The British government and Foreign Office recognised quite clearly that, "non-interference" notwithstanding, the army that liberated a country and above all its capital would call its consequent political tune. Hence the urgency of their requests for a Western advance to Prague. On 30 April, on Churchill's instructions, the British Chiefs of Staff requested that Eisenhower "take advantage of any suitable opportunity that may arise to advance into Czechoslovakia."[15] By 4 May the weakness of Nazi resistance on the Western front meant that such an opportunity had arisen and Eisenhower attempted to take full advantage of it. He cabled the US Military Mission in Moscow and asked them to inform the Soviet High Command that his forces were about to embark on a thrust into Czechoslovakia. Once they had reached the agreed boundary line, "we are prepared, if the situation so dictates, to advance in Czechoslovakia to the line of the Vltava (Moldau) and Elbe rivers, to clear the west banks of the rivers in conjunction with the indicated Soviet move to clear the east banks."[16] The Vltava flowed through the centre of Prague!

The Soviet response to this suggestion was predictable. Already at Teheran Stalin had recognised and accepted the social and political cleavage that would result from the military division of Europe. At the point of victory he and his generals were hardly likely to permit Western armies to penetrate into their zone of influence. General Antonov's restrained reply said that, "In order to avoid a possible confusion of forces, the Soviet command asks General Eisenhower not to move the Allied forces in Czechoslovakia east of the originally intended line."[17] This Eisenhower felt obliged to agree to, and he informed Antonov and his own Third Army accordingly.[18]

German military and political activity in the last phases of the war consciously aimed to provoke these kinds of conflicts amongst the Big Three. The Nazis recognised the peculiar character of the alliance that opposed them and tried to split that alliance, utilising the fears among the British and American ruling classes of the contagion of Bolshevism spreading through Europe. Politically, the Nazis attempted to conclude separate agreements with their Western opponents. Militarily, they shifted the whole emphasis to a defence of the Eastern front. By 25 March only 26 German divisions remained on the Western front, as against 170 on the Eastern.[79] In Czechoslovakia the Nazis made the advance for American troops easy, and even encouraged them. As Murphy wrote on 11 May, "German High Command strongly urged that USA forces should undertake such a mission [to enter deeply into Czechoslovakia] and the opposition to the forces would apparently have been insignificant."[20] Sections of the Protectorate government and various Czech bourgeois and officer groupings attempted to contact the US forces with a view to their entering Prague and establishing favourable political conditions for these elements.[21] Despite this and pressure from the State Department[22] Eisenhower stuck to his position, and ordered no US troops into Prague when the insurgents rose on 5 May or during the subsequent days of fierce battle.

Considerations of a general and more specific political and military character influenced this decision. On a general political level it was too dangerous for the United States to endanger the wartime coalition in such a direct way at this point. While for the British the war was virtually over, the USA still had to defeat the Japanese and in May, with the viability of the A-bomb in doubt, they were relying on the Soviet armies to aid them in this battle. Hence for the USA the military and anti-Nazi aspect of the coalition remained central, and more long-term political considerations had to be subordinated to this.

With regard to the rising itself, political factors again came into play. Early in the morning of 7 May the Germans officially surrendered at Rheims, yet 7 and 8 May were days of fierce combat in Prague. The Nazis fought tenaciously for Prague because many of their escaping armies had to pass through the city as they fled to American-held areas, and it was only on 9 May with the entry of Soviet troops into the capital that the serious fighting ended. Without breaking the agreement with the Soviet Chiefs of Staff, Eisenhower could have taken several steps to ensure an earlier cessation of hostilities. Dive bombers could have been sent in. Roadblocks could have been set up, refusing German troops entry into American-held areas and thereby removing the incentive for their flight. Eisenhower could have instructed Admiral Doenitz to broadcast an order to German troops to lay down their arms, a step taken only on 10 May. The cause of American indifference to the fate of the rising lay in their estimation of its political character. Despite the spontaneous origins of the rising, the control which the Czech National Council obtained over the radio gave the impression that it was firmly in command of the situation. Thus, in addition to their wider political considerations, it is probable that the Americans felt no urgent desire to aid a communist-dominated rising. American popularity among the Czech people fell to a low ebb, in contrast to the rapturous welcome which greeted the entry of the Red Army units into Prague.[23]

Above all else the episode highlighted the decisive role of international politics in determining the character of the new Czechoslovak republic. This was realised not only by the politicians and military chiefs of the Big Three but also by leading Czech politicians. In his autobiography Václav Kopecký recounts these days, when he was travelling with the Presidential convoy from Košice to Bratislava. As reports came to them of American troops reaching Western Bohemia and advancing towards Prague Beneš and Drtina cheered noticeably. Kopecký became depressed, for he considered that if American troops occupied Prague the Košice government would have to stay in Bratislava or Brno and that the republic would be split in two, as Germany later was.

When they arrived in Bratislava on 9 May, they learned that Prague had been liberated by Soviet troops that day, much to Kopecký's relief.[24] His fears and Beneš's hopes clearly illustrated the crucial political role played by the Allied armies. Kopecký did not believe the left was strong enough to guarantee the establishment of the National Front government in Prague, if the US army had been there. The rest of the communist leadership took a similar view. Therein lay the vital political significance to the question of which army liberated Prague. The Red Army victory gave the Czech communists a tremendous propaganda weapon and enormously heightened the sympathy and solidarity the Czech people felt for the Soviet Union. Above all, it ensured that the communist strategy expressed concretely in the Košice government and its programme could develop in conditions suitable to it. Not for the first time, nor the last, international politics was decisive in determining the course of Czechoslovakia's domestic development.

II
The National and Democratic Revolution

5
The Košice Programme

The Czechoslovak government returned to Prague on 10 May. Its Košice programme, and the government responsible for its fulfilment, embodied the concept of a national, democratic revolution, some aspects of which had already been developed during the war. Considered schematically, the issues of the orientation of Czechoslovak foreign policy, Czech-Slovak relations and the position of the German and Magyar minorities constituted the major "national" aspects of the revolution. The issues of state administration, the "physical" organs of the state, land reform and the ownership, control and management of industrial and financial enterprises represented the major "democratic" areas of the revolution. The programme was to be carried out by a National Front government of Czechs and Slovaks composed of those political parties which had drawn up the programme.

Already before their meetings in Moscow the representatives of the political parties in emigration had decided that there would be a limitation on the number of political parties permitted in the post-war republic. Four parties were to be permitted, based on the Czech Lands: the Czechoslovak Communist Party (KSČ); the Social Democratic Party (SDS); the National Socialist Party (NSS); and the Popular Party (LS). In Slovakia two parties were to be legally permitted, the Slovak Democrats (DS) and the Slovak Communist Party (KSS), which at this time was a separate organisation. The basis of this decision was that only those parties which had been involved in the fight for national independence had any right to operate as political organisations in the post-war republic. All those parties which had openly or implicitly collaborated with the Nazi occupation had forfeited their right to exist as such. This ban shifted the whole arena of Czechoslovak politics to the left, as it removed the pre-war conservative and neo-fascist parties from the political scene. The ban on these parties signified a breach of the pre-war liberal democratic order. No longer were parties permitted to exist *a priori*. The new concept of popular democracy, central to the national democratic revolution, meant that those parties whose policies and actions had threatened the independence and indeed the very existence of the nation were barred from participating in the new republic.

Having decided the political basis of the new republic, the four Czech-based parties, along with representatives of the Slovak National Council, agreed to the composition of the first postwar government during their meetings in Moscow from 27-29 March. Zdeněk Fierlinger, a Social Democrat and the government's wartime ambassador in Moscow, was chosen as Prime Minister, and there were five deputy Prime Ministers, one each from the other parties. Each party received three of the twenty-two ministerial posts, with non-party specialists or personalities of national significance named in the remaining four ministries.[1] As the communists were the strongest element in the country, they had choice of ministries; and as elsewhere in Eastern Europe, they selected the key posts of Ministry of the Interior (Nosek) and Ministry of Information (Kopecký), while Ďuris occupied the important Ministry of Agriculture. Thus central strategic posts in the government were occupied by communists.

Significantly, the government was composed entirely of representatives of the foreign resistance. In Moscow it was agreed that after liberation each party had the right to exchange its representatives in the government with personalities from the domestic resistance movement. No party made use of this right. This was due in some cases to a party's strength lying abroad; in the case of the KSČ and KSS it was due to the political positions that their domestic leaderships had adopted, which were at variance with those of the foreign leadership. Just as many of the policy demands of the domestic resistance were ignored at the Moscow meetings, so the claims of the leaders of that resistance to posts in the government were overlooked.

The programme delineated three major issues which had to be resolved if the Czechoslovak republic were to be guaranteed a permanent existence as an independent, national state. Firstly, a Slav line had to be the basis of the nation's foreign policy;

secondly, there had to be full equality in Czech-Slovak relations; thirdly, the German and Magyar minorities had to be transferred from Czechoslovak territory. These constituted the major "national" aspects of the revolution.

The twenty-year treaty of friendship between the USSR and Czechoslovakia was to form the basis of the republic's post-war foreign policy. With the memory of Munich and her betrayal by Britain and France, alliance with her powerful Slav neighbour was viewed as the most reliable guarantee of Czechoslovakia's future independence. The treaty with the Soviet Union was to be the bulwark against any revival of pan-Germanism; a bulwark whose efficacy had been highlighted by the successes of the Red Army. All sections of the Resistance approved of the treaty, which was very popular among the population as a whole. To the KSČ the treaty with the Soviet Union was a primary concern and its achievement was a major success, since it completely reorientated the direction of Czechoslovak foreign policy. The KSČ was seen as the main architect of the treaty and gained widespread popular support in consequence. In accord with its strategy, it argued for the treaty in terms of Slav solidarity, and in this way conceived of the alliance as one of the major components of the national revolution.

Another major task of the Košice programme was to remove the national conflict that had existed between Czechs and Slovaks in the first republic. This was done by ensuring that the new republic represented a common state composed of two equal nations, Czechs and Slovaks. The Slovak National Council was the constitutional representative of the Slovak nation and the legislative and executive authority on Slovak territory. The central government was to perform common tasks of the republic in closest co-operation with it. Discussions in June 1945 between a Slovak delegation and representatives of the government clarified the areas of competence devolving upon the Slovak National Council. These were initial steps taken to overcome the oppression which the Slovaks had experienced at the hands of the Czechs during the first republic, so that both could play an equal role in the new republic.

The third major "national" aspect of the revolution concerned the transfer of the German and Magyar minority populations. During his discussions in Moscow in December 1943, Beneš had gained Stalin's assent to the proposal to transfer Germans in Czechoslovakia to Germany at the end of the war. Anti-fascists, communists, democrats and all abroad who participated in the anti-fascist struggle from the ranks of the German population were to be exempt. Beneš stated: "The future republic shall be a state of Czechs, Slovaks and Carpathian Ukrainians. It shall be a national and Slav state."[2]

The KSČ leadership agreed with this policy. They, following the Soviet example, had attempted to rouse the Czech people to opposition against the Nazis primarily on a national basis. The main emphasis of their propaganda appealed to sentiments of Slav solidarity and national unity against German oppression. The logical corollary to this was to make nationalism and Slav sentiment a plank of post-war policy, and it was this that was agreed upon at Moscow.

The niceties and qualifications about anti-fascist Germans were quickly lost in the nationalist xenophobia encouraged by this policy. General Svoboda, in a speech to the officers of new Czechoslovak units in February 1945, stated: "The new republic shall be a better republic, more socially just. In it there shall be no place for Germans and Magyars."[3] *Mladá Fronta* proclaimed, "The whole German nation is responsible for Lidice."[4]

Article 8 of the Košice programme dealt with the position of the German and Hungarian minorities.[5] Since most of them had aided foreign aggression and participated in actions aimed at exterminating the Czech nation, the new republic had to take drastic action against them. A population transfer would solve the problem permanently. This policy was formally agreed by the Allies and incorporated into the Potsdam Agreement, the Allied Control Council being given the responsibility for the transfer.[6] The main bulk of the population transfer occurred during 1946 and by the end of that year it was estimated that 2,232,541 Germans had been transferred from Czechoslovakia since the end of the war.[7]

The policy of population transfer was enthusiastically welcomed by all classes of the Czechoslovak population. Their wartime experience at the hands of the occupying Nazi forces had hardened their nationalist, anti-German feelings. The Czech nation was to revenge Nazi brutality by expelling Germans from their midst. These strong nationalist feelings were encouraged and bolstered by the policy of the government, of all the political parties and by the press. They found expression among the Czech working class. The resistance journal *Boj o zítřek*, produced by the communist partisan group *Prokop Holý*, was rife with anti-German sentiment. The paper issued calls "against the German invaders" and to "prepare for the fight of the Czech nation against the hated Germans".[8] The factory council at the Zbrojovka arms works passed a resolution on 30 May 1945 calling for all Germans living in Brno to be interned, prior to their expulsion.[9] *Práce* pursued a similar line. A headline on the Potsdam transfer agreement commented, "Victory for our viewpoint. We get rid of all Germans".[10] The policy of differentiating anti-fascist Germans from the rest disappeared under the waves of nationalist hysteria.

Four-square behind this policy stood the KSČ. *Rudé právo* stated the position clearly on 2 August: "Away with the Germans from our lands! We shall clean our border (lands) with an iron hand."[11] Those anti-fascist Germans who had worked in partisan groups in Northern Bohemia were ignored; pre-war German communists who had spent the war in concentration camps or abroad often returned to find themselves ineligible for party membership; others who had been leading figures pre-war were given minor posts of responsibility.[12] When rank-and-file communists in Podmokly produced a dual-language newspaper *Rudý prapor/Rote Fahne*, the KSČ Central Secretariat quickly issued a statement saying that the periodical "was published without its knowledge, and on the orders of the Central Secretariat was immediately stopped".[13] The unity of the nation and Slav peoples had become more important to the KSČ than the unity of workers irrespective of their nationality. The KSČ attempted to justify this policy theoretically. At the Eighth Party Congress in 1946 Václav Kopecký, the leading party ideologue, said:

> And we are carrying out this most national, anti-German programme as communists, who have always proclaimed internationalism and who are not giving up and will not give up the idea of the international brotherhood of workers.
> We emphasise that our implacable anti-German viewpoint is not the expression of some kind of race hatred but is the product of our tragic experiences, is the expression of

the interest in security for our national and state future. Our anti-German viewpoint is identical with the interests of Slav solidarity, with the interests of freedom, with the interests of progress.[18]

Rather than countering the nationalistic, chauvinistic feelings prevalent among many Czech people at the end of the war the KSČ adopted a similar stance as a way of achieving easy popularity. In 1945 two main strands of thought can be discerned among the Czech working class: one was a nationalistic, anti-German strand; the other was a rudimentary, socialist strand. Quite often the two coexisted. Yet the defensive Popular Front strategy of the KSČ precluded it from developing the latter, whereas it fitted in neatly with the former. The logic of this resulted in the policy of wholesale population transfer. The alternative, that of putting on trial those accused of war crimes and leaving the remainder of the German population alone, was not considered. KSČ policy actually encouraged nationalistic ideas among the Czech working class. The political rationale for the policies of land reform and nationalisation sprang from these nationalist, anti-German, anti-Magyar premises. The limitations of the KSČ approach were clearly shown here. Not only, according to it, was this not the time for socialist revolution, but in the fight for KSČ policies the whole emphasis and character of their propaganda was such as to undermine the development of a socialist understanding among working people.

Democratising the state

The character of the new state administrative and security apparatus was one of the most crucial spheres of the revolution. The programme proposed a decisive rupture with the former state machinery. Popular democracy had to create new forms of power as the best method of guaranteeing its future development.

The reactionary attitude of most of the upper echelons of the state administration, highlighted by their frequent collaboration during the occupation, allied with the undemocratic character of the system, made its transformation one of the most urgent tasks facing the new republic.[15] The KSČ leadership laid great emphasis on this question and in particular stressed the vital role of national committees as popular democratic organs of local administration.[16]

During the war, following calls from the Moscow communists and Czechoslovak government in London, many illegal national committees were formed and worked closely with the resistance. On liberation national committees emerged throughout the country and took responsibility for all essential administration in the localities: the continuation of food supplies; the provision of security arrangements; safeguarding of health and welfare services; purging of Germans and collaborators from public service; renewal of production in the factories, and much else besides.[17] National committees were elected in every village and town, with parity among the candidates from the political parties, as there was in the government. A district and provincial structure was built up on this basis, and it was from the national committees that the Provisional National Assembly was elected. This met on 28 October 1945 and continued until general parliamentary elections were held in May 1946.

The national committees represented a new system of public administration based on democratic rather than bureaucratic principles, shown most clearly by open election as against the previous system of state appointments. The destruction of the pre-war administrative apparatus and its replacement by the national committees was an integral part of the national democratic revolution. National committees also helped to democratise other sections of the state apparatus, notably the local judiciary and police, these being purged of all collaborationist elements.

During any revolutionary social change a crucial sphere over which it is essential to gain control is the military. If the Czechoslovak working class and allied sections were to be the leading forces in the new republic, then the army along with other areas of the state apparatus had to be transformed. Although KSČ leaders at the time maintained a "low profile" on this question there can be no doubt that they understood its significance. At the Moscow discussions they staunchly defended their proposed military reforms against attack from NSS and LS representatives. The core of the KSČ's measures was incorporated into the Košice programme. Article 3 stated that "the organisation, equipment and training of the new Czechoslovak armed forces will be identical with the organisation, equipment and training of the Red Army", while "the government intends to put an end once and for all to the so-called non-political attitude of the armed forces". Education officers were to be assigned as deputies to every commanding officer.[18]

In accord with the programme, the new Czechoslovak army was purged of all officers who had collaborated. The education officers and military press helped to gain support for the national democratic revolution among the ranks. A policy of close cooperation with the Red Army was followed, with full use being made of the Red Army's military experience and the most able Czechoslovak officers being sent to the highest Soviet military schools, including the Military Academy, where they received technical and ideological training.[19]

These measures reduced the danger of the government succumbing to a right-wing putsch. They were also another indication that Czechoslovakia lay clearly within the Soviet Union's orbit of influence. The personal and organisational connections arising from this training had implications far beyond the realm of national defence. They strengthened the sympathetic orientation of the leading circles of the Czechoslovak army to the Soviet Union.

In the immediate post-liberation period some sections of the working class wanted the revolutionary guards to form part of the armed state apparatus. These armed detachments of workers had taken part in the final risings and then, along with the works councils, assumed responsibility for factory security and the purging of collaborators in the enterprises. Some sections wanted these revolutionary guards brought under ÚRO leadership in order to develop the national democratic revolution into a socialist revolution immediately.[20] This syndicalist current opposed the attempts led by the KSČ to bring the revolutionary guards under state control, and there was strong opposition to the policy of disarming them. On 16 May ÚRO issued a call for the establishment of revolutionary guards in all factories and considered these armed units to be the major force for internal security and under the control of ÚRO. This view was unacceptable to the KSČ, and Zápotocký and others argued against this position. After discussion the Ministry of the Interior issued an order on 16 June dissolving all armed units existing outside the army and police. It was agreed that ÚRO could establish factory militia, but their role and function was to be much more limited than that originally intended for the revolutionary guards.[21]

Internal security was to be under the strict control of the Minister of the Interior, Václav Nosek.

Land reform represented another sphere of the democratic revolution. The Košice programme declared that all land belonging to Germans, Hungarians and traitors was to be confiscated.[22] Almost all large landholdings were encompassed within this category and they were to be divided up into private smallholdings. The takeover of landed estates occurred as liberation proceeded, and their division into smallholdings was already being undertaken by the time the presidential decrees on the confiscation, allocation and settlement of land held by enemies and traitors were issued in June and July 1945. Under this decree 7,280,774 acres were confiscated, representing almost a quarter of the country's territory. Of this total 3,200,987 acres were forest land. About 300,000 proprietors lost their land, 239,000 of them in the border regions of Bohemia and Moravia, which were resettled with Czech and Slovak citizens.[23] The land reform policy was crucial in securing the support of the peasantry, small farmers and rural landless behind the national democratic revolution. It welded them into a closer alignment with the working class and other working strata than had existed previously. Thereby political space was denied to those who wished to use the rural strata as a base from which to challenge the Košice programme and the national democratic revolution.

6
Unity and Diversity: The Politics of Nationalisation

Overall a considerable degree of unity had been achieved both within the government and in the country on those aspects of the national and democratic revolution dealt with in the previous chapter. Widespread popular enthusiasm had been displayed for the Soviet Union, for the policy of population transfer, for the national committees and for the land reform. However, with another major "democratic" aspect of the Košice programme a variety of conflicts was to appear. The economic sections of the programme had been left vague, and it was on the issues of the ownership and control of industrial and financial enterprises, the degree of nationalisation and the functions of the workers' councils, that the sharpest conflicts of the immediate post-war months came, as the Czech working class pushed for measures to ensure that the national and democratic revolution assumed a wider social character. The presidential decrees on nationalisation and works councils issued on 24 October were to express the interplay of the differing class and political forces operating in this situation.

The participation of the Czech working class in the last days of the Resistance had revolutionary implications. The illegal trade unions were closely involved with the final rising, and with the demise of Nazi power, works councils, often aided by armed workers' militias, took control of the factories and enterprises. They purged the enterprises of Germans and collaborators and took the responsibility for the renewal of production.[1] Effectively, the works councils were assuming control of the enterprises and some rapidly set up national managements, like the Ostrava miners on 10 May.[2] On 19 May President Beneš issued decrees for the establishment of national managements in accord with Article 10 of the Košice programme, and with this the setting up of managements by works councils accelerated. In a short time some 10,000 national managements were operating in industrial enterprises. In the Czech Lands this amounted to 45 per cent of the total and accounted for 75 per cent of those employed in industry.[3]

However, national management was recognised as a temporary form of administration for these enterprises and a central political question concerned their future character. During the opening weeks after its return from abroad the KSČ leadership stuck to its original position. In his keynote speech to Slovak communist functionaries at Košice on 8 April Gottwald had maintained that the call should be for national management and that the demand for nationalisation should not be put at this time.[4] Speaking at Ostrava on 21 May Gottwald stated that national management was a first step, but that the fate of these confiscated enterprises would be decided by the next legislature.[5] Gottwald's speeches during May and June contained no explicit mention of nationalisation, while *Rudé právo*, the daily communist newspaper, did not print the statements of the SDS, the Minister of Industry, ÚRO or sections of workers, which came out in support of nationalisation at this time. The political rationale of their position was somewhat baldly stated by Antonín Zápotocký, who returned from six years in a concentration camp to be chosen as the Chairman of ÚRO on 7 June.[6] Addressing trade-union leaders on 21 June, he declared:

> Today we are in a period of national revolution. In the political direction the leading notion is revolutionary democracy; in the economic field we are going in the direction of state, national capitalism. We must not suppose we are already building a socialist state. The struggle against Nazism was the fight of all strata of the nation, which it was necessary to unite without regard of classes for its defeat. That also applies on a world scale.
> We are now in the period of revolutionary democracy, which is the first step to socialism. . . . Of course, right now when there is revolutionary democracy and national capitalism, the revolutionary trade-union movement stands in front of two dangers; radical sloganising, and the danger of retreats and complying with capitalism.[7]

Indeed, this was an overstatement of the official KSČ position, which did not consider "national capitalism" to be the main trend of economic policy. Yet Zápotocký was expressing KSČ policy in considering the main impetus of the revolution as national. Hence the key strategic need was for the working class to place itself at the head of the nation and to control and democratise political and state institutions.[8] By contrast, economic questions such as nationalisation were considered of secondary importance and could wait until a National Assembly had been elected. In addition, as they were likely to be divisive of the political unity of the National Front government, the KSČ leadership refrained from raising the issue, and its National Economic Commission did not discuss it.

Other left-wing elements viewed the matter differently. The Social Democratic Party was re-established inside the country on liberation and the policy statement of its Central Preparatory Executive Committee maintained a clear socialist position, with the party's aim being the creation of a socialist order. The statement gave full support to the government and its programme, and gave a firm commitment to the public ownership of the country's natural wealth and energy resources as well as "of key and heavy industry, mines and finance".[9] Already Bohumil Laušman, the Minister of Industry, had stated in a meeting with trade unionists that "in accordance with the intentions of the government, heavy and large industry especially has to be nationalised",[10] while in a speech at Hradec Králové on 10 June he also mentioned his intention of banks being included in the nationalisation programme.[11] The SDS Economic Policy Commission began research on the nationalisation of particular industries[12] while the demand for the nationalisation of the sugar industry and trade was raised.[13] To the SDS the public ownership of the major sectors of the economy was central to their political conception of the new republic, and they displayed none of the early hesitancy nor caution of the KSČ on this question.

At its first plenary session on 16 May ÚRO's position was outlined in the main report given by Jungmann. The trade unions would be the firmest prop of the socialist bloc of parties and would unite all working people behind the government and its programme. This programme included the nationalisation of all property confiscated from Germans, Magyars and collaborators and of all heavy industrial enterprises, institutions of finance capital, energy resources and other raw material resources.[14] Already Czech film workers had demanded the nationalisation of the film and cinematographic industries.[15] On 3 June a conference of the works councils of the mines in the Ostrava region passed a resolution calling for the nationalisation of the mines. On 5 June the Minister of Industry agreed that the district's Central Miners' Commission could formulate detailed nationalisation proposals.[16]

With these developments the KSČ leadership recognised that it had underestimated the strength of feeling on the issue.[17] Before it came out in favour of immediate nationalisation, however, it had to be certain that this would have the support of Beneš and the government, so that the unity of the National Front was preserved. While it was clarifying the position, the party press and leadership maintained their silence on the issue. Communist trade-union leaders adopted a similar stance, Zápotocký's radio broadcast on 14 June not mentioning nationalisation but rather the need "to take decisive industrial and financial enterprises into national management".[18]

The Slovak Democratic Party, Popular Party and the majority of the NSS were quite content to leave the matter for an elected National Assembly. These parties accepted nationalisation, yet wished to retain a considerable private sector within the economy, which could be more easily achieved once the existing popular radicalism had waned. Yet popular pressure would tolerate no delay and President Beneš, sensitive to the popular mood, recognised this. In a speech at the Škoda Works in Plzeň he mentioned nationalisation in an oblique fashion, stressing that it was a very complex question but that the country would shortly be in a position to undertake the appropriate measures. Škoda would be taken into "a new system of social production".[19]

While the attitude of the government remained unclear, calls for nationalisation increased. The finance section of ÚRO urged that private insurance be taken into public ownership, as it represented an important part of the national economy. They submitted their proposals to the government, the economic ministries and the political secretariats of all political parties.[20] Prague engineering workers discussed the question, and a deputation led by G. Kliment from the works councils of the fifteen largest metal factories in the city demanded the nationalisation of key industries and the planning of production when they saw Laušman on 3 July.[21] On the same day a conference of works councils from the West Bohemian quarries held in Plzeň came out unanimously in favour of the nationalisation of all mines and asked ÚRO to convene a conference to press this demand.[22]

As late as 2 July at a meeting of the National Economic Commission of the KSČ, Frejka, the leading communist economic spokesman, would only consider a proposal to nationalise the arms industry as a special case. When at a meeting of the three-party socialist bloc and ÚRO on 3 July ÚRO representatives asked for the nationalisation of armaments and banks, Frejka said he would have to consult Gottwald before these demands could be included in their joint programme. When the KSČ economic commission met again on 4 July Frejka stated that, "after conversation with Kl. Gottwald it was apparent that the situation has altered to the extent that today we can ask in the economic programme of the political bloc for the nationalisation of all key industry and large industry immediately."[23] Gottwald had reported to the Party Politburo on 3 July on his conversation with Beneš, during which the President had given his approval to nationalisation measures. With this assurance the Politburo passed a resolution giving its support to immediate nationalisation.[24]

Henceforth, the communist press and leadership gave prominence to the question of nationalisation. *Rudé právo* published stories of engineering workers and miners demanding the public ownership of key industries,[25] while on 15 July a lead article appeared, written by Frejka, which explained why nationalisation was the correct policy to pursue for moral, political, national and technical reasons.[26] Whereas calls for nationalisation previously had largely been spontaneous they were now reinforced by the weight and thrust of the KSČ.

Communists in the trade unions and works councils were encouraged to press for nationalisation, while Zápotocký reverted to the original ÚRO position on nationalisation, declaring: "It is in the (Košice) programme, we stand by it, it must be carried out and shall be carried out".[27] Yet the explanation and justification given by the KSČ leadership for nationalisation showed that nationalism rather than anti-capitalism was the impulse behind the policy. The class character of the issue was blurred. It was in the interests of the unity of the nation that the property of enemies and collaborators was to be taken into the hands of the state. With his first public mention of nationalisation on 9 July, Gottwald said that German and Hungarian enterprises were to be taken completely into public ownership,[28] while at a KSČ District conference at Ostrava he said bluntly: "The government wants this time to do away completely and definitively with the consequences of the (battle of) White Mountain".[29] In the same speech he vehemently denied that the communists wanted to nationalise wherever possible. Such a policy would have contradicted the entire KSČ political strategy, which included allying with that part of the bourgeoisie which had participated in the anti-fascist struggle. The nationalist emphasis of the argumentation for public ownership meant that those Czech bourgeois elements which had not collaborated were unlikely to find their enterprises nationalised and could continue to support the government and its national democratic revolution. As Gottwald said at a rally at Krč, Prague, nobody in the government intended to nationalise medium or small industry or craft trades, and that "whoever spreads such tales is involving himself with the spreading of enemy, anti-state propaganda". He assured his audience that alongside the nationalised sector private enterprise would have wide areas in which to operate, and that in these "it shall be fully supported by the government".[30]

What was at fault was not the KSČ's goal of uniting the broadest majority behind the government programme. The problem lay in the KSČ's caution in moving on from its wartime position and in seeing that opportunities were present in these months that could facilitate the transition to socialism. First, the KSČ underestimated the popular consciousness on economic questions. Secondly, when the party did recognise the mood, it argued the case for nationalisation almost entirely in nationalist terms.

On 11 July at a meeting at the Ministry of Industry, Laušman for the first time officially announced that key and heavy industry, mines and mineral wealth, finance, insurance and the banks would be nationalised.[31] His statement alluded to the pressures that had been brought to bear. Originally the government had supposed that the system of national management would be completely sufficient until a National Assembly was elected and could make its decision. So at first the Minister had made no preparation for nationalisation decrees. However, this had proved unsatisfactory, for "the nation has called for it". Since Laušman considered himself a servant of the nation, he, along with the rest of the government, had been unable to disregard this call.[32] The NSS, Popular Party and Slovak Democratic Party accepted that nationalisation was on the government agenda and the central political question shifted to its extent and exact character. On 18 July a central government working committee on nationalisation was set up with representatives from the political parties, ÚRO, the Central Association of Industry and technical experts. Laušman was its chairman and appropriate subcommissions were set up. Trade unionists headed several of these.

The popular groundswell of support for nationalisation that existed before the KSČ and the government had come out openly for immediate nationalisation now took on a tidal force, as all sections of the trade-union and labour movement put forward their demands. From trade-union branches, works councils, district conferences, district trades councils and national delegate meetings, calls for the implementation of public ownership poured into the government, the Ministry of Industry, ÚRO and the offices of the political parties. Three major phases can be discerned within this upsurge: first, resolutions were mainly concerned with mining and heavy industry; from the end of July resolutions came in on banking and finance; and finally, during mid-August, calls came for the nationalisation of industries that had not previously been considered as "key" sectors.

On 7 July a conference of works councils in the North Bohemian coalfields was held in Most, and this demanded the public ownership of coal. On 9 July a delegation handed their demands to Laušman. These were for the immediate nationalisation of all mines without compensation, and there was a warning that if this were not done then co-operation between the miners and the government could not continue.[33] Similarly, a miners' meeting in Kladno passed a resolution on 21 July welcoming government moves to nationalise key and heavy industry.[34] At an all-trade-union regional conference for Greater Prague held on 14 July in the Lucerna Hall the 1,500 delegates representing all sections of Prague workers passed a resolution backing the government and its programme, especially welcoming the proposals for nationalisation.[35] Further substantial support came at a large conference of national committees and works councils in Bratislava, where a motion was unanimously passed supporting the initiative taken to nationalise key industry, banks and insurance and declaring that Slovak workers would use all their strength in backing such measures.[36] Throughout July the core of the Czechoslovak working class expressed its wholehearted support for the proposals.

Towards the end of July and beginning of August a second wave of petitions and resolutions was sent to the government from factories, offices and localities, prominent among them being those from workers in financial institutions. The works council at Živnostenská Bank sent off a resolution to Fierlinger, Šrobár and Laušman after a meeting held on 17 July declaring that all the employees welcomed the proposal to nationalise trading banks as a further step in the economic reconstruction of the people's republic.[37] The employees of the Prague Credit Bank demanded the public ownership of the banks at a meeting on 6 August,[38] while on 10 August at a works councils delegates' meeting of all banks there was a unanimous vote for the nationalisation of all joint-stock banks.[39] A meeting of employees of the Czech Union Bank on 21 August supported the call for the nationalisation of the trading banks. At a huge gathering of works councils of Greater Prague in the Lucerna Hall on 23 August, Laušman confirmed that joint-stock banks were to be nationalised, since this complemented the proposals for key industry. The two went together, he maintained, and he then said that insurance was likely to be nationalised as well,[40] a demand that the 17,000 insurance workers of Greater Prague voiced a few days later.[41]

During the middle of August demands came to widen the areas of industry to be taken into public ownership to include the chemical, pharmaceutical, shoe, leather, rubber and gramophone industries. A meeting of works council delegates in the paper industry on 14 August unanimously passed a resolution demanding the nationalisation of all paper mills, 74 per cent of which were already under national management. They sent a delegation to Laušman, who agreed that paper mills were a key area of the economy, but said a decision as to their nationalisation was still to be made.⁴² The sugar workers held a conference of all works councils in the sugar industry in the Czech Lands in Prague and discussed the economic and social problems facing their industry. After a long, detailed debate it was agreed that this large, economically important industry, which had been in the hands of a reactionary, agrarian clique before the war, should be transferred into the hands of the state. The whole industry had to be nationalised.⁴³ A similar conference of all works councils in the distillery industry made a call for the immediate nationalisation of their industry.⁴⁴

The response of the parties

As the pressure from below for nationalisation mounted, and as workers increased the range of their demands, significant differences began to appear among the parties of the National Front. A considerable area of common agreement did exist amongst the parties on the question. The NSS management committee had reiterated its position in favour of the nationalisation of coal, energy, iron, rolling mills, engineering, arms and chemical industries on 10 September.⁴⁵ At the major government meeting on 13 September Stránský said that "the National Socialists at the meetings in Moscow reckoned completely on nationalisation".⁴⁶ At the same meeting Procházka of the Popular Party said: "We are for the nationalisation of the mines, energy, arms and key, large industrial enterprises",⁴⁷ while Ursíny gave the general assent of the Slovak Democrats. Beneš, similarly, agreed to the nationalisation of finance and heavy industry before the establishment of a National Assembly.⁴⁸ With the KSČ, SDS and ROH solidly backing the proposals, they were due to be decreed by 20 September. However, some technical delays occurred and, more significantly, opposition to several aspects of the proposals began to be raised. The formulation of the government decrees on nationalisation was to take more than a month, with the government meeting twice daily at times.

During this period the political trends contained within the government and the country as a whole emerged more clearly. There existed two fundamental groupings: one composed of the Popular Party, Slovak Democrats and many National Socialists, who, to varying degrees, desired a considerable sector of the economy left in private ownership; and that of the Communists, Social Democrats, trade unionists and some National Socialists, who desired widespread nationalisation. The left contained within it a further significant if somewhat ill-defined division. Elements of the trade-union and SDS leaderships supported nationalisation proposals which extended far beyond the bounds of the original Košice programme, proposals which did not subscribe merely to "nationalist" criteria. They supported those demands which came from workers in many industries and enterprises during August and September for their particular industry to be taken into public ownership. Against this the KSČ leadership and those areas of ROH, especially the ÚRO Presidium, where veteran communists held sway, were more concerned with preserving the overall unity of the National Front. They were very wary of supporting more extensive nationalisation proposals, whose enactment could threaten the class and political alliances on which the National Front was based. It was within the complex of discussions and agitation over the extent of nationalisation, the questions of compensation and of its timing, that these different political trends emerged.

There was broad acceptance among the parties of the National Front for taking into public ownership all mining industry and large enterprises in heavy industry. The precise details on these areas were discussed at later government meetings, but they were not to evoke major controversies. The question of nationalising the banks and insurance companies was the matter of greater disagreement. The Slovak Democrats and the Popular Party were opposed to the proposal, as indeed were the NSS.[49] Their statement of 10 September had not mentioned this. Yet given that the vague Košice formulation of placing industrial enterprises and the monetary and credit system "under state control" had been taken by National Socialist speakers to signify nationalisation, they were unable to oppose the proposal effectively. The considerable popular pressure for this demand, which bank and insurance employees had shown in August, continued, with many works councils and trade-union organisations including nationalisation of banks and insurance companies in the list of their demands.[50] Thus, while there were complications in the drafting of the decrees on banks and insurance, it was not the question over which the major conflicts arose. In his speech at

Brno on 24 September Prokop Drtina stated that the NSS supported the nationalisation of the banks as well as large industry,[51] and the decrees were drawn up without significant disagreements.

Further demands

It was on the issue of extending nationalisation beyond the strictly defined boundaries of the Košice Programme that the main battles were fought in the government. What was encompassed within the programme depended on the interpretation given to the phrase "key enterprises in industry". During September further sections of workers in industries which had not previously been considered as being within this category sent in resolutions to the government and to their trade-union leaders, demanding that nationalisation apply to the large concerns in their industries as well. The employees of the Královédvorská textile factory demanded the nationalisation of the whole textile industry.[52] At a conference of works councils and trade-union branches of employees of Prague trading houses, the situation in their trade, especially with regard to national management, was discussed in detail. A resolution was unanimously agreed upon, which called for trading houses to be nationalised as the only way to place them on a solid basis.[53] *Právo lidu* carried an article on 23 September supporting demands for the nationalisation of the pharmaceutical industry. Workers in Plzeň breweries convened a meeting on 4 September and sent a resolution to Laušman, Fierlinger, Majer and Gottwald supporting the nationalisation of key industries and banks. Their resolution went on to argue the case for the nationalisation of Plzeň breweries, one-third of which had been owned by Germans and another third by collaborators.[54] At a beer festival gathering in Prague on 20 September the chairman of the breweries' works council asked Majer to nationalise the industry.[55] From works councils and national managements in the foodstuffs industry came resolutions asking for their sector to be nationalised, and an article in *Rudé právo* stated that as a result the government would have to discuss these new proposals.[56] Further support for these proposals came from a meeting of works council delegates from chocolate and sugar factories in Bohemia and Moravia. The delegates demanded that all large enterprises in the foodstuffs industry be nationalised.[57] Popular pressure for nationalisation of the sugar industry mounted. At a national conference of sugar workers on 2 October organised by ÚRO, delegates rejected proposals for a co-operative system and demanded unconditional nationalisation.[58] Works councils from five sugar refineries sent in resolutions calling for the public ownership of their industry.[59]

Again, the response of the communist leadership to this further popular upsurge was cautious. Pursuing a Popular Front strategy, which at the *political* level meant alliance and co-operation with other political parties, also required, at the *economic* level, support for a multi-sectoral economy. While the KSČ supported some of the demands to extend the area of nationalisation, they opposed the more radical proposals which would have resulted in the public sector dominating the economy and thereby undermining the political framework of the National Front. An article by Kolár in late September gave communist support to the calls for the public ownership of large sugar works, distilleries and breweries,[60] yet no mention was made of other areas such as wholesale trade, while communist spokesmen maintained their position that medium enterprises were not to be affected. *Rudé právo* gave widespread coverage to the general resolutions works councils and trade-union branches were passing in support of nationalisation, yet was careful in its reporting of new demands. The calls for public ownership of trading houses and of the textile industry were not reported, nor was the initial call of the Plzeň brewery workers. Their omission cannot have been accidental.

Antonín Zápotocký fulfilled a vital role here. He was rapidly appointed to the KSČ Politburo[61] and as a veteran, trusted communist of long standing and experience he was part of the inner-party leadership. He was a key figure in ensuring that his party's strategy was carried out in the trade unions. He used the authority and power of his position as chairman of ÚRO to keep official trade-union policy closely aligned to the government. In this he was aided by other veteran communist trade unionists, notably Josef Kolský, Jura and Malík, who were co-opted to the ÚRO Plenum along with Zápotocký on 7 June.[62] At the ÚRO Plenum meeting of 18 July Zápotocký's restraining influence was apparent when he said, "We must keep to the government programme: the nationalisation of key industry. The rest shall be solved later".[63]

The National Economic Commission of ÚRO was extremely active on the nationalisation issue. One of its members, O. Mrázek wrote in a pamphlet published in August: "At the present time of transition our immediate task is . . . the creation of the bases of a socialist order, and that is first of all by nationalisation and consistent democratisation in the economic field".[64] This expressed the political approach of the commission which desired further extensive nationalisation and supported the demands of sections of the membership for this. At the ÚRO Presidium on 22 August Mrázek presented detailed proposals on the extent of nationalisation. He then added that wider nationalisation was necessary, and that key and large enterprises in other sectors of industry, notably liquor and sugar, should be taken into public ownership. "The request of Dr Mrázek that the Presidium authorise him to demand a broadening of nationalisation to further branches of industry was not complied with, since for the time being that would be hasty."[65] Despite this rebuff the National Economic Commission continued to press for further nationalisation measures, as growing rank-and-file demands were made. On 27 September it recommended the nationalisation of all trading houses employing more than 100 people and having an annual turnover in excess of 10 million crowns. Again the ÚRO Presidium refused to back the proposal, Zápotocký considering it to be politically inopportune.[66] The ÚRO Presidium refrained from supporting these more extensive demands and thus weakened their impetus. In accordance with the view of the KSČ leadership, the ÚRO Presidium considered it most important that the unity of the National Front government was not impaired. As Zápotocký wrote in *Práce,* "We refrain, therefore, we trade unionists, at this time, from all actions which would seek to extend the decrees concerning nationalisation to those branches with which nationalisation has not so far dealt".[67]

The Social Democrats came out with a much clearer position of support for extended nationalisation. At a meeting of their management committee on 7 September a resolution was passed which stated that the SDS would rebuff any attempts at compromise on the question of the nationalisation of the joint-stock banks. It went on to declare support for the nationalisation of further sectors in accordance with "the spontaneous call of the people and the demands of the trade-union movement".[68] Their representatives in the government were urged to support such proposals. In the following weeks *Právo lidu* gave an extensive coverage to the nationalisation demands of employees in the new sectors, notably textiles, wholesale trade, breweries, foodstuffs and sugar.[69] The position of the SDS leadership and their daily newspaper was much more combative on this question than their communist counterparts. However, within their ranks a rightwing grouping began to emerge, linked to Majer, and it was from this section of the SDS that opposition to the nationalisation of the sugar industry came.

In the government meetings, from newspaper stories and articles and the overall political campaign during September and October, it became clear that the LS, DS and significant sections of the NSS desired a weaker public sector than was being demanded by the left. At the government meeting on 13 September Procházka had asked for decisions on many industries to be postponed, and Ursíny supported this proposal.[70] Both the LS and the DS tried to limit the extent of nationalisation by arguing that it was going beyond the scope of the Košice programme, the Slovak Democrats being particularly opposed to the nationalisation of the banks and foodstuffs industry. More important was the fact that the NSS began to drift away from the Socialist Bloc. While Stránský at Plzeň on 16 September and Drtina at Brno on 24 September[71] urged speedy publication of the decrees, the NSS press began to emphasise the problems and warn against haste. Taking their cue from the DS and LS they also started openly opposing further nationalisation. Zenkl, as Mayor of Prague, had signed a memorandum asking that Prague power stations should not be nationalised, a proposal that had met a vigorous rebuff from a meeting of the works and enterprise councils of the thirteen major power stations in Bohemia and Moravia.[72] On 19 September in *Svobodné slovo* a strongly-worded article appeared which defended the NSS position on nationalisation. It maintained that it was firmly behind the Košice programme and its nationalisation proposals, and rejected any suggestion that it was holding up the decrees. What was responsible for the delay were the proposals from other industrial sectors for nationalisation, which were reaching the government daily. It was these new proposals exceeding the outlines of Košice that were holding back the decrees.[73] This theme was taken up by Stránský, who wrote on

16 October that the decrees were to be published shortly. He ascribed their delay in publication to the growing number of new targets for nationalisation, "against which even the chairman of ÚRO had to raise his voice in the end".[74]

Implicit in this argument was that the NSS opposed these new proposals and viewed them with hostility. This came out most clearly over the question of the sugar industry. While *Rudé právo* and *Právo lidu* reported the sugar workers' demands, *Svobodné slovo* covered the meeting of delegates representing 4,000 farmers in the Chrudim region who asked the government to run the industry on co-operative lines, with farmers, workers and the state having a say in the management. The same demand came from the Kutná Hora district.[75] The next day an article supported this proposal and considered it an appropriate method of management for the entire foodstuffs industry. The divisions on this question were clear and they had already been the subject of lively debate in the government.[76] The special commission that the government set up of Majer, Kopecký, Ripka and Hála was to arrive at a settlement formally agreed by the meeting on 17 October, which involved concessions by both sides.[77]

This was just one of several clashes in the government concerning the decrees. As a result of popular pressure the extent of nationalisation was broadened beyond the scope envisaged in the Košice programme. Laušman recognised this in a radio broadcast he gave on 19 September when he stated that all large enterprises and not just those in heavy industry, as originally proposed, were liable to nationalisation.[78] It was this development, which took the proposals beyond purely "nationalist" criteria, that evoked the strongest opposition and saw the Czech and Slovak propertied classes begin to organise to defend their interests. Laušman admitted the clashes when in a newspaper interview he said that while "all parties are for nationalisation in principle . . . in some cases we have been at variance with each other".[79]

Yet their room to manoeuvre was considerably restricted by the innumerable demands for nationalisation that came from all sections of the working class throughout September. District and area KSČ organisations encouraged their members to push for these in their factories, pits and plants, while many Social Democrats and unaffiliated socialists took similar initiatives. From works councils, trade-union branches and area organisations resolutions came in support of the nationalisation proposals. The industrial core of the working class — those working in large units of production — reaffirmed their identification with the proposals. Kladno miners sent a deputation to press their demands.[80] Workers in the iron foundries and plants in Prague and Kladno called for the speedy nationalisation of key industry, banks and insurance.[81] Large engineering plants came out in favour of similar demands,[82] as did power-station workers.

A huge number of resolutions, telegrams and letters poured into government, trade-union and newspaper offices daily.[83] *Svobodné slovo* felt compelled to deny allegations that the NSS was responsible for the delays. A meeting of Škoda workers at the start of October sent a telegram to Fierlinger demanding immediate nationalisation.[84] Large demonstrations in Bratislava and Košice on 2 October were organised by the Slovak trade unions.[85] These called for speedy publication of the nationalisation decrees and for the foodstuffs industry to be included in them. The resolution at the SDS Prague District Conference unanimously called for "the nationalisation of large industry, banks and private insurance without delay".[86] A similar call was made by workers at the huge Zbrojovka works in Brno.[87] In this situation the left retained the initiative in the government. They ensured that the decrees were published in one go and presented to the temporary National Assembly. This represented a shift from the earlier position of the KSČ, SDS and ÚRO, when they were in favour of delaying a decision until a proper National Assembly had been elected. While some of the other parties wanted the decrees published in stages, they were unable to present a united front on this question, with the National Socialists in particular being split on the issue.[88] On 24 October President Beneš signed the decrees. Their content signified the dominance of left forces in the government.

The decrees and their scope

A total of 16.4 per cent of enterprises, employing 61.2 per cent of persons engaged in industry, were nationalised (see Table 1).[89] The differences in the extent of nationalisation between industries were a consequence of the diversity of criteria applied to the individual sectors.

Table 1
Nationalised Industries in 1945

Industry	% Employed in nationalised sector	% of Technical Units in nationalised sector
Mines	100	100
Steel furnaces	99.4	97.8
Energy	99.1	88.5
Chemicals	76.4	25.7
Engineering, iron and metal	72.6	22.2
Glass	67.4	10.8
Stone and Ceramics	63.4	24.3
Paper	60.7	19.3
Leather	58.5	6.5
Textiles	54.3	22.1
Clothing	13.1	2.7
Woodworking	26.3	5.7
Sawmills	15.8	5.7
Building	13.4	2.8
Printing	2.7	3.8
Waterworks	0.7	2.5

Table 2
Nationalised Enterprises in the Foodstuffs Industry

Industry	No. of enterprises nationalised	No. employed	% of production held
Sugar beet factories	81	13,819	76%
Distilleries	31	1,601	15.3%
Margarine factories	5	4,472	75%
Confectionery factories	7	2,935	25%
Breweries	6	3,152	30%
Mills	7	947	15%

A separate decree was promulgated for the controversial foodstuffs industry (see Table 2) while further decrees stated that joint-stock companies engaged in banking and financial transactions were to be nationalised,[90] as were all private insurance interests.[91]

In analysing the decrees we can evaluate the success of popular pressure in ensuring the fulfilment both of the original demands and their extension. The continuous pressure from the working class for the nationalisation of all significant sectors of heavy industry and finance committed all parties in the government to the policy. Wherever there was any sign of hesitancy in these areas, further swift expression of workers' attitudes (as in the cases of insurance and the power-stations) ensured that the commitment was upheld. The pressure for more widescale nationalisation succeeded to an extent, notably with the decree that all industrial enterprises employing over 500 people be nationalised and with the decree on the pharmaceutical industry. The calls for widespread public ownership of the paper, sawmill, textile and foodstuffs industries were met to a considerably lesser extent, while wholesale and domestic trade remained entirely within the private sector. As Macura, a leading trade unionist in the foodstuffs industry, noted, "The govenment did not fully accept our proposal and so only parts of the food supply industry were nationalised".[92] Here and elsewhere considerable areas of private enterprise remained, bases on which the Czech and Slovak entrepreneurs aimed to rebuild their strength.

Overall these decrees marked a considerable victory for the left, yet some notable concessions had been made to those who wanted a weaker public sector and who were more sympathetic towards private capital. While the functionaries of the Economic Commission of ÚRO wanted no compensation to be given, the KSČ supported a more restrictive interpretation.[93] Compensation was not to be granted on property owned by: the German Reich, or the Kingdom of Hungary, or their political parties in Czechoslovakia; persons of German or Hungarian nationality except those loyal to the republic; or any Czechoslovak collaborationists.[94] Patriotic Czech and Slovak proprietors were to receive compensation which was to be paid either in cash, in government bonds, or in other stocks and sums to amount to the current price of the property according to the official prices.[95] This had been the demand of the National Socialists and Slovak Democrats. The Communists agreed, stating that the granting of such compensation was proper, as Czechoslovakia was experiencing a national and democratic revolution, not a socialist one.[96]

The possibilities for the renewed growth of private enterprise were secured by a clause in the decrees which ensured that they were not to be retrospective. Article 2 stated that "the regulations of this decree do not apply to enterprises . . . if the conditions for their nationalisation have not obtained until after the day when this decree comes into force".[97] This clause referred to those industrial sectors where enterprises were to be nationalised according to the size of their labour force or of their technical capacity.

Enterprises below the limit which later were to grow beyond it would not be liable for nationalisation. This represented a victory for the right-wing grouping within the National Front, as did the section dealing with the management of the national enterprises. Article 18 stated that "National enterprises should be run according to the rules of commercial enterprise. The State does not vouch for their liabilities",[98] while Article 20 outlined relatively orthodox management procedures. Considerable power was vested in the hands of the managing committees, and they were instructed to operate the enterprise "along sound business lines",[99] the powers of the employees, especially of the works councils, being considerably restricted.

On 24 October the presidential decrees on nationalisation were published, and the following day huge demonstrations were held in 120 towns throughout Czechoslovakia in support of the decrees.[100] In Prague an estimated quarter of a million people crammed into Wenceslas Square to hear President Beneš and political and trade-union leaders.[101] All the major industrial centres in the country had similar demonstrations.

In Kladno 30,000 attended the demonstration. At the rally organised in Ostrava over 100,000 packed into Stalin Square; in Plzeň there were 50,000; in Olomouc 20,000 took part; a similar number attended the demonstration in Mladá Boleslav; while in Bratislava the chairman of the Slovak trade unions addressed a crowd of over 20,000. Other major industrial centres to hold demonstrations included Liberec, Jihlava, Hradec Králové, České Budějovice and Most.[102] The extent of support for the demonstrations illustrated the widespread enthusiasm felt for nationalisation.

The broad character of the decrees reflected the weak position the Czech and Slovak bourgeoisie found themselves in. At the end of the war they were in a state of serious disarray, undermined at a political and ideological level by their attitudes to Munich and the occupation, and at an economic level by wartime German control of the economy. So considerable were these weaknesses that although they had begun to regain their political balance by September, aided by the influx to their parties from those active in the resistance abroad, the political parties which wanted a much more vigorous private sector were never able to form a cohesive bloc. The DS were unable to go beyond the defence of local propertied interests, notably in the banks and food industry, and link up with Czech parties hostile to nationalisation in these spheres. Their provincialism highlighted the political disarray of the propertied classes. Similarly, the LS, where the dominant current was one desiring a strong position for medium-scale enterprises, was unable to link up effectively with like-minded elements within the NSS. The NSS displayed the most complex position, for while it expressed general support for the proposals, the divisions within it emerged when it came to discuss specific problems. By September right-wing trends were becoming apparent and opposing the demands of trade unionists and economists within the NSS, who favoured more extensive nationalisation.[103] It was on the questions of further nationalisation, their retrospective character and compensation that it became evident the NSS was taking up positions pointing to its objectively fulfilling the role of the Czech bourgeoisie, although at this stage they were unable to make these elements cohere. Indeed they approved of the decrees as a whole both because they followed to a marked degree NSS "nationalist" aspirations, and because they hoped that their publication would mark the end of the revolutionary mood. While Ripka gave a positive assessment of the NSS attitude to nationalisation,[104] it is fair to say that their position overall was one favouring a mixed economy. Once matters returned to normal, they hoped the disparity between the public and private sectors could be rectified.

Beneš pursued a similar position. He recognised that "all

modern wars must inevitably assume revolutionary aspects", and hence that the Czech "national, *anti-German* revolution" would result in "some changes in the economic structure of our state".[105] The decrees represented "the beginning of the construction of new forms of ownership *alongside* private ownership and co-operative ownership".[106] Beneš's position remained the same as that he had outlined to Feierabend:[107] he accepted the necessity for changes in the republic's social structure, yet hoped to contain the reforms within a framework which would permit Czech private capital to re-establish itself. Like the NSS he hoped that over a period the disparity between the public and private sector would be equalised and a stable, social democratic republic emerge.

The publication of the nationalisation decrees signified a tremendous victory for the left-wing forces in the republic. The political parties and mass organisations of the Czechoslovak working class — KSČ, SDS and ROH — ensured that all the major centres of industry and finance were placed under public ownership. With over 60 per cent of the economy nationalised, no significant large-scale agglomerations of private capital remained. Above all, the monopoly segment of the pre-war Czechoslovak bourgeoisie had disappeared. As Gottwald wrote in *Rudé právo*, "With the nationalisation of the main sections of our national economy, the widest strata of the nation are given the guarantee that the results of their difficult construction work shall not go to the benefit of individuals or exploiting groups, but rather to the benefit of all".[108]

The achievement of such widescale nationalisation, while the unity of the National Front was maintained, was viewed by the KSČ as an enormous political victory. It could be argued that this victory justified the cautious pragmatism that characterised their whole approach to the nationalisation issue. What was achieved in the way of nationalisation was the optimum that could have been gained without fracturing the unity of the National Front and provoking the government crisis which the Gottwald leadership feared.[109] However, the argument is not really tenable. During the first two months after liberation, while the KSČ refused to raise the issue publicly, the SDS, ÚRO and workers in various industries demanded immediate nationalisation. If the KSČ had given a similar lead during this time, the revolutionary tempo would have been considerably increased, especially as this was the period when right-wing forces were in greatest disarray and widely discredited. The two-month delay gave these forces a breathing space, and by September they had regrouped sufficiently to be able to defend some of their interests.

The question here is not whether the whole economy could have been nationalised with the KSČ taking the matter up earlier, but rather of approaching the issue in a qualitatively different way, which would have emphasised class criteria as well as national ones. Such an approach was best expressed by Mrázek. He wrote that the key pillar of the national revolution against fascism had been the working class, and it saw "the definitive securing of our independence only in a socialist order". This was not possible at present, so the demand was for a programme which would lay the basis for such an order by consistent socialisation.[110] This outlined the connection between the present policies and socialism, whereas in the statements and propaganda of the KSČ no such links were made. The main thrust of the argument for nationalisation was based on nationalism rather than anti-capitalism. Thus Kolár, in the Communist Party magazine *Tvorba*, wrote: "We speak in the economic field of our state life about the nationalisation and democratisation of the economy as the application nationally of revolutionary principles for the economy. By nationalisation we understand the transfer of the property of Germans, Hungarians, traitors and collaborators to the hands of the Czech and Slovak nation".[111]

There were theoretical reasons why the KSČ did not pursue this alternative approach. Contemporary communist theorisation on socialist societies viewed them as monolithic social formations. Following the existing Soviet model, the complement to a socialised economy was a single-party state. Yet if at a political level several different parties were in existence, then there had to be a multi-sectoral economy, since each party was considered to represent fundamentally differing class interests. The possibility of several parties operating within an economy dominated by the public sector was not envisaged by Communist politicians. Thus to have supported further extensive nationalisation would have inevitably threatened the unity of the parties within the National Front and undermined the whole strategy which the KSČ was pursuing.

Primarily, it was because this alternative approach threatened

KSČ strategy that it was rejected. It was an approach that implicitly went on to the strategic offensive, whereas, for the reasons analysed in Chapter 3, the KSČ leadership considered a defensive application of the Popular Front strategy based on the wartime anti-fascist unity, at both a domestic and international level, to be most appropriate. To have taken a position of strategic offensive might have resulted in splitting with some sections of the National Front, and the KSČ leadership could not permit this. Adhering to their overall political strategy, the KSČ leadership attempted to ensure that the calls for further nationalisation were contained within the framework of the national democratic revolution.

Despite this reluctance by the KSČ to grasp the initiative more decisively, the extent of nationalisation was a notable success for the left-wing forces and dealt an extremely severe blow to those hoping for a strong private sector within the economy. The decrees were an expression at an economic level of the political strength which the working class and its various representatives had established.

Two major qualifications have to be made to this evaluation. With the signing of the decrees, the immediate post-war revolutionary period was concluded. The major social and political issues arising from the war had been settled and the general political situation stabilised in consequence.

Within the economy quite considerable areas of private capital remained, especially in the consumer industries, distribution and trade, and in the more stable conditions that were now to prevail the possibility existed of these areas of private capital growing in strength. A more offensive policy could have restricted their base and would have had wide working-class support. Secondly, the entire rationale for nationalisation at both a popular and theoretical level had been underpinned by nationalism. This weakened the socialist understanding of the working class and other sections of the working population, and made them more susceptible to non-socialist ideas which other parties propagated. It was in these two spheres that right-wing forces were to attempt to rebuild their strength and influence in the following years.

7
Works Councils and Trade Unions

For the Czech working class, one of the central questions it confronted with liberation was that of its own organisation. The prewar fragmentation of the working class and its organisations had had disastrous consequences for the labour movement. The unity which the trade unions began to forge in the resistance pointed the way forward to post-war developments. At the founding meeting of ÚRO in Prague on 1 May 1945, the chairman, Cipro, recalled the role of the revolutionary trade unions in the struggles of the domestic resistance. With final victory near, he promised that in building the new trade-union movement in the liberated republic, "We shall learn from the past and the experiences of our movement. . . . The unification of the working class in one undivided, strong body"[1] was essential. In the immediate post-liberation period the opportunity existed for the Czech working class to mould its own institutions in a new way. The new organisational forms evolved and the relationships between them were central to the long-term development of the working class as a whole.

To the KSČ the unity of the working class and its mass organisations were a vital concern, for only if these were achieved could the working class be the major effective social force in the post-war republic. Their politico-strategic understanding of the question was based firmly on the resolution passed at the Seventh Congress of the Communist International:

> Emphasising the special importance of forming a united front in the sphere of the economic struggle of the workers and the establishment of the unity of the trade union movement as a most important step in consolidating the united front of the proletariat, the Congress makes it a duty of the communists to adopt all practical measures for the realisation of the unity of the trade unions by inquiries on a national scale.

The Communists are decidedly for the re-establishment of trade union unity in each country and on an international scale; for united class trade unions as one of the major bulwarks of the working class against the offensive of capital and fascism; for one trade union in each industry; for one trade union centre in each country.[2]

Although these goals were not achieved before Munich, the KSČ maintained its adherence to this perspective. The article by Jan Šverma in *Československé listy*, published in Moscow on 1 June 1944, expressed the point of view of the Moscow leadership of the KSČ as regards the building and tasks of the united trade unions in liberated Czechoslovakia. Šverma recognised that the greatest cause of the weakness of the trade-union movement before the war lay in its own internal divisions and the placing of party political interests before those of the unity of the movement. This had led to trade-union leaderships failing to mobilise their members in defence of their economic and social interests, with consequent working-class disillusionment, while the whole set-up encouraged bureaucratisation within the unions and their secretariats.[3]

In the new popular democratic republic, the trade unions would be founded on a new basis. "We shall build a united trade-union organisation in order to serve the entire working class as a whole." This would be constructed "on the basis of a genuine workers' democracy", in which the old bureaucratic hierarchies would have no place. "The united trade unions shall be independent organs of the working class and must not be instruments of party political policy — but that does not mean that the unions have nothing at all to do with politics."[4] Herein was contained the main Communist exposition on trade-union organisation: they were to be united, democratic and independent of political party. Yet some of the more complex problems of the internal character of trade unions and their autonomy from political parties were avoided, while the question of factory councils and their relationship to the trade-union movement was not dealt with at all. The main outlines of Communist policy on trade-union organisation were clear. In the factories during the occupation, and especially with the liberation, Communists heeded the call to "organise one trade-union organisation of all workers and employees".⁵ However, the lack of theoretical clarity and leadership on some of the more complicated questions, notably the role and scope of the factory councils, resulted in confusion during the summer of 1945.

In the Košice programme the parties of the National Front refrained from interfering in the internal organisation of the trade-union movement. Article 14 guaranteed "all employees, workers by hand or brain . . . the right to combine voluntarily in trade-union organisations and to freely elect their representatives."⁶ Works committees were to be elected in factories, workshops and offices, and these and the trade-union organisation were to be the legal representatives of employees on matters of wages, work and social policy.⁷

All three parties of the Socialist Bloc adopted a positive attitude towards a united trade-union movement when they returned to Czechoslovakia. As early as 11 May, KSČ Gerenal Secretary Slánský held discussions with ÚRO representatives on the tasks facing the trade-union movement. Overall agreement on the major areas was reached, with special attention being focused on the necessity of trade-union unity.⁸ On 7 June an eight-strong NSS delegation led by Zenkl, David and Ripka held a similar discussion with ÚRO leaders. After a full, detailed debate the NSS stated "its completely positive attitude to the unity of the trade unions", and a joint statement called for "the closest working relations" in the future.⁹ In the first major SDS declaration produced by its Central Preparatory Executive Committee, full support for the united trade unions was declared.¹⁰

The entire structure of the pre-war trade-union movement had been destroyed by the Nazi occupation, but with the downfall of the Nazis their corporatist union federations effectively collapsed. Thus conditions were exceptionally favourable for the revolutionary trade unions, which had developed in illegality, to construct a new trade-union movement on lines most favourable to the working class. The revolutionary upsurge in the final days of the war accelerated this process, as throughout the Czech Lands works councils sprang up and along with works militias assumed control of factories and enterprises. At the Škoda works in Plzeň a revolutionary works council was formed on 5 May and took control of the factory and responsibility for its security.¹¹ At the Zbrojovka arms factory the works council performed a similar role and began to ensure the renewal of production.[12] In the vast majority of large-scale enterprises, works councils assumed decisive control in these immediate post-war days.[13] It was on this basis that a new, united working-class organisation was to be built.

Some of the principles of future trade-union organisation had been sketched out by Cipro at the founding meeting of ÚRO. The trade unions were to follow the principle of industrial unionism, rather than being based on trades and professions. All employees in an enterprise were to be members of the same union, thereby strengthening their united power. No distinction was to be made within the enterprise between manual and non-manual workers.[14] Already these organisational directives had been sent out to the illegal district trades councils.[15] These steps were aimed at overcoming the internal divisions which had hamstrung the trade unions during the First Republic.

No analysis of the role of the works councils was attempted, however, nor of the distinction between them and trade unions. Whereas works councils embrace *all* the workers in an enterprise *a priori* and are concerned primarily with ensuring the greatest possible degree of workers' control over the production process, trade unions are voluntary organisations whose main sphere of activity is the furtherance of the economic and social interests of their members. In a society where the majority of enterprises are socially owned the tendency would be for works councils to defend the interests of workers as citizens, and the trade unions the interests of their members as employees. Given this division in the character and functions of the two institutions, they needed to remain organisationally separate. The works councils would be new, independent organs of working-class power, ensuring popular democratic control of the major units of social production. Obviously this would entail close co-operation with the trade unions. In addition, the works councils would operate within the context of the national plan decided by the political parties in the government. Yet they would retain their autonomy, thereby enabling them to act independently.

No section of the Czech left developed a theoretical and political approach in accord with this perspective. What emerged in the moulding of the new organisations of the working class were two major trends: a confused syndicalism, especially prevalent in the immediate post-liberation period; and a rigid, administrative approach which sought to contain the factory councils within the orbit of the trade-union movement. The syndicalist tendency saw the works councils as forming the base of the trade-union organisation and failed to recognise the distinction between the two institutions. They also saw the trade-union movement, rather than political parties, as the primary agents of social change and the determinators of production. The KSČ were the main opponents of this line, which they countered by advocating restrictions on the role of the factory councils. Their political attitude, which had its theoretical roots in the stalinist concept of mass organisations being "transmission belts" for party directives,[16] was one of having united, centralised mass organisations which could be controlled. Hence they opposed strong, autonomous, decentralised works councils and tried to restrict their role in relation to both workers and management, and to ensure that they were brought within the trade-union structure and subordinated to it. The KSČ correctly recognised that the basis of trade-union organisation had to be a trade-union branch and not a works council,[17] yet they sought to contain working-class organisations within a bureaucratic framework. This became clear in the policy of the KSČ and the leading Communist trade unionists pursued during the summer months.

It was the syndicalist trend that dominated ÚRO policy in the immediate post-liberation period, as the ÚRO leadership was influenced by the tremendous upsurge of works councils. On 12 May ÚRO issued directions for the procedure for elections of works councils. These were to be set up in all enterprises and offices with more than 20 employees. In those with between 5 and 19 employees a kind of shop steward was to be elected instead of a council. Everyone employed in the enterprise over the age of 18 was eligible for election and could vote. Members of the council were chosen at works meetings at the individual enterprises and could be removed whenever there was a majority vote against them. The size of the works council was dependent on the number of workers.

These directives reflected the popular mood in favour of democratic organs of workers' control. Yet the syndicalist bias was apparent in the statement that works councils were "the primary organs and representatives of the unions of the working people."[18] An identical position was taken by *Práce,* which declared that "the free, revolutionary trade-union movement shall be created on democratic bases and shall rest on the revolutionary works councils of workers and employees",[19] while the first issue of the *Věstník závodních rad* (Bulletin of Works Councils) stated that "Factory councils are the basis of the whole organisation (i.e. ROH)."[20]

By the time President Beneš issued the temporary decree on national administrations on 19 May, works councils had been set up and had taken charge of management in many enterprises. The powers they assumed were extensive. Their main task was to ensure the transition to normal life in the factory. They were competent to cover "the control of the working and management of the enterprise", and were the legal representatives of the workers "on all questions of wage, work and social policy," with the right to inspect all the trading books of the enterprise.[21] Such was the scope of the works councils in these early weeks. Aside from the implicit confusion between their role and that of the trade-union branch, if works councils had continued to develop in this way they would have become significant, autonomous institutions exercising popular control at the point of production.

The syndicalist tendency considered works councils to have a more extensive role. This was most clearly expressed by Jungmann at the first session of the ÚRO Plenum on 16 May. He said that "works councils shall be the power on which the whole economic structure of the state rests".[22] Speaking about rebuilding the economy, he said that "we must not rely on specialists, but we must try to rest this economic construction on workers, who must have control of management and production. Therefore we are trying to get works councils superior to national managements . . . so that they could control them."[23] This syndicalist formulation, with its failure to appreciate the role of political parties and the government, did not attract much support, yet the confusion between the works council and trade-union branch remained. At a meeting with journalists on 4 June, Erban indicated that "the building of trade-union groups shall be carried out from below", and "factory councils, which are formed on the principle of 'one factory, one organisation' are the foundation".[24]

However, with the return of veteran Communist trade unionists a shift in ÚRO policy occurred. At the ÚRO Plenum on 7 June where Zápotocký was elected as the chairman of ÚRO, Jungmann spoke of the need to build united factory organisations and did not mention works councils.²⁵ Zápotocký in a short speech on trade-union unity made an oblique reference to syndicalist tendencies: different opinions had to be discussed and if no agreement was reached, a democratic vote had to be taken and "to this decision we must submit in a disciplined fashion". Otherwise anarchy would result.²⁶ At this plenum veteran Communists Kolský, Jura and Malík were co-opted to the Presidium, along with Zápotocký and the National Socialist Wünsch.²⁷ Their influence was immediately felt. In a radio broadcast on 13 June Zápotocký urged the formation of united trade unions and emphasised the factory trade-union branches as constituting the basis of the movement.²⁸ A statement from the ÚRO Presidium on 14 June spoke of the need to build and create factory trade-union branches. Such branches "shall be the basis on which the whole structure of the united free trade unions shall rest",²⁹ thereby reversing previous ÚRO policy.

Yet during June and July this policy remained unfulfilled, as works councils continued to dominate most enterprises. Zápotocký himself defended them, although he viewed them very much as part of the machinery to renew economic life.³⁰ Confusion remained within the movement; an article in the June edition of *Věstník závodních rad* described "democratically elected works councils (as) the fundamental organs of the revolutionary trade-union movement".³¹ A section of the trade-union movement wanted the works councils to retain wide powers. As Mrázek of the ÚRO Economic Commission said, "It is not just a question of the protection of the economic interests of the working people but indeed a question of control of the entire production and operation of the whole enterprise".³²

In these months the number of works councils established was much higher than the number of factory trade-union branches.³³ The KSČ recognised the seriousness of this position and by August felt strong enough to push for the implementation of their perspective as regards works councils. The Communists pursued a dual theme: the necessity to encompass the works councils within the trade-union structure and subject them to its control; and to limit the scope of works council activity.

In a major article in *Práce* Josef Kolský outlined the relationship between factory union branches and works councils. The former were the basis of the trade-union movement and fundamental to its growth. The works council had to be closely linked to the trade-union branch so that it could act as its instrument in the fulfilment of legal tasks in the area of public management, while elections to it were to be run by the union. As Kolský bluntly stated, "The factory trade-union organisation . . . cooperates with the factory council, controls its activity".[34] Gustav Kliment, another pre-war leader of the Red Trade Unions who returned to become head of the Metalworkers' Union, emphasised the same point in *Rudé právo*.[35] As Zápotocký declared in a radio broadcast, "Works councils are and shall be important in the future, but always as auxiliary organs of the labour and trade-union movement".[36] In attempting to explain why this was so, Zápotocký lapsed into illogicality. Trade unions had long experience of struggle during the Habsburg Monarchy period and in the First Republic, which the works councils did not have. He then stated that the rights of works councils were created by the strength of the trade-union movement. Yet as he continued by asking why trade-union branches were developing so slowly — in comparison to works councils — his argument was completely contradictory.[37] The real reason for subordinating the works councils to the trade-union structure lay in contemporary Communist thinking, which conceived of working-class organisation as a conveyor belt set in motion by Communist directives.

This entailed not only containing works councils within the official union structure but also restricting their scope and sphere of independent activity. As Zápotocký said at a plenary session of ÚRO on 18 August:

> The works councils do not run production or guide the administration. In the management of production and administration they share in control. . . . The control does not mean that works councils are review or supervisory organs of the enterprise or office. The aim of the control activity of the works councils is to inspect production, trade and administration so that it is not abused against the interests of employees and the state.

The co-operation lies in the fact that the works council has the right to put suggestions, make objections, put . . demands concerning production and administration of the enterprise and office, but of course it does not have the right to publish independent orders and to make its own decisions in matters of production and administration.

The management of the enterprise or office carry the responsibility for the correct course of production and administration.[38]

This limitation of their role was the logical complement to their subordination to the trade unions. As Zápotocký concluded, "the works council is chosen at the suggestion of the trade-union organisation and its activity is regulated by the trade-union organisation".[39] The contrast between the role envisaged for works councils and what many experienced just three months previously could not have been starker. The strong, autonomous organs exercising popular control over production were no longer. Prime Minister Fierlinger supported Zápotocký's position in a speech at Brno. Works councils did not have the competence to manage production, a competence which, he declared, "belongs exclusively to the responsible commercial and technical directors. . . . It is necessary to limit the scope of works councils by law".[40] It was clear that the administrative approach to the question of working-class organisation which dominated KSČ policy had gained the political ascendancy within the Czechoslovak labour movement.

One of the questions posed by this is why the KSČ was able to gain the acceptance of its position so easily, given the widespread backing for works councils in May and June. Undoubtedly the firm and resolute way in which the KSČ stated its attitude was important. They adopted a clear policy concerning the relationship of works councils to trade-union organisation and pursued it. This policy was transmitted to Communist party factory branches, who were instructed "to support trade-union organisation, to support trade-union unity".[41] As the KSČ was the strongest and best organised working-class political party, Communists were in a good position to persuade their fellow workers of the correctness of their policy.

Of exceptional importance was the role played by veteran, pre-war Communist trade unionists, who had spent the war abroad or in concentration camps. In the immediate post-liberation period none of these leaders of the pre-war Red Trade Unions were on ÚRO; but as they returned, they occupied prominent posts in the key areas of the trade-union movement. Macura became chairman of the food employees; Špic of the chemical workers; Křivánek and Vycpálek were on the central committee of building workers; Babulík was chairman of glassworkers; Havelka was chairman of the tribunal responsible for screening all those who had worked in the apparatus of the Nazi trade-union syndicates during the war; Kapoun was chairman of the district trade-union organisation in Brno; Veselý in Ostrava; Kučera in Olomouc and Bílek in Prague. In addition Jura led the transport workers, Malík the miners and Kliment the metalworkers, all three being on the ÚRO Presidium along with Zápotocký and Kolský, who was responsible for organisational work.[42] These experienced Communist trade unionists formed the decisive core leadership of ROH. In consequence, as Kolský has written, they were able to guide the many young people who had entered important positions in the movement, "who had no experience of trade-union activities" and whose "incorrect (i.e. syndicalist) tendencies were quickly overcome thanks to the sagacious policies of the KSČ".[43]

The KSČ viewpoint was accepted also because no coherent opposition to it was expressed. There was no clear exposition of the specific role of works councils in nationalised enterprises or of their relationship to industrial unions. This hindered any attempt to develop them as autonomous organisations. The theoretical weaknesses of the Czech left resulted in two alternatives presenting themselves: a muddled syndicalism; or a subordination to the trade unions. Given that the main working-class party adhered to the latter policy, its success was predictable.

This restriction on the role of the works councils encouraged more right-wing elements, for example, Stránský and the NSS, to limit them further.[44] When the presidential decrees were issued on 24 October, along with those on nationalisation, their sphere of activity had been strictly circumscribed. Amongst the most important decrees were:

1. The duties of factory councils are to protect the economic, social and health interests of employees, to control working conditions in the interest of the com-

munity and to take part in management in an *advisory* capacity.

3. The appropriate organs of the trade-union organisation will direct the activities of the factory council as far as their own regulations allow.
6. The works administration is obliged to negotiate all questions concerning employees with the factory councils and must allow the council access to records of work and wages.
7. The factory council will take part in planning and controlling production.
8. The works administration must consider proposals put forward by the factory councils as regards production and administration and give monthly reports on the situation in the works.[45]

Thus the works councils had been accommodated within the trade-union structure. They were to be elected by secret ballot on the basis of candidate lists proposed by the united trade-union organisation. At least 80 per cent voting had to support this list if the works council was to be elected.[46] The limited scope of their influence, as against that delineated in the ÚRO directives of 12 May, was clear. This was in accord with those sections of the nationalisation decrees which dealt with the management of national enterprises. Article 20 declared:

1. A national enterprise is administered by a managing committee presided over by the manager. . . .
4. The manager acts on behalf of the national enterprise. . . .
6. The managing committee and the manager have to run the enterprise along sound business lines,

while Article 21 stated that "part of the members of the managing committee and their substitutes are representatives of the employees".[47] The factory councils were not to be organs of workers' control in the nationalised enterprises, for these were to be run on orthodox lines. As the central committee of the Metalworkers' Union informed its members, "neither the factory council nor the factory's trade-union branch committee takes away the tasks of direction and management of the enterprise".[48]

The KSČ, wary of the potential independent power of the works councils, had succeeded in circumscribing their range of activity and channelling them into the trade-union structure so that the trade unions effectively became the controlling organs for the works councils. This bureaucratic solution to the works councils was to undermine seriously the possibilities for independent working-class initiatives in the future.

The expansion of trade unions

Within the ranks of the working class there was much less confusion over the character of trade-union organisation. No significant opposition was raised to the position taken by the ÚRO leadership on this question. Their policy was in accord both with what Šverma had argued for in 1944 and Cipro and Jungmann in the illegal movement. As Evžen Erban expressed it in a leading article in *Práce*, "We are building the trade unions as a united movement including all wage-earning working people. . . . What (they) have in common is primary and fundamental, whereas the special interests of individual categories of working people are derivative and secondary".[49] According to the editorial in the first issue of *Věstník závodních rad*, "the basis of the organisational composition of ÚRO is all working people without difference of job in workshops, offices, transport, trade, in field or forest. . . . There can be no division between manual and white-collar workers".[50] All sections of the trade-union movement agreed that ROH was to be built upon the principle of industrial unionism, with one union representing all members in any one enterprise. The call was *"jeden závod — jedna organisace"*: one factory, one organisation. In this way the fragmentation which the trade unions had suffered before the war was overcome.

The trade-union movement was to be internally democratic. "On all fundamental problems in the organisation the majority decides in democratic, elected organs".[51] ROH was also to avoid the party political divisions that had affected the trade unions pre-war. Zápotocký declared that "the trade-union movement . . . organises and associates in its ranks all employees without regard of political conviction".[52] That did not mean the movement was apolitical, however, for it supported those parties which followed trade-union policy and interests.

These principles were expressed in the organisational structure of the trade-union movement which ÚRO decided upon in August. Every aspect of ROH was covered: the proposals were to apply until their ratification or alteration by the First ROH Congress. The spheres of activity for the central, district and factory organs of the ROH were delineated and the whole structure was based on industrial unionism, with the unions independent of political party and under the direction of the central organ, ÚRO. The structure agreed upon was similar to that which the Seventh Congress of the Communist International had called for in 1935.[53]

By the time these directives were issued, a considerable degree of trade-union organisation had already been achieved. A major part of working-class action in these months centred on destroying the Nazi trade-union apparatus, purging their ranks of collaborators, transferring their members into a new, united, trade-union organisation and enlarging its membership. In the immediate post-liberation weeks the trade unions grew slowly, as the main focus of working-class activity were the works councils. During May and June ROH made a net increase of only 23,551 members.[54] However, despite the confusion over the relationship of works councils to the trade unions, the district ROH organisation began to develop. As early as 27 May a district conference of 400 trade unionists from all the large factories in Moravská Ostrava and adjoining areas was held. Erban outlined the new tasks and organisation of ROH, a resolution was passed in support of the united trade-union movement, and a District Trades Council (*Krajská odborová rada* — KOR) was elected.[55] At the ÚRO Plenum on 7 June it was reported that 75 per cent of Ostrava workers were already members of the united trade union and a radical purge of all collaborators had been carried out.[56] A similar conference with 1,500 delegates representing all sections of Prague workers was held on 14 July and at this a 60-strong KOR was elected.[57]

The strength of ROH among the working class can best be gauged by investigating the developments in several important trade unions in these months. As experienced Communist trade-union leaders returned to the movement and ÚRO strengthened its grip on the situation, so trade-union organisation and membership developed.

On 26 June Malík called a meeting in Prague at which former secretaries of the Miners' Union with long experience were invited. This meeting set up a central committee representing all employees in the mining industry, as the temporary central organ of a united miners' union. The committee saw one of its priorities as the incorporation of those miners formerly in NOÚZ into the framework of the new trade-union branches and an expansion of the membership. This had stood at 28,529 in May and had barely increased by July. The central committee organised meetings and conferences and issued publicity material on the principles so that the last half of the year saw a doubling in membership.[58]

ÚRO took a similar initiative in the metal and engineering industry, ensuring that basic, central union organisation was established. To begin with, the central committee of the Metalworkers' Union, headed by Kliment, limited its activities to the Prague region, Kladno and Central Bohemia, yet from July onwards was able to extend its range. By the end of the year 19 district committees had been set up and in 17 of these there was a total of 1,258 factory trade-union branches. Building the union on the basis of "one factory — one organisation" the membership of the metalworkers' union grew from 161,000 in July to 298,460 by 31 December.[59]

Josef Špic and František Janata were given the responsibility by ÚRO for establishing the trade union in the chemical industry. A temporary central committee was elected at a Prague conference in June. On 26 August a much broader conference was held with delegates participating from all of Bohemia and Moravia. The conference discussed the role of the united trade union and current organisational tasks in their industry. A proper central committee was set up with the veteran Communist Špic as Chairman. By the end of the year 306 trade-union branches had been set up in the chemical industry with 38,000 workers unionised. Over twenty thousand Czechs remained unorganised, mainly employed in small enterprises, while no attempt was made to organise the similar number of German chemical workers.[60]

The union of workers in the foodstuffs industry had developed in embryo in the last months of the occupation. The first working meeting of the central committee was held in Prague on 26 June, and a presidium was established with Macura at its head. The meeting set itself the task of building a strong union in the industry; meat, fish, breweries, distilleries, grains, cereals, sugar, confectionery and dairies were amongst the sections encompassed. By the end of 1945 the union had 76,708 members and was very firmly established.[61]

These four examples illustrate the rapid gains made by ROH in this period. They highlight the influences of the left in gaining the adherence of the working class to a united centralised trade-union movement. Trade-union membership rose steadily, reaching almost one and a half million by the end of 1945.[62] Accompanying this increase came the growth of factory trade-union branches. Whereas there were only 2,995 on 31 July 1945, by the end of the year there were 8,030.[63] Although this was still below the number of works councils, which stood at 11,131 on 31 December,[64] this disparity was much smaller than it had been in July, showing the influence of ÚRO policy on trade-union branches. 66.6 per cent of the total workforce in Prague, 78.1 per cent of that in Kladno and 69.6 per cent of that in Brno were unionised,[65] figures which further emphasise the strength of ROH and the rapid organisation of the working class into the united trade unions that occurred after liberation.

By the end of 1945 the Czech working class had a strong, united, centralised trade-union movement, the ROH. The other mass working-class organisations, the works councils, were under the effective control of the ROH. This level of trade-union organisation, combined with the wide-ranging nationalisation, showed the strength and influence of the working class in the new republic. Yet the restrictions which the dominant political force in the working class, the KSČ, imposed upon the works councils weakened their capacity to act as independent working-class institutions. The locus of power within the working class lay in ROH, and there, it was firmly centred in ÚRO. The united weight of the trade-union movement, organised and centralised in ÚRO, was destined to play a decisive part in the political and class conflicts of the following years.

III
The Calm

8
The Determinant Force

At the central committee meeting of the KSČ on 18 December 1945 it was decided to hold a party congress from 28-31 March 1946. In conjunction with this a call went out to achieve a party membership of one million by the time of the congress.[1] The decision for a congress was the central committee's response to the political uncertainty that affected the country at the end of 1945. The presidential decrees on nationalisation and works councils marked the end of the revolutionary wave and thereafter the political tempo slowed. The main impetus of the Košice programme had been exhausted. Conservative groupings and ideas began to emerge more strongly than hitherto.[2] As they gazed hesitantly towards the future, all sections of the left assessed the outcome of the revolutionary events of the summer and drew conclusions for their future strategy.

The KSČ leadership had greatest cause for satisfaction at the course events had taken, for in all fundamental respects the national and democratic revolution had followed their strategy. On this point there is general agreement bewteen Communist and Western historians of the period. As Kozák has written, "The establishment of the National Front and the adoption of the Košice programme . . . were related to the idea of a government of the Popular Front, anticipated by the Seventh Congress of the Communist International".[3] This strategy, formulated at a time when the overriding necessity was defence against fascism, continued to be the basis of official Communist policy throughout Europe in the early post-war years, despite the altered political situation. As some of the earlier chapters showed, this strategy was challenged by sections of the communist and working-class movement. Yet at no stage were these elements able to formulate a coherent, alternative strategy. The position of the Soviet Union and its Communist Party within the international communist movement exerted its decisive influence on the Czechoslovak left.

No significant challenege to the theoretical premises of Soviet policy was made by any section of the Communist or non-Communist left. "The men of 1929", who constituted the inner leadership of the KSČ had little difficulty in maintaining a united party supporting their strategy.

This strategy of the KSČ had as its basis the sharing of political power within a coalition government. In harmony with contemporary Communist theory, this had to be complemented by a mixed economic system containing public, private and co-operative sectors. The KSČ leadership, therefore, was cautious in its handling of the issues of nationalisation and workers' councils. As has been illustrated, the KSČ sought to contain workers' demands within this framework, and incipient conflict was resolved fundamentally in accord with KSČ policy, the boundary walls of the framework being extended but never breached. Nevertheless, the widescale nationalisation and land confiscation measures made huge inroads into the economic power of the large bourgeoisie and aristocracy. It was apparent that, in comparison with the situation in the pre-war republic, the organisations of the working class had become the dominant political and social force within the country. This combination was by no means secure or necessarily permanent, yet it weighted future class conflicts in favour of the left, while nationalisation deprived right-wing forces of a major social base. They were also denied support from the army and police by the grip which the left exerted on these crucial areas of the state apparatus. With Nosek in charge of the Ministry of the Interior and the army maintaining its close relations with the USSR, those elements that wished to reverse the political situation and its existing leftward trend were unable to turn to the military and police forces for reliable support. There can be no doubt that by autumn 1945 the KSČ leadership had achieved all the major objectives they had set in emigration as regards the immediate post-war period, and were in the decisive position for influencing future policy.

Implicitly they recognised that the entire domestic situation was underpinned by the international position and that the maintenance of the wartime anti-fascist coalition was essential to the continuation of the National Front. In November 1944 Stalin had stated that "the alliance between the USSR, Great Britain, and the United States of America is founded not on casual, transitory considerations but on vital and lasting interests,"⁴ and it was on this mistaken assumption that the post-war strategy of communist parties was based. Communist participation in national anti-fascist coalitions complemented the coalition of the Big Three powers and enhanced the possibility of continued co-operation, whereas revolutionary conflagrations would have ruptured the Allied coalition.⁵

As we have seen, the KSČ pursued such a strategy, yet is possessed certain strategic advantages in comparison with other communist parties. Unlike its French, Italian and Belgian counterparts, the KSČ had the advantage of operating in a country within the Soviet sphere of influence, a matter of considerable political importance, as all the manoeuvres concerning the liberation of Prague indicated. But unlike communist parties in parts of Eastern Europe, the KSČ had played a leading role in the resistance, enjoyed considerable popularity and had quickly built up a mass membership, especially among the industrial working class.

However, it still pursued a similar line to the other parties, pinning its policy on a maintenance of the international *status quo*. The KSČ ignored the signs of disintegration within the Big Three, which emerged on the issues of Poland and Germany and at the conferences of Yalta and Potsdam.⁶ Indeed, a lead article on the Potsdam conference in *Rudé právo* asserted:

> The great allied coalition still shows, even after the end of the war in Europe, its vitality. The close co-operation of the allies at Potsdam is a hard-blow to all those reactionary circles which were hoping for the disintegration of the coalition. The Soviet Union, the United States and Great Britain again demonstrated their desire for united advance in the peaceful construction of the world.⁷

In reality the unity of the Allied coalition, bound together only by the overwhelming necessity to defeat Nazi Germany, had already splintered. It was only in the spring and summer of 1947 that the underlying conflicts flared. In the meantime East-West relations drifted, with minor but increasing tensions becoming apparent. Until East-West relations broke, KSČ strategy remained the same; the relative calm of the international scene forms the key to an analysis of events in Czechoslovakia from late 1945 until mid-1947. In this situation the KSČ's approach retained its validity, since its fundamental premise, that of inter-Allied co-operation, had not been completely undermined. The task facing the KSČ as the leading working-class political organisation in the country was to retain the initiative which it had achieved in the political life of the country.

One of the reasons why the policy the KSČ pursued was so decisive to the political development of the country was that it was the largest, most influential party. There had been a general recognition among the Communist leaders in Moscow during the war that in industrialised countries communist parties needed to have a mass membership. If they were to pursue their aims successfully, the social character of these countries demanded that they build a mass party.[8] The KSČ was in an excellent position to do this. Unsullied by Munich and having taken a leading part in the domestic resistance, it was the party which working people saw as the one most likely to fulfil their radical and socialist aspirations. In addition the KSČ had been alone in maintaining itself as an organised political force during the occupation and was in a position to grow rapidly on liberation. The summer months saw an enormous growth in KSČ membership. The party leadership convened 18 district conferences to ensure that the organisational measures necessary to cope with such an influx of members were undertaken, as well as to explain the party's policy.

The party's rapid expansion and mass base was illustrated at these district conferences. At the conference at Zlín 800 delegates attended; at Havlíčkův Brod 900; at Kolín and Kladno 1,000; at Ústí 1,100; at Brno 1,936 delegates. The Brno conference reported that there were 1,147 branches in the district; the Ostrava conference reported 400 branches with over 40,000 members; and in Plzeň there were 764 local and factory branches organising more than 52,000 members.[9] With 28,000 members on liberation the KSČ gained half a million new members in the following two months. By the end of September it had grown by half as much again, with its more than three-quarters of a million members organised in over 9,000 local and 2,000 factory branches.[10]

The increase in KSČ membership in the revolutionary turmoil of the immediate post-war period is shown most dramatically by the graph. The rate of increase slowed considerably after this, although a steady rise continued in the first half of 1946 in the pre-congress and pre-election periods. In the calmer political conditions prevailing, KSČ membership stabilised. A "screening" in the latter half of 1946 resulted in a fall in membership which was partially recovered in the first half of 1947, yet at no stage did membership fall below one million.

Not only did the KSČ succeed in becoming a mass party but also one which found its major base of support among the industrial working class. At the Zbrojovka arms works, 52 KSČ branches with a total of 3,000 members were operating within two months of liberation.[11] At the Škoda engineering works there were 46 party branches with 6,548 members by 21 June.[12] At the Eighth KSČ Congress it was stated that there were 4,200 members in the Poldina steelworks, while at the Pelikan agricultural machine factory in Bradys over half the workers were members.[13] By the time of the congress there were 577,000 industrial workers who were KSČ members, representing 57.7 per cent of the membership.[14] The proportion varied according to the social character of the region. For example in the Ostrava district, which contained 48 per cent of the country's industrial production at the start of the Two-Year Plan, 86.9 per cent of the membership were industrial workers.[15]

The social composition of the remainder of the party membership consisted of 13 per cent peasants and small farmers; 9 per cent intelligentsia; and 17 per cent others, including state employees and housewives.[16] The KSČ was clearly the largest political party in the country. The NSS had a membership of 574,648 in April 1946; the SDS had 352,840 by mid-1946; and the LS may have had half a million members before the election.[17]

Compared with these parties the KSČ also had by far the largest component of industrial workers in its ranks, measured both numerically and proportionately. There were about 100,000 industrial workers in the NSS, constituting around one-sixth of their membership, and approximately 120,000 in the SDS, comprising around one-third of theirs, while it would seem that in the LS the proportion of industrial workers barely reached 15 per cent.[18] With 577,000 workers in its ranks the KSČ exerted the decisive political influence within the industrial working class, while its significant degree of peasant support — 129,000 mem-

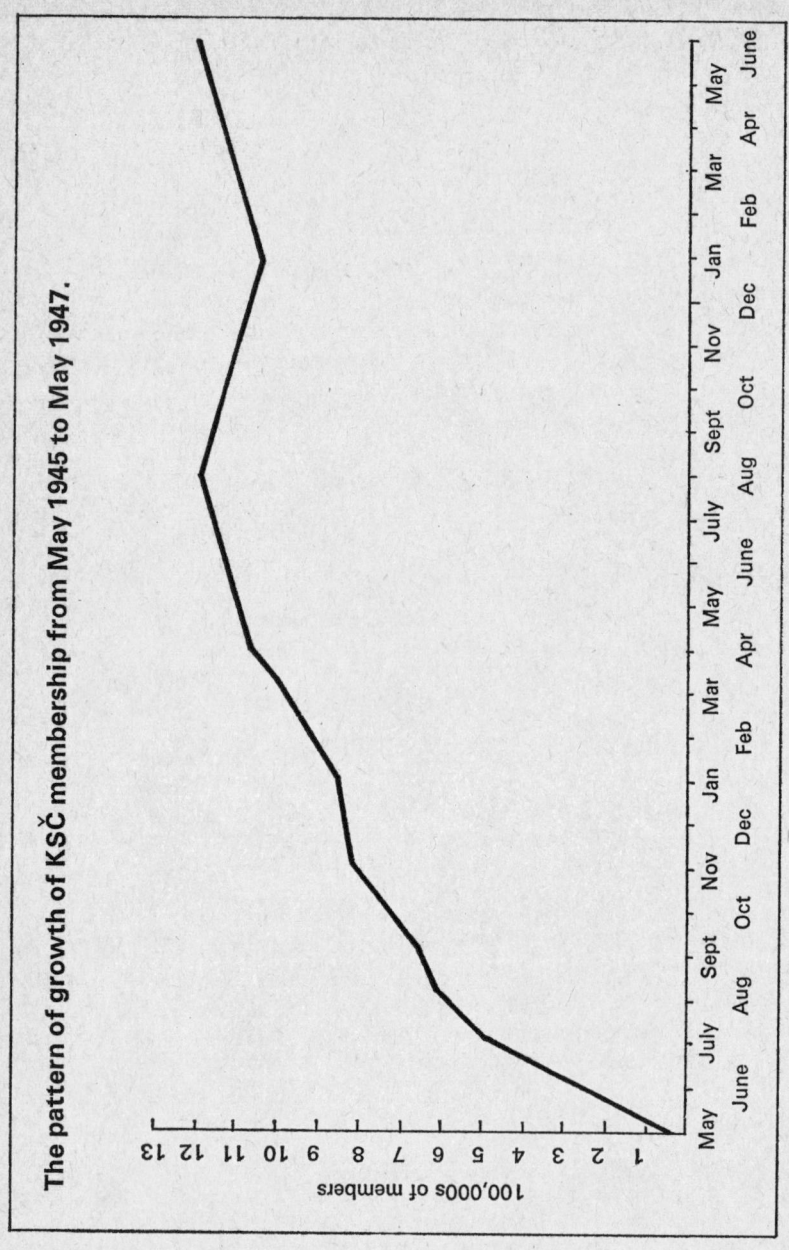

bers — meant that it was in a position to forge the alliance of working people of town and country that was central to its strategy.

The Eighth KSČ Congress

From the above it is clear that the KSČ held the key to political developments within the country. Its Eighth Congress evoked widespread interest. The Communist theme was clearly stated in Gottwald's report on "The Current Situation, the Policy of the Party and its Action Programme". Above all, he declared, the task must be to consolidate the present course and to strengthen its popular, democratic character.[19] The entire congress concentrated on this theme of consolidation.

Gottwald's speech was the focal point of the congress. The continuation of the National Front government was central to its perspective. As Gottwald said, "The new, democratic, popular republic and its *political* and economic structure correspond to the interests of all the working strata of our nation".[20] At no stage during the congress was it ever suggested that the existing National Front would be reconstituted. Representatives of the other political parties within the government were present at the congress and spoke,[21] while a friendly letter was taken to President Beneš.[22] At a political level the continuation of the National Front coalition was fundamental to KSČ policy.

Within the economic sphere two major areas were emphasised. In accord with their political strategy the KSČ pursued an economic policy of "full support for small and medium enterprises",[23] as an open letter to all members in January 1946 expressed it. At the congress Gottwald confirmed Communist support for the petty and middle bourgeoisie when he said that "next to the nationalised sector of the economy there shall continue a broad private sector, and small and medium private enterprises shall participate in our economic system and shall enjoy the full support of the National Front".[24] No opposition to this support for "a broad private sector" was voiced by any delegate.

With changes in social relations of production precluded, the main emphasis of KSČ policy in the economic sphere centred on renewal and reconstruction. Gottwald stated that for Czechoslovakia to recover its pre-war standard of living and then to raise it higher "more and more work, more and more effort, more and more sweat"[25] was required. The main task before the Czechoslovak working people he saw as *"Republice více práce, to je naše agitace* ('To the republic more work, that is our agitation'). This is not just an electoral slogan — in it is expressed the essential part of our whole programme for the construction of a new republic."[26]

It was around this theme that many delegates spoke. Delegates from engineering works spoke on reorganising and renewing production and on the lead the KSČ branches had given on this; a miner spoke of the importance of competitions between workers as a method of boosting production and working morale; the delegate from the Bat'a works dealt with their technical and production achievements and problems; the speaker from Hradec Králové expressed this overall theme most clearly when he said, "Our party in the district has concentrated its forces on carrying out economic tasks".[27] This was in accord with the leadership's directive for, as Švermová stated in her report on party organisation, the main emphasis of the party's district and area committees was to be laid on the problems of economic renewal and reconstruction.[28]

In the ideological and cultural sphere, the emphasis was placed on a renewed Slavism. Czechoslovakia's future was declared to be dependent on the brotherhood of Slav nations.[29] Kopecký, the party's chief ideologue, stated that general cultural developments were part of this overall Slav policy and that those cultural elements which Czechoslovakia had in common with other Slav countries were to be emphasised. This policy was viewed as the contemporary expression of the nation's heritage and traditions. The conference hall displayed portraits of Hus, Smetana, Kollar and Palacký,[30] while Kopecký spoke of "the great personality and great historical role of T. G. Masaryk",[31] especially in the formation of the first Czechoslovak state. This nationalist and populist approach was but the expression in the ideological arena of the KSČ's Popular Frontism, or rather its opportunist application of the strategy.

To say this is not to argue against the harnessing of a nation's progressive traditions and culture to the socialist movement. Similarly, a movement serious in its revolutionary intentions must aim to win sizeable sectors of the non-working-class strata of the population to support its policy. What left the KSČ open to criticism was that its tactics on these issues bore no real relation to its vision of Czechoslovak socialism. The party's future perspectives were assimilated into the tactics, although the extent to which these perspectives were clearly worked out is itself open to question. In consequence there existed no room for the development of KSČ policy in these areas, only policy statements relating to the present situation.

With regard to the forthcoming elections, three major points emerged from the Congress. First, that the KSČ was not proposing any measures which would disturb existing ownership patterns. The KSČ supported a broad private sector in industry, trade and agriculture, and vehemently rejected any suggestion that it would undermine the position of artisans, traders, working farmers or medium-sized enterprises. Secondly, the KSČ emphasised its opposition to the Munich diktat and its leading role in the national resistance.[32] They linked this with fierce anti-German sentiment, which flourished at the Congress and was the complement to the KSČ's nationalist, Slav policy.[33] Such a policy was considered electorally popular. Thirdly, the KSČ reaffirmed their support for the National Front and considered that its main task was to guide the rapid economic reconstruction of the republic. As Gottwald declared, "We stand before the nation as the party of honest work, the party of clear conscience, and with clean hands".[34] On this basis the KSČ leadership felt confident of gaining wide popular support in the elections for the National Assembly.

With regard to the wider strategic perspective expressed at the congress, two fundamentally differing interpretations have been made. Czechoslovak Communist politicians after the events of February 1948 declared that these were the logical culmination of the political strategy which had been laid down at Košice and consolidated at the Eighth KSČ Congress. In his speech to the Central Committee in November 1948, Gottwald declared that February was the climax of the general line which the party had pursued since 1945. Czechoslovak historians have generally accepted this view of continuity. Kozák writes that "the transition to socialism in our country . . . was realised by way of a national and democratic revolution . . . and by its gradual evolution into socialist revolution,"[36] while the official KSČ textbook declares that Gottwald's speech at the Eighth Congress laid "the clear direction of the party for the further gradual transition to socialism".[37] This interpretation considers that the KSČ had a clear strategy for the transition to socialism, that it expressed this strategy in its political discussions and that the particular policies it pursued between 1945 and 1948 were integrally linked to this strategy.

By contrast, the emigré and Western literature on the subject has considered that the "democratic" line which the KSČ pursued between 1945 and 1947 was merely a stratagem, a means by which to deceive their partners within the National Front. Bolton writes that "the communists were collaborating with the three other parties for the sake of tactical advantage,"[38] while Korbel states the case even more baldly. Until mid-1947, "behind the relatively tranquil scene it (the KSČ) methodically followed the policy of deepening and widening its position of power". The KSČ's policies, " 'operation grant deceit', a carefully-prepared plan to capture the minds of the great masses, produced at least in the first two years after the war remarkable results".[39]

Neither interpretation gives an adequate analysis of Czechoslovakia's development in these years. The latter is merely another version of the conspiracy theory of history which, while appealing to US State Department officials past and present, has little to offer serious analysts.

However, the official Communist interpretation is also inadequate in that it fails to analyse the social and political forces operating during the period and how the contradictions sharpened over time. The interpretation is completely linear, declaring the transition to socialism to have followed a smooth and straight path naturally culminating in February. It offers a classic example of historical interpretation being nothing but an instrument of political propaganda.

There is no recognition of the existing international situation and its relation to internal Czechoslovak politics. The continuance, however fragile, of the Big Three coalition was the linchpin of Communist strategy at this time, in Czechoslovakia as well as the rest of Europe. As long as the possibility of inter-Allied co-operation existed, this was the strategy that the USSR advised and encouraged Communist parties to follow. As the Communist Party of the Soviet Union declared in its message of greetings to the Eighth Congress, "as the party of the working class, representing the interests of broad strata of the working people, the Communist Party (of Czechoslovakia) is one of the leading parties of *the democratic coalition*. The Communist Party is fighting with success for a strengthening of the people's democratic state, for the development of the national economy and culture of Czechoslovakia, for a strengthening of the union and friendship between the Czech and Slovak nations, for the definitive destruction of all remnants of fascism and reaction, for strengthening the co-operation of Czechoslovaks with the Soviet Union and *all democratic states* and for securing firm and lasting peace for its people."[40] Therein lay the perspective and rhetoric of the CPSU. In 1946 the KSČ, in harmony with the outlook of the CPSU, considered that further significant co-operation within the National Front was a real possibility. The entire content, outlook and spirit of the Eighth Congress reflects this political strategy. Even the most cursory glance at Gottwald's address to the congress shows that what was envisaged for the forseeable future was a continuation of the existing political and economic structure, and not its socialist transformation. In no way did the Eighth Congress lay the ground for a policy of exclusive communist control of the government and state.[41]

By reaffirming its previous strategy and basing itself squarely — even if only implicitly — on the existing international equilibrium, the KSČ was acting in accord with its fraternal parties and like them, under Soviet guidance, it evolved a concept of its own road to socialism. In August 1946 Stalin had told a British Labour Party delegation that there were two roads to socialism, the Russian road and the parliamentary one, the latter being a longer process but involving no bloodshed.[42] In November Thorez, General Secretary of the French Communist Party, was explaining to the correspondent of *The Times* that "the progress of democracy throughout the world . . . permits the choice of other paths to socialism than the one taken by the Russian Communists. In any case, the path is necessarily different for each country".[43]

The introduction by Gottwald in autumn 1946 of the concept of a specific Czechoslovak road to socialism[44] was in line with contemporary Communist thinking. Nowhere were the theoretical aspects of this concept clearly expressed, so it remained unclear as to whether all it involved was a different *way* to power or whether an alternative *model* of socialism was involved. What was common to all proponents of the concept was that the transition to socialism was viewed as a very gradual process.

This was epitomised by the Eighth Congress, with its themes of unity of the nation, unity of the Slav people, unity with small and medium capital and unity with the other parties in the National Front. The link in revolutionary strategy between the national democratic and socialist revolutions had become so tenuous as to be non-existent. All the KSČ leadership could offer was a continuation of present policy, allied to more work, more effort and more sweat. Later proponents of the view of continuity in KSČ policy maintained there was no "Chinese wall" between the two stages of revolution.[45] In fact the policy and propaganda of the KSČ leaders showed that they expected it to be a very long march.

The congress also cast light on the internal functioning and organisation of the KSČ and the character of its leadership. The enormous distortions of Lenin's principles of inner-party democracy which occurred under Stalin were not confined just to the Soviet Communist Party. Stalinist practices had been transmitted through the Comintern to all member parties. No draft resolutions were circulated to districts and branches before the congress, merely a letter from the Central Committee which supported government policy and said little else, other than "a strong Communist Party is the best guarantee of a strong and happy republic".[46] The congress itself was presented with no resolutions around which debate and discussion could focus. Slánský, Gottwald, Švermová, Kopecký, Nepomucký and Horn gave the six main reports to the congress, yet not one of them dealt with the crucial questions posed by the contemporary political scene: the Great Powers' coalition and its significance for domestic Czechoslovak politics; the political trends developing in the other parties of the National Front; the political position and role of President Beneš; the strengths and weaknesses of ROH and the works councils; the transition to socialism. All that was said of political opposition was subsumed under the generic term "reaction". Not surprisingly, speakers from the floor followed suit, and in consequence no coherent political discussion took place at any session of the congress. In its place there was a series of speeches from district and area delegates on how well they were working to strengthen the republic, often completely unrelated to the report supposedly under discussion. The party leadership had decided already on the main policy outlines, and the whole nature of the congress operated against any attempt to alter that policy. The policies were implicit in the main reports, and rather than being a policy-making body the congress was reduced to the status of a rubber-stamp. In the final session Dolanský presented the report of the Policy Commission. He asked formally that congress accept that the reports of Gottwald and the other five should represent the political direction of the party, and that the Central Committee should take the necessary measures to ensure their widest support amongst the working people. The proposal was accepted unanimously; the Central Committee had its free hand.[47]

In the absence of a functioning internal democracy, the leading functionaries of the KSČ inevitably assumed a preponderant political weight and influence. The two features were complementary, each reinforcing the other. As has been discussed earlier, this process was intimately linked with the "Bolshevisation" of the KSČ by the Comintern in 1929. By the Eighth Congress these features had solidified into accepted inner-party norms.[48] The implicit attitude of the mass of members was that the line of the leadership was — and indeed had to be — correct, and hence no opposition was expressed to the lack of debate or to the proposed new Central Committee, which was accepted unanimously.[49] The authority of the leadership was immense, and this strengthened the centralist tendencies within the party.

The Central Committee was heavily weighted towards those who had had long-standing membership of the party. 38 of the 101-strong Central Committee were founder-members of the KSČ.[50] Great emphasis was laid on experience, indeed 398 of the 1,038 delegates at the Eighth Congress had been members since before 1930, when the membership had been very small.[51] This quest for "experienced" cadres was a political question, since it was considered that those who had been tested through previous policy shifts would be most amenable to the policies decided by the inner leadership and least likely to display the independence of mind and policy which, for example, the domestic resistance in the Czech Lands and Slovakia had more than hinted at.[52]

The decisive policy-making body was the Presidium of the Central Committee, commonly known as the Politburo,[53] and here the "men of '29" dominated. The Politburo chosen at the Central Committee meetings on 31 March 1946 consisted of Václav David, Jaromír Dolanský, Josef Frank, Klement Gottwald, Gustav Kliment, Václav Kopecký, Ladislav Kopřiva, Josef Krosnář, Zdeněk Nejedlý, Václav Nosek, Rudolf Slánský, Josef Smrkovský, Marie Švermová, and Antonín Zápotocký.[54] Široký and Ďuriš attended as well, although the KSS was a separate organisation. Dolanský, Kopecký, Krosnář, Nosek, Slánský and Švermová had all become members of the Central Committee for the first time in 1929. All were supporters of the Comintern's policy and were part of the bloc which aided Gottwald and ousted the former leadership. By the Seventh Congress in 1936 this bloc had consolidated its position with the new Politburo including Slánský, Kopecký and Široký, as well as Zápotocký and Gottwald.[55] Borne to leadership at the insistence of the Comintern, these politicians viewed the interests of the Czechoslovak working class as being umbilically linked to the defence of the world's first socialist state. Under their leadership KSČ policy altered in accord with the shifts in Soviet policy, and with an extremely centralised, strictly disciplined party the new line imposed from above was passively accepted by the membership.[56]

The distortions in the internal functioning of the KSČ culminated in the boundless adulation which was heaped on Klement Gottwald, the party chairman and to a lesser degree on Rudolf Slánský, its general secretary. This phenomenon of cultism cemented the party, with its forces marshalled, disciplined and led from above.

Thus Klement Gottwald led the major working-class party in the country. The KSČ held the central position within the National Front government and intended to continue its Popular Front strategy. Heading an exceptionally centralised party, Gottwald and his colleagues formed a dominant, cohesive leadership which exercised enormous authority over the party and was able to shift its policy rapidly, yet unitedly. This was a very important feature of the KSČ. Similarly important was the manner in which such swift policy shifts could be reflected in other organisations, especially those with a mass character, and above all in the trade-union movement. Stalinist practices had embedded themselves not only within the party but also in its relationship with other organisations.

9
The Main Transmission Belt

The upsurge in activity of the working class after the war was reflected in the trade-union movement, which developed exceptionally rapidly. Such was the strength and influence of ROH that it was able to hold its first national conference in Prague from 11-13 January 1946 with 930 voting delegates present.[1] This was a prelude to the First All-Trade-Union congress which ROH held from 19-22 April 1946. Delegates were elected on the basis of one for every 2,000 members or part thereof. In factories employing 2,000 people or more election was direct; otherwise delegates were chosen at district trade-union conferences.[2] These were held on 13 and 14 April. In all there were 1,237 Czech and Slovak delegates registered with voting rights at the conference, the Czech delegates representing 1,679,000 members of ROH, while the 182 Slovak delegates represented 240,000 Slovak trade unionists.[3] The political weight of the trade-union movement was highlighted by the presence at the conference of Fierlinger, the Prime Minister; Svoboda, Minister of Defence; Šoltész, Minister of Finance; and Masaryk, Minister of Foreign Affairs. All spoke, as did representatives from the parties of the National Front: Petr for the LS; Šivera, deputy chairman of the NSS; Vilím, general secretary of the SDS; and Gottwald, chairman of the KSČ.[4] Their attendance signified a recognition of the crucial role which ROH had in determining the future political course of the republic.

Crucial to the development of ROH had been the organisational structure which it had evolved. The question of internal trade-union organisation was one of the most vital matters which faced the Czech labour movement at the end of the war. The historical experience of the catastrophes wrought by the divisions and fissures of the pre-war years merged with the outlook of the Communists, who favoured a very centralised trade-union movement. The provisional proposals which emerged from the ÚRO organisational commission in August 1945 reflected this coalescence and the domination of the KSČ within the trade unions. Accepted by the ÚRO Presidium, these proposals formed the skeleton of internal ROH organisation and were in broad outline the proposals which the congress accepted.

In essence the proposals attempted to overcome pre-war union disunity by centralisation. Decisive weight was given in the structure to central, all-trade-union bodies. ÚRO was the executive body of ROH between congresses. The First Congress agreed that this 120-strong body meet three times a month. In between times responsibility lay with a 42-strong management committee, a central body whose vital importance was highlighted in the original proposals. These stated that "This organ directs ROH and decides on all fundamental questions of the trade-union movement".[5] However, by the First Congress the locus of power within the central apparatus had shifted to the 14-strong Presidium. Responsible for the day-to-day functioning of ROH, with its own secretariat and with all specialist central commissions answerable to it, the Presidium was the body from which almost all policy initiatives came.

The three key trade-union organs were ÚRO, the management committee of ÚRO and the Presidium, in ascending order of significance. The decisive mechanism in the structure for transmitting central directives to the membership was the district trades council (KOR — *krajská odborová rada*). These bodies, at least 20-strong and elected at all-trade-union district conferences, had overall responsibility for the development of all spheres of trade-union work within their district. They were responsible for setting up area trade-union councils, for the work of district union committees, for growth in membership and for the fulfilment of ROH policy. The diagram shows clearly the centralised character of the whole movement, with the separate trade unions playing an extremely subordinate role to the all-trade-union bodies at both a national and district level. As stated in part 3 of the 21-part resolution[6] which the organisational commission put to the First ROH Congress, trade unions were not independent bodies but inseparable parts of a united organisation. Their activity in the solution of specialist questions had to be decided in accordance with the common interests of the working people.

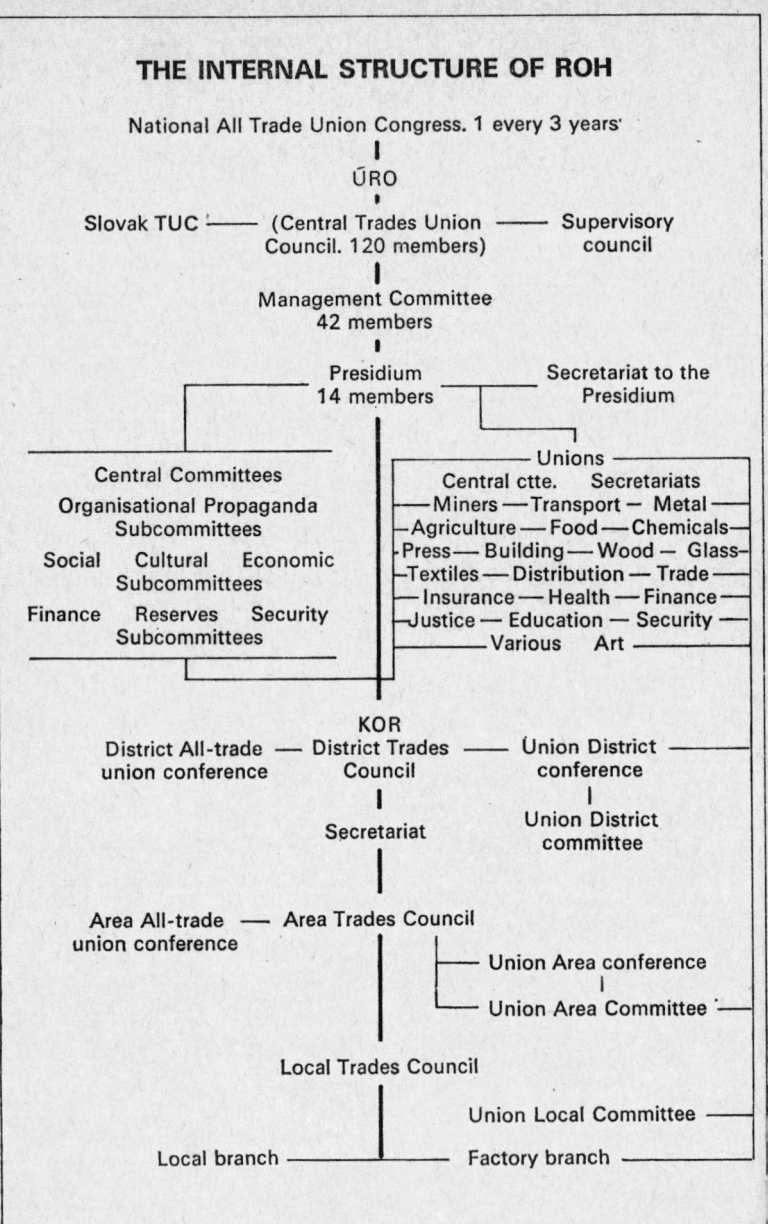

It was to ensure as far as possible that this occurred that the structure of ROH was so centralised. The resolution stated that the current level of unity among the working class was sufficient to permit a certain decentralisation and for trade unions with functioning executive and district committees to be established.

What was exemplified here and characterised the resolution as a whole was the belief that political and ideological differences within the working class would disappear if the trade-union movement was united as an organisation. Erban, ROH's general secretary, declared to the congress that the unity of trade-union organisation was the key to unity of trade-union policy,[7] while the resolution stated that trade-union organisation had to consistently preserve both the organisational and ideological unity of the movement. Entire union policy for all sections would be directed by ÚRO on the principles of democratic centralism. "This new form of organisational construction of the trade unions has proved to be *the politically effective defence* against all attempts of reaction to subvert or weaken trade-union unity."[8] The question of political and ideological unity was viewed primarily as an organisational matter.[9] As the report to the Second ROH congress in 1949 explained:

> In order that the new, united organisation should be capable of fulfilling the tasks of the trade unions and overcoming internal professional, craft and political influences, in order that it should be simultaneously capable of resisting the attempts of reactionary political forces to disrupt the unity, it was necessary to build the organisation on the principles of democratic centralism. This means that all organs of the movement are democratically elected, that the majority makes the decisions and resolutions in all groups whereas the minority abides and accepts the majority resolutions, and that the resolutions of higher organs of the movement are binding on the lower organs.[10]

At the base the principle of industrial unionism was pursued,[11] opposition to this policy being negligible.[12] The demand for greater trade-union autonomy from central organs received more support,[13] yet since ROH was already operating along principles of democratic centralism and its central bodies had assumed preponderant importance, the balance in favour of accepting the leadership's organisational proposals was inevitably overwhelming. At the congress the matter was deal with by the organisation commission, there being no debate on the major issues at stake. Not surprisingly, therefore, the question aroused little interest. Only three speakers mentioned the issue, all registering their support.[14] When the resolution of the organisation commission was presented on the last day of the congress, it gained unanimous endorsement.[15]

The strength of ROH

The trade-union structure adopted placed considerable organisational emphasis on the district trades councils (KOR), and an appreciation of ROH's strength can be gained by investigating these bodies. By the congress there were 21 functioning KORs covering the entire Czech Lands.[16] In Plzeň, a district with large-scale engineering, foodstuffs and brewery industries, the KOR had held 1,856 meetings, which 137,573 people had attended.[17] In Pardubice, an area of medium and small enterprises with metal, textile and footwear industries, the KOR had organised 2,230 meetings at which 146,819 people had been present.[18] Olomouc KOR organised 3,190 members' and factory meetings in their district, where medium-sized enterprises predominated, and 192,000 people attended these meetings. In addition they held 26 area conferences attended by 9,200 members and established 7 area trade councils in the district;[19] while Plzeň KOR established area trade councils in all 8 political constituencies in the district.[20]

The KORs also played a decisive role in encouraging trade-union participation in economic renewal and reconstruction. In Brno, a district with major metal, textile, building, wood, chemical and foodstuffs industries, the KOR set up an economic commission which had specific responsibility along with its sub-committees for encouraging intiative in reconstruction, in planning and with voluntary brigades.[21] In Moravská Ostrava, the most important industrial region in the republic with major coalmines, coke ovens, power stations, gasworks, steel plants, engineering and chemical industries, the KOR had encouraged labour competitions as a means of boosting production.[22] In Most, with important mines and considerable iron and steel making, the economic commission checked production developments and the progress of new methods.²³ The KOR secretariats also assumed responsibility for developing individual unions. In Brno a conference of works councils in the metal industry was held as early as 22 May 1945, and a union district committee was established.²⁴ In Ostrava the KOR took a similar initiative, and by the end of 1945 the metalworkers' union had 38,000 members organised in 87 factories in the district.²⁵ These examples, along with Table 3 below,²⁶ illustrate the range of KOR activity and the rapid growth of the trade-union movement. On 31 December 1945 ROH membership was calculated as 1,442,816, and at the

Table 3
The state of trade unionism in the Czech Lands on 31 December 1945

KOR	Membership	% of workforce	Works Councils	Shop Stewards*	Trade Union Branches
Prague	344,050		2,516	3,003	—
Brno	100,000	70%	1,607	1,014	1,070
České Budějovice	20,516		470		177
Hradec Králové	76,695		719	625	542
Jihlava	25,000		478†		—
Karlovy Vary	3,453‡		120	105	—
Kladno	67 989	80%	476	406	432
Klatovy	26,080	48%	308	261	193
Kolín	76,000	58%	604	536	431
Liberec	25,000‡		484†		202
Mladá Boleslav	47,638		485	502	272
Moravská Ostrava	127,900	65%	640†		488
Most	29,357‡		483	180	229
Olomouc	75,000	64.6%	659	556	448
Pardubice	60,536		494	374	—
Plzeň	101 117		396	293	324
Šumperk	12,325		99	156	105
Tábor	45,000		413	402	—
Ústí	15,968‡		265	155	299
Zlín	—	58.9%	538†		316
Znojmo	—		154	130	168

* In workshops employing less than 20 people a shop steward was to be elected rather than a works council.
† Combined figure for the works councils and shop stewards.
‡ Area heavily populated by Germans. No attempt was made to unionise them.

congress Zápotocký declared that trade-union membership in Bohemia and Moravia was 1,696,698, representing 73.5 per cent of the total labour force.[27]

Another significant feature of ROH was that it unified the Czech and Slovak sections of the working class in one organisation. This unification, confirmed at the congress, was especially important, as it lessened the possibility of right-wing and catholic elements gaining support among Slovak workers. The social structure of Slovakia was markedly different from the rest of the republic, the last pre-war census showing that only 19.1 per cent of the population worked in industry while agriculture accounted for 56.6 per cent. The corresponding figures for Bohemia were 41.5 per cent and 25.6 per cent.[28] With a smaller industrial base, the working class in Slovakia was significantly weaker, both absolutely and relatively, than its Czech counterpart. Of the 1,626 factories in Slovakia on 1 March 1946, 1,192 engaged less than 51 employees, while in none were there more than 5,000. Against this 12.6 per cent of all employees in industry in the Czech Lands worked in enterprises of over 5,000.[29] Hence the trade-union movement faced a harder task in Slovakia, and this was further complicated by the character of Slovakia's wartime experience and the considerable influence which clerical ideology retained amongst wide strata of the population. There was early recognition by the left that the unification of the Slovak trade unions within ROH would strengthen the position of the unions in Slovakia. The ROH leadership argued that as a result the Slovak working class would pursue policies in accord with the overall interest of the working class in the whole republic rather than fall prey to sectional, autonomist policies.

Discussions between Czech and Slovak unions began as early as 18 June 1945 in Prague.[30] A meeting in Bratislava on 20-22 July led to an agreement being signed at Piest'any declaring common unity behind the government programme.[31] A further meeting held at Banska Bystrica on the anniversary of the Slovak National Rising led to an agreement that representatives of both trade-union centres should meet monthly, alternately in Slovakia and the Czech Lands.[32] The conference of Slovak trade unionists at Turčiansky-Martin on 13-14 October laid the basis for uniting the two organisations,[33] and a 12-man Slovak delegation was present at the ROH conference in January 1946. Zupka, head of the Slovak unions, addressed the conference and emphasised the common interest of the Czech and Slovak working people.³⁴ Detailed negotiations were undertaken in the following months, and at the congress the Slovak trade unions were formally incorporated into ROH.

The foregoing illustrates the extent to which ROH entered its First All-Trade-Union Congress as a strong, united body. As Erban stated in a preview article in *Práce*, the congress — "this parliament of the working class" — would resolve the further policy direction of ROH, as well as unifying Czech and Slovak union organisation and deciding ROH's internal structure.³⁵

ROH's left-wing leadership had already outlined its main policy aims at the first national conference in January, and these correspond closely to KSČ thinking.

The fulfilment of the main aspects of the Košice programme had wrought fundamental changes on the character of Czechoslovak society, and in consequence the role of trade unionism had both altered and broadened. Trade-union activity was no longer restricted to the fight for better wages and conditions, but was extended to include taking part in major decisions on all aspects of national economic and social life. The nationalisation decrees laid the basis for this new trade-union politics, for they permitted long-term national planning which would involve ROH. The leadership felt that with nationalisation it was also possible to forge co-operation between manual workers and those employees engaged in organising production, and that it was easier to encourage workers to make increased efforts to boost production.³⁶ From this reasoning it followed that the question of production was the major matter on ROH's agenda. As Zápotocký told the first national conference:

> I limit myself again and again to the question which I consider as the most topical task of our trade-union policy at this time, and that is the question of production, production and again production. In the solution of this question lies the key to a successful solution of all other questions.³⁷

In the period between January and April ÚRO began to tackle this question,³⁸ and it was to this theme that Zápotocký returned when he delivered his main address to congress. The aim of ROH was "to build the republic, to renew production".[39] He placed the matter within the context of a long-term economic plan, the basis of which "must be the total needs of the nation".[10] To ensure fulfilment of the aim, the slogan which had to guide trade-union policy and which expressed the movement's fundamental demands was: "Renew production: make more products, better products and cheaper products".[11] This would not be an easy task, and Zápotocký warned that to revitalise the economy and raise the standard of living of the working people would entail a new, enthusiastic working morale and considerable sacrifice. Social attitudes to work would have to change, and a shift of labour to the more productive sectors of the economy was necessary.[42] The major part of his address was devoted to "the organisation and planning of production, the main task of our trade-union work and activity".[43] Success in this sphere was crucial, for it held the key to the possibility of fulfilling the movement's other demands. This view was reiterated in the resolution which the head of the political commission, Kliment, presented to the congress. The resolution, which was unanimously accepted, stated that nationalisation permitted the establishment of a planned economy with planned production: "Therefore, it is the most fundamental task of ROH to renew and increase production, especially primary production, to secure transport, to provide more, better and cheaper products".[44] This would be achieved by removing remnants of Nazi-influenced working morale and by invoking voluntary working enthusiasm and a spirit of solidarity and co-operation.

Within the context of the overall theme of the renewal of production four major interrelated questions were posed: how best to obtain a steady labour supply; by what means to boost the workers' enthusiasm: how to ensure that wage increases were related to a raising of productivity levels and thereby avoid inflation; and how to preserve the right of trade unionists to strike yet also ensure that sectional interests were not constantly placed above those of the movement as a whole. By the end of its First Congress the trade-union leadership had attempted, at various times, to grapple with all of these problems and had formulated its basic approach, which was to guide it in the following months.

Concerning the supply of labour and the shortage consequent on the expulsion of the Germans, the main emphasis was placed on bringing women into the productive process.[45] There were powerful economic as well as ideological pressures which encouraged Communist and left-wing trade unionists to call for the removal of all obstacles to women's entry into social production.

The congress's political resolution, using phrases often to be repeated, declared that ROH would mobilise and organise all the creative forces of the working people for the construction of the republic. The means by which this was to be achieved were national competitions; these competitions were to be organised in the factories and workshops by production committees.[46] In their efforts to renew and increase production ROH laid their entire emphasis on these appeals to workers to work harder rather than combining these exhortations with a policy encouraging specialist technical development and new investment. In this their policy was identical with that which the KSČ Congress had called for three weeks previously. Its shortcomings and inadequacies were to dog the economy in the future.

With the major sector of the economy under public ownership, the trade-union leadership recognised that ROH's approach to wages issues had to be different from what had been the traditional trade-union approach. This had to be so despite the low and inadequate wages which many workers received. ÚRO had fought against any demands for large increases in wages or salaries, since the state of the national economy meant that these would not have led to real increases in the standard of living, but rather to inflation. As Zápotocký told both the first national conference and the first congress, only when the problems of production had been resolved would it be possible, with sufficient wealth being produced, to overcome the inadequate level of wages.[47]

Intimately related to the wages question was that of strikes. Not only would strikes disrupt the process of reconstruction but also, if they resulted in wage increases unrelated to productivity, they would begin to undermine the entire economic programme. The essence of the trade-union leadership's solution was to preserve the right to strike yet make it difficult to exercise *at a local level*. As Macura explained at the first national conference, a strike decision could not be decided on by the local organisation alone, but had to be agreed on by the area and district leadership, and if necessary ÚRO. Only then was it possible to resort to a strike, "the last weapon of the working class".[48] At a plenary session of ÚRO on 14 March 1946, a resolution on strikes was passed. It reserved the right of union members to strike, but stated that it did not wish to provoke them, and felt that the influence and strength of the trade-union movement, along with the goodwill of the government, meant that such conflicts were unlikely. The resolution went on to warn all organs and members against any ill-considered strike action, reminding them that all channels had to have been worked through and the agreement of the central trade-union bodies obtained before any such action could be undertaken.[49] In this way the centralised ROH structure was used to discipline the membership. This discipline from above could be exerted in a dual fashion, for as Zápotocký declared to the congress, ROH would use the strike weapon if provoked by reactionary elements,[50] and all its sections would be bound to obey a strike call emanating from its central committee.

In its broad aspects ROH policy was very similar to that which the KSČ was pursuing. Like the KSČ, the trade-union leadership considered that the coalition of parties in the National Front government would continue for the forseeable future and based their policies on this assumption. Just as the KSČ Congress had done, so the ROH congress saw its main task as being to renew economic life and increase the gross national product, this being the fundamental way to safeguard and develop the national and democratic revolution. Indeed, the only noticeable difference of ROH from the KSČ — and this was one of emphasis not strategy — was its tendency to mention socialism more clearly and definitely as their goal. Zápotocký concluded his address to congress by saying that the united trade unions along with the National Front government would bring "a new epoch of popular political and economic democracy, leading to socialism";[51] the congress slogan and title was "By struggle and work to the victory of socialism"; and the report of the central national economic commission to the congress stated that "Industry must be built on a scientific and socialist basis, it must be planned".[52]

Given the preponderance of support among the industrial working class for the KSČ, it was predictable that the ROH would adopt a similar policy. There existed a corresponding Communist dominance in the personnel of the trade-union leadership. Ninety-four of the 120-strong ÚRO were KSČ members,[53] and many of these had experience of "the practical school of the old labour movement" and had been steeled by it.[54] This applied above all to the leading Communists who dominated the trade-union movement, Zápotocký, Zupka, Kolský and Kliment being the most prominent. Antonín Zápotocký, the chairman of ROH and its dominant personality, had been an active left-wing leader in the SDS before the formation of the KSČ. A leading member of the KSČ from its foundation, he had such standing in the Communist trade unions that he was elected to the executive committee of the Red International of Labour Unions (RILU) in 1928 and became secretary of the Red Trade Unions in Czechoslovakia in 1929. From 1929 until the war he was on the KSČ Politburo, a position he reoccupied on his return from Oranienburg concentration camp. František Zupka, ROH's vice-chairman and head of the Slovak trade unions, was a founder member of the KSČ in Slovakia and had been a prominent Red Trade Union functionary after 1929. Josef Kolský, the deputy general secretary of the ÚRO with major responsibility for organisational matters, was another founder member of the KSČ. Active in the Metalworkers' Union, he had been sent to Moscow from 1932-36 as the representative of the Red Trade Unions to RILU and was to return to the Soviet Union as an émigré after Munich. Gustav Kliment headed the country's largest union, the Metalworkers, and was a member of the ÚRO management committee. After being involved in the anarchist movement as a locksmith's apprentice, he joined the KSČ at its foundation. He became a Communist deputy in the National Assembly from 1929-38, while continuing to be involved in trade-union activity in Ostrava.[55] The entire political understanding and experience of these leaders was one which led them to see their role as being to gain the speediest implementation of KSČ policy within the trade unions. Their training in "the practical school" had equipped them well for their task.

Not only did ROH pursue the same policy as the KSČ and have a similar, veteran Communist leadership, but also in its internal functioning undemocratic methods, identical to those in the KSČ, were practised. No pre-congress resolution was circulated by ÚRO, and at the congress no debates were held. The political arguments were confined to the four commissions, political, organisational, electoral and mandatory, which had to prepare the congress documents. These were presented to the congress on the final day for formal acceptance.[56] The only possibility for debate at the congress came in the session after Zápotocký's speech. A Czech historian, analysing the congress, has written that Zápotocký's report evoked "a rich discussion",[57] yet he fails to point out that the discussion was entirely unstructured and that no opportunity for serious debate of matters at issue within the trade-union movement was offered at the congress. The main resolution placed before the congress was drafted in the political commission and based primarily on Zápotocký's report. Minor alterations to it were possible, but the entire procedure ensured that no important policy changes were made. There was no way in which major political differences could be brought to the floor of congress. This pinpointed the fact that the congress was not designed as a policy-making body. In the ROH structure, although it was nominally the sovereign body, a congress took place only once every three years and therefore, inevitably, policy was agreed upon and decided elsewhere. In effect congress was a propaganda rather than a policy-making occasion. The first congress devoted only one day to discussion, with 51 delegates taking part. The first day of the congress was taken up with speeches by ministers, spokesmen from political parties and mass organisations, and fraternal greetings from foreign trade unionists, while on the second Erban and Zápotocký delivered the two major congress reports. The short final day was occupied by the main commission reports and a concluding speech by Zápotocký. Thus discussion at the congress was strictly limited and the whole affair structured to avoid any airing of critical opinion. All these features meant that the stature of the congress as the highest decision-making body of ROH was completely devalued.

However, the most serious matter concerned the organisational structure of ROH, a structure which had been confirmed by the congress and the implications of which did not become apparent to the Czechoslovak working class and trade-union movement until much later. As far as can be seen, there was no serious criticism from the left of the decision to establish a democratic centralist structure for the Revolutionary Trade-Union Movement as a whole. This was the policy of the KSČ. They were the main force in gaining the acceptance of the congress for this proposal — a proposal which was to undermine the autonomy and vitality of the trade-union movement and the popular initiatives which workers were able to take within it. Thereby the *active* participation of the working class both in the revolutionary events of February 1948 and the post-February period of socialist construction was to be severely restricted.

In order to understand why these organisational developments were so serious and yet why they took place, it is necessary to investigate the specific functions of trade unions and communist parties and the relationship between them. Trade unions are spontaneous organs of the working class. Wherever workers have been drawn together in large-scale production units they have attempted to combine together to defend their immediate, sectional interests. They have waged this collective economic struggle in order to gain better terms for the sale of their labour power, for better living and working conditions. This has inevitably been a trade-union struggle, since working conditions, the character of the employers, the profitability of the industry and each industry's specific situation differ between industries: consequently workers' economic struggles can only be based on *trade* organisations. What emerges from this is that within the entire working class there exist strong, centrifugal forces tending to disrupt unity by placing the immediate interests of a particular section of workers above the interests of the class as a whole.

On the other hand the task of the party is to unify the working class in pursuit of its hegemonic and permanent interest — the establishment of socialism. To this end the party has to subordinate the temporary or sectional interests of the working class.

It follows logically from these different functions that the character and structure of the two organisations differ. Where trade unions are mass organisations which tend to encompass the bulk of the working class, the party embraces only the most advanced, class-conscious elements. It encompasses only a minority of the working class. This was true even of mass communist parties on the Czechoslovak, Italian or French scale. They recognised that in fact only a minority of the working class would actively work for the policy of the party and thereby be eligible for membership, although they expected to gain the support of the majority of the working class. In trade unions, membership is open to all workers in that particular trade or industry and the union wants as large a membership as possible within those limits. In contrast, party membership is defined by an individual's political understanding and support for the party's programme of socialism. What unites communist party members is precisely this socialist consciousness. They are united as revolutionaries, whereas trade-union members are united by their job.

Given their different function and character, the internal structures of the organisations vary. A communist party operates on the lines of democratic centralism. This means that after broad intra-party discussion, the highest executive organ of the party takes a policy decision which is binding for the whole party and which members have to argue for publicly, even if they personally disagree. In broad outline an *individual* trade union usually adopts a similar procedure, although, since it is a mass, voluntary organisation with its membership defined by trade rather than political viewpoint, it cannot direct its members to argue publicly for the majority view. However, for the *united* body of the trade-union movement, representing all the different unions, to adopt a democratic centralist structure by which the decision of the highest executive organ becomes binding on all affiliated unions completely undermines the premises of trade unionism. The organisational structure adopted by the ROH meant that the Czechoslovak trade-union movement lost its distinctive character. By this step the sectional distinctions within the working class were suppressed. The policy was an attempt to overcome the centrifugal forces within the working class by an administrative, centralising measure, and as a result the ability of Czech trade unions to act in defence and furtherance of the immediate interests of their members was denied. No longer able to fulfil their original role, the individual unions at national, district and branch level were to become quiescent organisations, whose role was to carry out the directives decided centrally by ÚRO.

Although in opposition to the classical marxist-leninist tradition, KSČ thinking was in complete harmony with the formulations which Stalin had outlined in his work *The Foundations of Leninism*. Stalin had written:

> The party is the organised detachment of the working class. But the party is not the only organisation of the working class. The proletariat has a number of other organisations . . . But how can a single leadership be exercised with such an abundance of organisations? What guarantee is there that this multiplicity of organisations will not lead to divergency in leadership? . . . Where is the central organisation which is not only able, because it has the necessary experience, to work out such a general line, but, in addition, is in a position, because it has sufficient prestige, to induce all these organisations to carry out this line, so as to attain unity of leadership and to make hitches impossible?
>
> That organisation is the party of the proletariat . . . the only organisation capable of centralising the leadership of the struggle of the proletariat, thus transforming each and every non-party organisation of the working class into an auxiliary body and transmission belt linking the party with the class.
>
> The party is the highest form of class organisation of the proletariat.
>
> This does not mean, of course, that non-party organisations, trade unions, co-operatives, etc., should be officially subordinated to party leadership. It only means that the members of the party who belong to these organisations and are doubtlessly influential in them should do all they can to persuade these non-party organisations to draw nearer to the party of the proletariat in their work and voluntarily accept its political leadership.[58]

Herein were contained the elements that were to dominate Communist thinking and practice for the next three decades. Assuming that the party's policy was always right, its approach to mass organisations was one of getting them to "carry out this line". These mass organisations were the one-way transmission belts by which the party ensured that its policies were adopted by the working class. This approach was pursued by parties during the struggle for socialism, and inevitably, once communist parties gained power, these mass organisations degenerated into bodies completely subordinate to party leadership. Mass organisations were the passive beneficiaries of party policy.

In essence the KSČ followed this practice. ROH's declared aim was the establishment of a socialist order. The KSČ considered that the unity of the working class necessary for this was primarily an organisational problem, and consequently they sought to resolve a fundamental political question by administrative means. There were numerous organisational measures, above all industrial unionism, which could cement workers' unity and were an expression of it. Yet its achievement was *primarily* a political and ideological task. The KSČ failed to appreciate the crucial distinction between coercion and persuasion. Since trade unions were voluntary organisations, and as each union represented one sector of the working class, the only effective long-term method of achieving the active agreement of all sectors to a united policy was by persuasion. Propaganda, discussion, debate and the practical implementation of policy had to be the primary means of gaining the assent of workers for a particular course. It was only in this way that sectional, craft and professional attitudes could be genuinely eradicated. By placing their major emphasis on organisation and the use of a centralist structure to enforce working-class unity, the Communists were suppressing rather than removing differences within the working class. Such an administrative solution weakened the political understanding of the rank and file and lessened their initiative. They were no longer part of a genuine decision-making process. In these conditions the trade-union movement became steadily bureaucratised, while it also developed its own leadership cults. By their failure to recognise the twin polarities of force and consent, and that within trade unions the latter had to dominate, the Communists placed ROH in a bureaucratic strait-jacket.

The great majority of SDS trade unionists accepted this position. The KSČ exercised ideological dominance over wide sections of the non-communist left, as well as within its own ranks. The decline and "dogmatisation" of marxist theory, characteristic of the Stalin period, resulted in an ideological sterility throughout the left. No serious theoretical discussion of these complicated issues occurred, and leading SDS trade unionists such as Erban and Cipro simply adopted the Communist position.

The degeneration of marxist theory meant that complex theoretical problems requiring sophisticated political handling were vulgarised and oversimplified. In a socialist state the party was to provide the "single leadership" that would "make hitches impossible". Conflict between this state and the trade-union movement was inconceivable. In discussions between the three socialist parties at Košice, Stránský of the NSS had raised this question, declaring that the trade-union movement's independence from the state and government and its genuine autonomy needed to be guaranteed, even if at any time the unions went against national interests.[59] Nosek, for the KSČ, side-stepped the issue but Fierlinger (SDS) baldly answered Stránský by saying, "As long as we carry out a policy for the working people there cannot be conflict".[60] This expressed the essence of the left's position; their view of a socialist state was monolithic, and hence the possibility of a clash between workers and the state was nonexistent. This view contrasted markedly with that of the Bolsheviks. In January 1921 Lenin had written that "the trade unions no longer have to face the *class* economic struggle but the *nonclass* economic struggle, which means combating the bureaucratic distortions of the Soviet apparatus, safeguarding the working people's material and spiritual interests in ways and means inaccessible to this apparatus, etc. This is a struggle they will unfortunately have to face for many more years to come".[61] The Tenth Russian Communist Party Congress rejected calls for trade unions to be deprived of their autonomy and absorbed into the machinery of government. Despite the enormous strains their state was under after the civil war, the congress recognised that the working class needed its mass organisations to defend itself when necessary and to pressurise the administration. The socialist state had to give scope to a plurality of interests and influences.[62] The Bolsheviks had outlined in a rudimentary form a framework for handling the delicate relations between a socialist state and its working class, ensuring that the organisations of the latter retained their independence and initiative.[63] In June 1945 Zápotocký had declared, "The leading organs of the united trade unions must always be influenced and controlled from below by the initiative of the masses".[64] Yet the theoretical understanding and political perspective of Zápotocký and the leading Communist trade unionists precluded just such a possibility, for it was not amenable to administrative control. They relied on organisation and centralisation to achieve the solidarity and unity of the working class, battalions to be brought into action when the central leadership thought it necessary. Such an outlook, and its acceptance by ROH, strictly limited the role the working class was to play in the events culminating in February 1948 and in the subsequent period.

10
A Period of Consolidation

The KSČ and ROH congresses were a prelude to the election campaign. The elections for the Constituent National Assembly were due on 26 May; 300 deputies were to be elected to the single chamber. Czechoslovak citizens of both sexes, over the age of 18 and of Czech, Slovak or other Slavonic nationality were eligible to vote. The elections were to be held according to the principles of universal, direct, equal and secret vote with the number of deputies for each party decided on the basis of proportional representation.[1] Despite their agreement to continue with a National Front government after the election, all the parties recognised that they would be an important indicator of the political feeling in the country, the first parliamentary test of support for the measures of the national democratic revolution and the parties of the National Front. The weeks before the election saw increased political tension and rivalry.

The KSČ election programme adopted the policy and tone of its congress.[2] While the programme did state that the KSČ followed the principles of scientific socialism, of marxism-leninism within the spirit of the Czechoslovak heritage,[3] class terminology and socialist declarations did not figure prominently in the text. The document was aimed at securing KSČ support among all strata of urban and rural working people. The main task was "the maintenance and bolstering of the present course of our domestic and foreign policy, of its people's democratic character".[4] For this a united National Front government was essential, and the programme warned of the danger of reactionary elements penetrating other political parties and disrupting the unity of the National Front from within.[5] The KSČ saw a major task of the next government as the declaration of a new constitution which would codify and guarantee the main results of the national democratic revolution, especially the nationalisation decrees and the national committees. Another key sphere was economic recovery, and considerable emphasis was placed on the need for working people to increase their work effort.

Confident of securing a considerable part of the industrial working-class vote, the programme concentrated on policies aimed at winning other social strata. Support for the mechanisation of agriculture was pledged to compensate for the decrease in the agricultural labour force and to ease the burden of work, especially on peasant women, while all possible aid was promised to those Czechs and Slovaks who settled in the border regions previously populated by Germans.[6] No policy for further nationalisation of industry or trade or for collectivisation of agriculture was proposed. The KSČ sought to appeal to all social strata — the working class, public and state employees, the intelligentsia, urban and rural petty-bourgeoisie — by appealing to their patriotism and nationalism. The election programme stressed the KSČ's resolute opposition to Munich and how it, alone of the political parties, had called for alliance with the Soviet Union and the defence of the republic. On this issue and in the struggle for liberation, in which the party lost 24,920 members, the KSČ had shown its real worth to the nation.[7] The document declared its full support for transferring the German and Hungarian minorities from the republic and expounded the KSC's national programme:

> We propagate the most beautiful thought: the new Slavism. The Slav states are today the most progressive states in Europe as far as their political, economic and social system goes. That opens up new horizons for Slav thought and Slav politics in a progressive spirit.[8]

This interpretation of "marxism-leninism within the Czechoslovak heritage" was aimed at winning wide electoral support from non-proletarian strata. The genuine admiration and sympathy which many of these people felt for the KSČ as a result of its pre-Munich policy and actions in the resistance was to be maintained by the KSČ's "new Slavism". Their complete support for the expulsion of the Germans and their specific electoral references to help for the settlers in the vacated border regions were aspects of a policy aimed at winning the "national" vote. On the strength of its achievements the KSČ expected to emerge from the elections as the strongest party in the republic, and its electoral programme took great care not to antagonise any section of its strategic alliance between the working people of town and country.[9]

The election programme of the SDS[10] expressed the party's firm commitment to socialism and viewed the working class as the chief bearer of this new society. The document stated that "Socialism is the aim of the political and economic efforts of Social Democracy", and that "in the people's democratic system the workers are the most secure guarantee of the path to socialism".[11] It was also necessary, however, to gain the allegiance of other working people — farmers, the intelligentsia and artisans — if socialism was to be achieved.[12] The programme gave full support to nationalised industry, the National Front government, the united trade-union movement and the alliance with the USSR.[13] The SDS gave their complete approval to these main planks of the revolution, and the entire tenor and spirit of their programme was one of continuing and deepening these revolutionary changes.

This was not the position taken by the other two Czech parties, NSS and LS, which occupied the right of the political spectrum. The popular revolutionary tide had reached its zenith with the nationalisation and works councils decrees, and the more conservative sections of the National Front felt that with the situation stabilised they could assert themselves more effectively than hitherto. They considered the national democratic revolution to have been concluded, and hoped that after a temporary period some aspects of it could be revised so that Czechoslovakia would re-emerge as a more orthodox bourgeois-democratic republic, comparable to its character after the first world war.

The whole terrain of Czechoslovak politics had shifted dramatically to the left; the task facing these conservative elements was correspondingly difficult. However, with the immediate post-war revolutionary impetus exhausted, and the political situation less turbulent, there was an opportunity for right-wing forces within the country to regroup. The election campaign offered an occasion for the right to assume a clearer identity and to dissociate itself from those within the National Front who called for the strengthening of the national democratic revolution and its eventual evolution to socialism.

Several factors aided their task and encouraged them. Internationally, cracks in the Big Three coalition were appearing, most dramatically heralded by Churchill's "Iron Curtain" speech at Fulton, Missouri in March 1946. Such developments boosted the confidence of the right, and those who had been quiet in the post-war months began to engage in political activity. Attempts were made to re-establish the leading, banned pre-war right-wing parties — the Agrarians in the Czech Lands and the "Catholics" in Slovakia — though these failed. However, the NSS and LS attempted to court former Agrarian supporters, as the DS did with former Hlinka supporters in Slovakia. The NSS allowed into their ranks former Agrarian Party functionaries, including Feierabend, Suchý, Novák, Dvořan and Krček.[14] Effectively what happened was that instead of the old right-wing parties being re-established, former members and functionaries linked up with right-wing circles inside the NSS, LS and DS, and consequently these parties moved to the right.[15]

At a more general level the right was aided by the political outlook of President Beneš. While he supported co-operation with the Communists and left-wing Social Democrats, he nevertheless remained essentially a bourgeois politician. His realism and sophistication, along with the trauma of Munich, had led him to support the Košice programme, yet he opposed any further socialist development of the revolution and indeed hoped that some of its more radical measures would be rescinded. Later in the year he was pleased to tell Steinhardt, the US Ambassador in Prague, that "moderates are making steady progress in leading the country back to democratic ways".[16]

Beneš had been a National Socialist before he had been elected President of the republic in 1935 and he shared a common political outlook with the NSS leadership, which in turn looked to him as an ally.[17] The NSS leadership was composed of people whose entire education and outlook was based on the Western world. It was from there that they, like Beneš, drew their political inspiration, had their main contacts and found their political identification.[18] They wanted Czechoslovakia to develop along the lines of a Western democracy: a society operating a multi-sectoral economy with the private sector stronger than it was after the nationalisation decrees; a foreign policy which maintained close ties with Western powers; and a society which recognised the right of the individual and encouraged his or her initiative. The emergence of this alternative, non-socialist perspective was an uneven, complex process. As long as political divisions at an international level remained blurred by continued, if increasingly fragile, Big Three co-operation, and until the Czech middle bourgeoisie regained a certain degree of economic vitality, the right remained constrained and did not directly attack the main changes brought about by the Košice programme. Rather, it attempted to bolster its own economic and ideological bases within the framework of the National Front. Its emphases differed markedly from the left's, as the election campaign illustrated. A clear right-wing grouping was in the process of formation, but for the present it was not to break from the National Front.

This right-wing trend showed up clearly within the NSS and its election programme.[19] This stated that the NSS was a democratic party folowed the philosophy of Palacký and Masaryk, and that it was the party of the "Czech little man".[20] While the document did not challenge any of the measures of the Košice programme, it emphasised the party's future (non-socialist) perspective and some of the social groupings whose support it was trying to secure. Backing was given to co-operative enterprises, by which it was possible to change the economic structure "by a democratic path, without class struggle and revolutionary upheavals".[21] The programme paid particular attention to the problems faced by state employees, declaring that the 1926 law on their pay was a classic document of how high bureaucracy viewed its relations to its subordinates. The NSS pledged to "consistently support all just demands of the state and public employees".[22] This dual emphasis on the non-public sector of the economy and on white-collar workers reflected both the class base of the NSS and its political orientation. It was from among these strata that the NSS was hoping for widespread support. The NSS statement on trade and the necessity for Czechoslovakia to have trading relations with countries throughout the world[23] was significant for its omission of any references to the USSR. Czechoslovakia's pre-war trade had had a primarily Western orientation, and the NSS desired a return to this situation. Ripka had reported to Steinhardt in April the details of his trade negotiations in

Moscow. He was very satisfied at their outcome, since no restrictions had been placed on developing trade with the West, especially the United States.[24] In foreign policy the NSS supported the alliance with the Soviet Union and also the links with Western democratic powers. It attempted to defend its pre-war policy, declaring that the Little Entente and the agreement with France did not fail as a policy but rather it was failed by those for whom the agreements became a shred of paper.[25] The significance of this argument lay in it being an attempted justification for a policy of Western orientation in foreign affairs that the NSS leadership was eager to renew.

The Popular Party, as the only expressly non-socialist party in the Czech Lands, was more conservative. As its election programme declared, "The Popular Party rejects class politics",[26] and instead appealed to all citizens to work in a united nation. The LS was a Catholic party, and it considered the fundamental keystone of society and state to be the family. Their programme stated:

> Where the family is in decay, so the end of the state is near. All economic and social functions, which create the content of state life, have their beginning in the family. Authority, the concept of right, understanding of duty.[27]

Popular Party policies stemmed from this twin ideological stance. In the economic sphere their main platform was support for the rural and urban petty and medium bourgeoisie. "Private owners must have full security of ownership,"[28] their programme asserted, and must be allowed to develop productive initiatives. The private sector was not to be discriminated against in relation to the public sector, and the economic plan had to be one "in whose framework individual industrial branches would be able to develop freely".[29] The LS programme, reflecting the party's agrarian base, exaggerated the economic importance of agriculture to the republic, yet it forcefully reaffirmed LS support for rural property-holders:

> Agriculture in the republic is built on the principle of private ownership and only as such can it prosper. Farmers must be left the greatest productive freedom so that they would be able to develop fully the individual initiative so important for the variety of agricultural work.[30]

The document declared that the LS would put its full weight behind the protection of private ownership in agriculture, and gave an unqualified statement of support to all rural property-holders irrespective of size. A similar declaration was made with regard to private industrial enterprises.[31]

The LS programme also appealed to Catholics. Claiming that the Catholic church had been the guardian of the spiritual culture of the nation for the past thousand years, the programme called for complete freedom for the church, especially in the field of education.[32] Like the Democratic Party in Slovakia, the Popular Party attempted to mobilise the Catholic clergy behind its platform. These two parties represented most forcefully the non-socialist section of the Czechoslovak political spectrum; they were the parties most eager to halt the swing to the left and revert to the model of the pre-war republic. As the election campaign progressed, like-minded elements in the NSS came increasingly to the fore, isolating more socialist members of the leadership such as David and Wünsch.[33] The election campaign accelerated the formation of a right-wing bloc, as the NSS concentrated its main attack on the Communists, while berating the SDS for their close alliance with them. Within the SDS a similar right-wing grouping began to develop. In response to this the KSČ Central Committee meeting of 3 May agreed to the proposal for a Two-Year Plan of economic renewal. In his report Slánský said that this would show the electorate the positive, constructive attitude of the KSČ, in contrast with some of the negative statements emanating from other parties. To this end the KSČ national economic committee had already begun formulating detailed policy for the plan.[34]

This announcement undoubtedly helped consolidate the KSČ's electoral support, and in the elections on 26 May they emerged as the strongest party in the Czech Lands, as Table 4 shows.[35] There was no suggestion that the ballot was anything other than fair and free. As Steinhardt noted, "The election was held without incidents or disorder of any kind throughout the country. . . . All experienced observers are agreed that the vote recorded was the expression of the will of the people in a democratic manner".[36]

He reiterated this opinion two days later when he cabled:

Table 4
Results of the General Election in Czechoslovakia on 26 May 1946

Party	Bohemia Votes	%	Seats	Moravia Votes	%	Seats	Total Votes	%	Seats
KSČ	1,541,852	43.3%	65	663,845	34.5%	28	2,695,227	38.0%	114*
LS	580,004	16.3%	24	531,005	27.6%	22	1,111,009	15.6%	46
SDS	533,029	14.9%	23	322,509	16.7%	14	855,538	12.1%	37
NSS	898,425	25.2%	38	400,555	20.8%	17	1,298,980	18.3%	55
		Slovakia							
DS	999,557	62.0%	43				999,557	14.1%	43
KSS	489,530	30.4%	21					see note	
Freedom	60,200	3.7%	3				60,200	0.9%	3
Labour	50,214	3.1%	2				50,214	0.7%	2
"Blank ballots"†							32,164	0.3%	—

* Combined figure for KSČ and KSS.
† These were votes recorded for those who supported none of the permitted parties.

> There have been no aspersions of unfairness and it cannot be said that the rather strong Communist trend is attributable to intimidation by the Communists or their control of the election machinery. Leading persons are convinced that it was a secret and fair ballot, having been controlled at the polling places by representatives of all the leading parties.[37]

The "rather strong Communist trend" must be seen as confirming popular support for left policies. In the eyes of the electorate the KSČ was the party least tainted with the past and the strongest prop of the new order. Having been the most resolute opponent of Munich and having provided the leading core of the resistance, the KSČ was also the architect of the Košice programme and its foremost proponent. This record, accompanied by a policy of furthering the national democratic revolution, was the basis of the KSČ's electoral success. As well as winning wide support among the industrial working class the KSČ gained many votes in the villages. Expropriation of landed estates, granting land to those who tilled it and settling Czechs and Slovaks in the border regions, had been forcefully advocated by the KSČ, and these measures had been undertaken by the Communist Minister of Agriculture, Ďuriš. Gottwald's post-election analysis at the General Committee meeting on 30 May[38] emphasised the importance of the party vote in the countryside, while the KSČ's vociferous support for population transfer as a complement to its settler policy secured it above-average votes in the border regions.[39]

In alliance with the SDS there was the barest majority for the left in the assembly, the KSČ and SDS having 151 of the 300 deputies. Yet continued close support for the KSČ within the SDS was by no means certain, as a right-wing grouping emerged opposing this policy. Gaining momentum from their poor election results, this grouping, led by the SDS district leadership in Plzeň and backed by the Ostrava, Hradec Králové and Prague districts, wanted a special congress to discuss the election and alter SDS strategy.[40] Although this move was blocked, it was a sign of increasingly sharp internal conflict, and the resolution of this conflict was recognised generally as being one of the keys to future developments.[41]

The main right-wing forces had failed to secure their strategic objective in the election, and for the moment had to draw back. Their most notable success was in Slovakia, where the DS emerged as an exceptionally strong force. Their large victory aroused serious concern in the KSČ,[42] which recognised the potential danger of an alignment of the DS with the Czech right-wing parties. The Popular Party was disappointed with its result, despite its considerable support in the rural areas of Moravia, and the following months saw sharp internal differences.[43] The hopes of the National Socialists had been similarly dampened: they got several hundred thousand less votes than they had expected. Their inability to obtain a larger share of the rural vote particularly disappointed them, but they had emerged as the second largest party and viewed the future with some optimism.[44] The elections had not swung the country decisively to the left and its future course remained uncertain, subject to decisive influence by international developments. As the US Chargé in Prague, Bruins, was informed by leaders of the right-wing parties, it was impossible to judge whether Communist strength had peaked and would begin to wane or would be consolidated. Bruins cabled to the Secretary of State:

> The more judicial minded of the moderates believe that no satisfactory prediction can be made as to which trend will prevail. They think that the answer must be found in political developments outside of Czechoslovakia, particularly the future relations between Russia and the Western Powers. The moderates point out that their position would be greatly weakened if Western Powers were to adopt an attitude of indifference and non-co-operation towards Czechoslovakia.[45]

Again the decisive weight of the international dimension was felt.

For the moment, before the break, each side jockeyed for the best position within the National Front. Emerging from the elections as the largest party, and with their position further bolstered by their success in the elections to the national committees held shortly afterwards,[46] the KSČ seized the initiative. Their Central Committee meeting of 30 May agreed to the Politburo's suggestion that the party claim the position of Prime Minister and form the government.[47] The government's programme was to continue the work of its predecessor, with special emphasis being laid on the Two-Year Economic Plan. The programme would be as specific and as concrete as possible, in order to bind all parties within the National Front to it.⁴⁸ It took Gottwald, whom Beneš asked to form a government, a month to gather one together around an agreed programme. The government was named on 2 July and presented to parliament on 8 July, its composition being similar to that of its predecessor.

The KSČ, in accord with its position of leading party, maintained the key ministerial posts of Interior, Finance, Information and Agriculture. The programme which Gottwald announced to the Constituent National Assembly had been agreed upon by all the parties of the National Front after much hard bargaining and compromise. Its linchpin was a Two-Year Plan of economic reconstruction, the exact details of which were worked out in the following months: the Assembly formally approved the Two-Year Economic Plan Act on 25 October 1946, the plan to commence on 1 January 1947.

The Gottwald government's "Construction Programme" outlined proposals for a new constitution, reaffirmed existing foreign and defence policy and dealt with social and educational matters,⁴⁹ but it centred on the Two-Year Plan. The KSČ's original suggestion for a plan had met with some opposition in right-wing circles before the election;⁵⁰ but with the temporary political stabilisation consequent on the election result, all the parties of the National Front adopted a more co-operative attitude. The SDS response was positive, while the NSS leadership and its economic advisers agreed to the general framework but emphasised the need to give full support to the private sector, a position similar to that maintained by the LS.⁵¹

Since the primary aim of the plan was the restoration of the economy to its pre-war level of activity, it was to be of two years' duration only. The Explanatory Memorandum stated that the plan was in principle a sectoral one, containing the plans separately worked out by the various branches of industry and co-ordinated by the Central Planning Commission. Concentrating on production, the plan emphasised four crucial sectors: power production, comprising coal, electricity and fuel; the basic industries of iron and steel, along with the artificial fertilisers vital to agriculture; capital goods, including railway rolling-stock, trucks, tractors and agricultural machinery; and the principal consumer goods, especially clothing and footwear.⁵² Overall, the plan's aim in industry was for "the level of production by the end of the year 1948 to show an increase of 10 per cent over that of the year 1937", while in agriculture the target was for "the pre-war level of production to be reached by the end of 1948".⁵³

The plan was an expression in the economic sphere of the KSČ's continued adherence to a cautious Popular Front strategy. Full equality in the plan was guaranteed to all forms of enterprise whether nationalised, co-operative or private, all being accorded the same opportunities and conditions for the development of their economic activities. This was especially important to the NSS and LS, who hoped that economic recovery would strengthen the private sector in relation to the nationalised sector. Hence it was also significant that in his address to the Assembly on 8 July Gottwald declared that the government "considers the campaign of nationalisation in production to be concluded".⁵⁴ This was not just a concession on the Communists' part to the right-wing parties, significant though their pressure was; rather, the KSČ considered the nationalisation decrees to have been sufficient for the moment, and still sought the support of small and medium private enterprises.⁵⁵ The plan was predicted on a continuation of the alliance of political forces on both a domestic and international scale which had made the national democratic revolution. Since the country had an insufficient raw material base, it had to engage in a considerable degree of foreign trade, exporting manufactured products to pay for raw material imports. The Gottwald government programme envisaged strengthening economic relations with the USSR and all other Slav states but also with the United States, Britain and her empire, France and other Western countries.⁵⁶ It was assumed that friendly relations between the major powers of the anti-fascist coalition would continue.

While the KSČ leadership was aware of some of the difficulties of this strategy, especially as regards the growth of an economically more powerful private sector, it considered the fulfilment of the Two-Year Plan as the most effective way of consolidating the achievements of the Košice programme and evolving towards socialism. For the initiators and architects of the plan its success was vital to their political standing and perspective. As

Gottwald reminded the KSČ central committee at its meeting in September 1946 every social system had, in the final analysis, justified and maintained itself by producing better material results than its predecessor, that is, by producing more, better and cheaper. That was the task that faced the KSČ and the working people: to show that their popular, democratic system — a transitional stage on the road to socialism — was a more viable economic system than that of the First Republic.[57] Gottwald reiterated the point in a speech to leading party industrial members several days later: "The fulfilment of the Two-Year Plan shall be an important stage on our road to socialism".[58]

The active co-operation of the working class was vital to the success of the plan, and the response of the trade-union movement to the announcement of the government programme was immediate and positive. The resolution of the ÚRO management committee meeting on 9 July welcomed the new programme and declared that the trade unions would ensure it was consistently fulfilled.[59] The resolution agreed with the government "that it is necessary to consider the nationalising of our industry at an end",[60] though the transfer of some confiscated enterprises into the public sector remained to be done. All trade-union organisations had to see that their production targets within the Two-Year Plan were met, a point that Zápotocký ceaselessly stressed.[61] The ROH leadership did not attempt to hide the difficulties of this period of economic reconstruction and that sacrifices would have to be made by working people. Their resolution of 9 July accepted this so long as these sacrifices were temporary and borne equally, and so long as the basis was thereby being laid for the future improvement in the standard of living of their members.[62] In the overall political context ROH was prepared to accept this situation because they saw the Two-Year Plan and government programme as part of the advance of a people's democratic republic towards socialism, and trade-union attitudes towards production, economic renewal work and wages therefore differed from what they had been before the war.[63]

The resolution was a concrete expression of ROH congress policy and, as with the KSČ, the plan's success was essential to validate the left course which the trade-union movement was pursuing. ÚRO took steps to publicise and popularise the plan as widely as possible among its membership, and in October and November it organised a series of politico-economic conferences in all major industrial centres of the republic.[64]

As the trade-union leadership recognised, the success of the plan was threatened by some of the economic and social consequences of the war. While the material war damage suffered by Czechoslovakia was by no means comparable to that of some other East European countries, six years of systematic Nazi exploitation had nevertheless caused damage equivalent to several times the annual pre-Munich national income.[65] Replacement of equipment and machinery had been minimal; in this period of economic recovery the capital reserves necessary for massive industrial investments were not available. Any imports of machinery would have needed to be balanced by comparable exports and were therefore unlikely, while the plan was not based on the foreign credits with which industrial machinery might have been purchased.[66] Thus to a large degree the rate of economic recovery was dependent on the increased efforts of workers and employees. Their burden was made greater by the expulsion of the German population. With their removal Czech industry lost over 230,000 workers, about 20 per cent of its labour force, while in particular industries the proportion lost was higher.[67] These workers tended to be highly skilled with many years of industrial experience, yet despite their removal from the labour force the plan's target for total industrial output was 10 per cent in excess of the pre-war level. This output was to be produced by a working class which during and immediately after the war had experienced considerable mobility of employment, in both area and occupation, which had many new, largely unskilled, recruits in its ranks and whose working morale and discipline had been undermined during the Nazi occupation.[68] This was the inauspicious setting for the Two-Year Plan, and its realisation was to test severely the political maturity and discipline of the working-class movement. In particular the movement was to have to deal concretely with the inter-related problems of labour supply, production, wages and strikes, and on its success in these fields depended the fulfilment of the plan's targets.

The labour requirements for the plan called for an addition of 590,000 workers to the labour force: 270,000 were required for industry; 90,000 for the building trades; and 230,000 for agriculture and forestry.[69] Such a large influx of labour was necessitated by the removal of the Germans, as both Gottwald and Zápotocký recognised,[70] though this disruption caused neither them nor any other political figure to question the policy of population transfer. The trade unions placed considerable emphasis on transferring workers from non-productive to productive sectors of the economy, so that a greater proportion of the workforce was directly engaged in the creation of material wealth. The distortions in the economic structure brought about during the Nazi occupation needed readjustment, while disparaging attitudes to physical work had to be overcome.[71] The civil service, local government administration, the railways, commerce, trade, insurance and banking were all areas where it was felt the labour force could be pruned and redirected to industry. However, the question proved much more complex than the ROH leadership had anticipated, and despite considerable efforts no significant shift of white-collar workers and clerks into industry occurred.[72]

Another key source of labour was the recruitment of new workers. As far as industry was concerned, the plan met with complete success, the original target for 202,000 new workers in 1947 being overfulfilled by 61,000.[73] The main source of this influx came from the countryside. This massive spontaneous shift of farmers, agricultural workers and rural youth into the towns resolved the labour requirements of industry but at the price of severe dislocation within the agricultural sector. By 1948 the economically active population in agriculture was only two-thirds of the 1937 figure,[74] and industry had not sufficiently recovered to produce the agricultural machinery which could repair the loss of labour by increases in productivity.

Labour was also drawn from those who had not previously been engaged in social production, especially women. Zápotocký's speech to the ROH Congress had stressed this point,[75] as did Gottwald in his programmatic address to the National Assembly.[76] Equal rights for women in economic, social and cultural life had been one of the demands of the Košice programme;[77] an act passed on 4 July 1945 had guaranteed certain basic rights and equal pay for work equivalent to that done by men.[78] This measure encouraged women to enter production. ROH welcomed this and attempted to ensure their rapid integration into the labour force.

Specialist women's committees were set up within unions, and these had responsibility for developing similar organisations at the workplace.[79] Although the report to the First ROH Congress declared that "all the activity of women in the factories . . . must aim at boosting working morale, at increasing and improving production,"[80] there was a partial recognition of some of the specific problems which female workers faced, and the factory women's committees did concern themselves with the provision of works canteens, factory laundries and nurseries.[81] The overall inadequacy of trade-union understanding of female labour was shown in the congress resolution. This recognised the importance of women in production and the trade unions and declared, "it is necessary to rouse working women from their present passivity and insufficient interest in organisational work, which has been caused by many years of social oppression."[82] Thus while accepting the specific oppression of working women, the resolution offered nothing else but exhortation. An effort of will to rouse working women was suggested as the solution, rather than tackling some of the major problems which prevented many women from working and which hampered those at work from developing their skills to the full. This inadequate theorisation of the problems of female labour meant that ROH was only able to deal in part with the question. As more women entered production and the organisation of ROH improved, so female membership increased. On 31 December 1945 there were 195,036 women in ROH; a year later the female membership was 328,569 and by the end of 1947 it had reached 528,370, an estimated 24 per cent of the total membership.[83] The number of women on trade-union branch committees also increased, yet the higher positions and organs of the trade-union movement remained male-dominated. For example in the Ostrava district at the end of 1946 there were 900 works councils but only 11 of them had female chairmen,[84] while in the metal industry where women were 20 per cent of the workforce, there was only one woman on the union's twenty-seven-strong central committee.[85] Information contained in the report to the First ROH Congress showed that there were only sixty-four women on the KORs, five women on the 120-strong ÚRO and two women on the forty-two-strong management committee, a situation which Erban recognised as unsatisfactory in his speech to the congress.[86] Considerable though ROH's efforts were, they only partly succeeded in integrating women workers into the trade-union movement. Obviously the difficulties faced by women in industry slowed down the number of others going to work. This problem was a cause for concern to the government, as well as ROH, since it was infinitely preferable to resolve industry's labour shortage by recruiting women to the labour force than by using former agricultural labour. A degree of success was achieved, however, for 55,750 women joined industry in the first half of 1947 and 73 per cent of these had previously been engaged only in household or domestic work.[87]

It was primarily from these two sources, agriculture and women, that the industrial labour requirements of the Two-Year Plan were met. Total employment in manufacturing industry reached its 1937 level by the start of 1948, although sharp fluctuations in occupational structure occurred during the Nazi occupation and post-war.[88] The Two-Year Plan's emphasis on heavy industries was reflected in the increased labour force in mining, metals and chemicals as against the 1937 figure, while textiles, clothing, leather and ceramics registered a decline. Over the period the working class in Czechoslovakia had experienced severe disruption and then undergone a process of re-formation with its German segment removed. This process meant that while there was a firm core skilled at its work and experienced in trade-union activity, the considerable wartime and post-war mobility in employment and the entry of unskilled and previously non-proletarian strata into the working class affected the homogeneity of the class. The consequent overall decline in working-class skills and disparity in its class experience and consciousness were further factors exacerbating the problems of fulfilling the plan's production targets.

Despite this the working class gave an impressive response to the call by the ROH leadership to increase production and to the example set by some of the country's major industrial enterprises. The main emphasis of ROH's activity was on this question, for as Zápotocký constantly reiterated, more strenuous and intensive work was necessary if the nation was to achieve a higher standard of living. ROH had to mobilise all the skills and resources of the working people. Voluntary brigades and national competitions were two expressions of this aim.[89]

In the immediate post-war months and in the summer of 1946, with the dislocation that arose from the transfer of the Germans, serious labour shortages threatened to disrupt the entire economy; voluntary brigades of workers were formed to avert the danger. These brigades were concentrated in the coal industry and agriculture, and played a significant part in overcoming the immediate difficulties both these sectors faced. Metalworkers were especially prominent in these brigades, while in 1946 the Prague works councils organised 19,000 workers and students into voluntary coal-mining brigades.[90] Mechanical brigades were also set up, with skilled industrial workers travelling to villages at the weekends to repair agricultural machinery. More than a thousand such brigades were active in the first six months of 1946.[91] As well as providing useful economic help, these brigades were seen by ROH as expressing the political unity of workers in industry with those in agriculture.

In its activity on this question ROH placed its main emphasis on the establishment of production committees. They wanted these committees set up in all large factories and their task was to secure "the development of the working initiative of all employees."[92] National competitions were seen as a way of stimulating this initiative, with individual workers and enterprises competing to achieve the highest productivity and output. The original idea for production committees had come from iron and steel workers, the first committee being set up in the Prague engineering plant of Českomoravská Kolben-Daněk (ČKD). As early as 24 January 1946 a conference had been held in the Libeň factory of ČKD with delegates from forty-five major enterprises in the engineering industry.[93] This important conference agreed to set up production committees as widely as possible, discussed how to remove obstacles to increased production and initiated various competitions between enterprises.[94] Although only thirty metal factories took part in the first series of national competitions, 397 participated in the second, involving more than 150,000 workers. The third series of national competitions in the industry was held from April to August 1946; an additional 150 factories with 90,000 more employees took part.[95] By the time of the metalworkers' conference in June 1947 over 700 production committees were operating in engineering and metal enterprises in the republic.[96] These committees, as well as promoting national competitions within their enterprises, co-operated closely with the trade unions and works councils in improving morale and discipline, and made suggestions for improvements in the organisation of the production process. The positive response by this key section of the working class to the problems of production set a clear example to the rest of the trade-union movement; by January 1948, 2,340 production committees were in existence, spread throughout the republic.[97] These committees, along with the rest of ROH's activities in the sphere of production, made a vital contribution to the fulfilment of the plan's industrial targets.

However, these measures were all of a short-term character. While necessary in the immediate post-war period, these methods offered no solution to the general question of increasing the nation's gross national product. They were a copy of the Soviet methods of extensive development, with the emphasis placed on physical exertion and labour. These methods did not correspond to the mature level of Czechoslovakia's productive forces, whose development required the intensive application of specialist technical and scientific knowledge by skilled personnel. In this regard the ROH leadership, like that of the KSČ, showed a lack of understanding and imagination. While short-term sacrifices could be called for, after a period the underlying deficiencies of such an approach were to become apparent. Indeed, in their own specific ways all the economies of Eastern Europe have experienced persistent problems of this kind in the last thirty years.

Within the trade-union leadership it was accepted that workers' wage demands had to be tied to the level of production. The ROH Congress had accepted this policy, and Zápotocký continued to stress that wages and salaries had to be related to production — otherwise there was an acute danger of inflation. In a speech at Brno in October 1946 he declared that "only with increased, improved production can we gradually settle wages and salaries."[98] Kliment spoke in similar vein when addressing the Prague metalworkers' conference in April 1947. He agreed that many workers' wages were too low, but said that only when the post-war economic, financial and industrial difficulties had been overcome would adequate wage rates be achieved.[99]

Although the share of wages and salaries in the national income had risen by 67 per cent in 1946, as against the 1937 figure of

59 per cent, since national income was much smaller than pre-war the average wage for each employee was only 92 per cent of the comparable 1937 level.[100] Within this, variations were considerable: some sectors had improved their standard of living compared to the pre-war period. Although detailed analysis is complex, unskilled workers had gained by the general levelling in wage rates between particular grades which occurred during and after the war,[101] as had those engaged in arduous physical work. However, it has been estimated that almost 40 per cent of working-class families were in the situation where their wages were insufficient to cover their living costs, while a considerable section of public and state employees and the technical intelligentsia faced a similar plight.[102]

This unsatisfactory situation could only be resolved ultimately by the recovery of the nation's production to and beyond its pre-war level. Yet the pressure demanding immediate wage increases was inevitably strong, despite the attempts by the trade-union leaders to explain that temporary sacrifices were necessary if a sound basis was to be laid for the future growth of the economy and improvements in the standard of living. The other main pressure on wage levels came as a result of the labour shortage. The quickest, easiest way to attract labour to a particular industry was to increase its basic wage rates. Especially in the first year of the plan, in attempting to fulfil targets many managements exceeded the declared wage directives in order to attract a larger labour force to their enterprise.[103] This, allied with a greater degree of piecework, ensured that wage rates rose rapidly in the period.[104]

In almost every industry the hourly wage rate in the second half of 1947 was considerably higher than that for the first quarter of 1946. The overall wage developments in this period showed a marked degree of independence and did not correspond to increases in productivity. This posed severe difficulties for ROH, especially since many of the wage increases came in the private sector. However, wherever possible ROH attempted to maintain its wages policy and continued to discourage strike action by its members over wages. Although reserving the right to strike — the National Socialist Minister of Justice had attempted to make any strikes during the Two-Year Plan a criminal offence — ROH assured the government that no strikes disrupting the plan would occur, while it would encourage its members to exhaust all possible channels of negotiation before resorting to strike action.[105] This was the essence of the resolution which Prague metalworkers agreed to in April 1947,[106] and strikes over wages were rare in this period. Thus while wage rates did rise ahead of productivity, it would appear that ROH's policy and propaganda exerted a considerable influence over their members and that wide sections of the working class accepted and supported this policy of restraint.

The positive response of the working class was central to the republic's economic recovery. Whereas in December 1945 industrial production had been only 55 per cent of its 1937 level, by November 1946 it had risen to 80 per cent, and by June 1947 was 97 per cent of the 1937 level.[107] The recovery of productivity levels was not so rapid; despite a rise by a quarter from 1946-1948, the resulting figure was only 99.7 per cent of the pre-war level.[108] This was hardly surprising, given the state of machinery and plant and the lack of new investment. Indeed, the increased productivity and output that was achieved reflected creditably on the success of the ÚRO leadership in harnessing the energies of its members in fulfilment of the plan. The example set by the most class-conscious sections of the membership, notably the metalworkers and miners,[109] acted as a spur to the rest of the working class. The ÚRO leadership understood the economic and political realities of the situation, and knew that the continuation of their left course depended on the successful realisation of the Gottwald government's programme. ÚRO bred no illusions among its members about their standard of living, and constantly stated that these inadequacies could only be overcome by means of considerably increased production. The structure of the trade-union movement helped it impose from above the discipline on its members which the situation demanded, yet many sections understood its necessity and were prepared to accept it voluntarily. Despite the exceptional dislocation it had experienced, the Czech working class, under the firm guidance of its trade-union leadership, made significant progress in this period towards rebuilding the republic.

This task was complicated, however, by the growing fissures in the class alliance on which the government had based its programme. At both an international and domestic level strains developed as class antagonisms became more acute. These tensions threatened to undermine the Two-Year Plan and the entire political basis of the National Front.

Tension between the United States and the USSR developed throughout 1946 and at times spread to Czechoslovakia. Given the composition of its government and the orientation of its foreign policy, it was not surprising that Czechoslovakia adopted the Soviet standpoint on matters of contention. When this occurred at the Paris Peace Conference in September 1946, Byrnes, the US Secretary of State, cabled instructions to Washington that the $50 million credit which the US had granted Czechoslovakia to buy US army surplus property in Europe should be immediately withdrawn.[110] He also asked that negotiations in Washington with Czechoslovak government officials for a $50 million dollar reconstruction loan should cease. Ambassador Steinhardt had counselled consistently against the granting of such a loan,[111] and on 28 September the State Department officially informed the Czechoslovak government that negotiations for a loan had been suspended.[112] The US government only intended to give loans to countries sympathetic to it. When Washington asked the US delegation at the Paris conference for advice as to how to explain the position to Czechoslovak officials, they received a classically brash American reply: "Tell him [the Czechoslovak official, Hanč] from here on out we intend to assist our friends. . . . You should add that we will sell surplus to the Czechoslovaks for cash on the barrelhead."[113] The tone was sharp and the trend was clear. Any possibility of drawing aid from both East and West was dwindling rapidly. As the antagonisms sharpened between the leading representatives of the world's two main social systems, Czechoslovakia's room for manoeuvre grew increasingly restricted.

This period also saw a sharpening of class divisions within the country. With relative economic stability the capitalist sector of the economy revived; as it accumulated capital, it sought to expand its share of the gross national product. The uneven character of the republic's industrial development, with widespread small and medium industrial and trade enterprises existing alongside large-scale plants and factories, meant that a considerable capitalist economic base remained after the nationalisation decrees. In Czechoslovakia there was a sizeable petty bourgeoisie of small producers. In December 1946 there were 177,119 trade enterprises in Bohemia and Moravia, to be found especially in textiles, clothing, food-processing, metals, services, woodworking, leatherworking and building.[114] In all 564,820 people worked in trades, 87.7 per cent in enterprises employing less than 20 people. But although small enterprises were dominant numerically, the top 3.84 per cent of trade enterprises accounted for 40.3 per cent of total trade income.[115] Rapid differentiation within these producer trades was occurring and a significant, if small, medium bourgeoisie developing. With private enterprise dominant in retail, wholesale and foreign trade, there existed a sizeable economic base from which the capitalist sector could be expanded.

Already in 1946 the demands of the petty and medium bourgeoisie began to be voiced through the Central Committee of Trades and other organisations. Policies were requested that were at variance with the needs of the working class, and the class and political unity of the National Front began to fracture. The participation of tradesmen in the black market, high prices for consumer goods in short supply and increased profits caused consternation among the working class. On the other hand there was resentment at the need to observe social measures which restricted the entrepreneur's freedom of enterprise, while overall government economic and social policy discriminated in favour of the industrial working class.[116]

As the international and domestic situation evolved, the rightwing grouping which had developed in the pre-election period developed a much clearer identity. The divergent trends within the National Front began to crystallise, the right consolidating its position within the NSS and LS and by early 1947 weakening the hold of the left within the SDS.[117] This right, as well as supporting and encouraging the growth of the existing private sector, caused a sharp political clash as it attempted to secure the attachment to the private sector of the confiscated enterprises.

Confiscated enterprises were comprised of those factories which had previously been owned by Germans, Magyars or collaborators but, because they had been below a certain size or capacity, had not been affected by the nationalisation decrees of October 1945. Their fate remained uncertain, and they were placed under temporary national management until it had been decided whether to attach them to national enterprises, to the co-operative sector or to return them to private owners. 3,931 medium-size and large factories fell into this category of confiscated enterprise, and they employed 13 per cent of the industrial labour force. They accounted for approximately one-eighth of industrial production, many of them being concerned with making supplementary and component products for the major industrial enterprises.[118] Hence they occupied a strategic position in the process of production: their return to the private sector would have strengthened considerably the economic base of the bourgeoisie.

During autumn 1946 the right-wing political parties began a sharp campaign to ensure the return of these enterprises to private hands, thereby revitalising the nascent bourgeoisie. The newspapers and journals of the NSS were a major influence in the campaign, arguing the necessity and benefits of capitalist competition. In September 1946 the NSS management committee, along with its economic advisory body, declared their opposition to attaching the confiscated enterprises to the state sector.[119]

This was in direct conflict with the policy which the ROH Congress had agreed[120] and which the ÚRO management committee had reaffirmed in its resolution of 9 July welcoming the new government. The issue was developing into a major political conflict, and was discussed at the ÚRO Plenary session of 13 and 14 December. The congress position was reaffirmed, though ÚRO emphasised that this applied only to medium and large enterprises, and that there was no intention on the part of ÚRO to nationalise small trades or artisan workshops.[121] If attempts to transfer confiscated enterprises to the private sector were made, the trade unions would take appropriate counter-action, a position which the KSČ fully endorsed.[122] Despite this clear warning, the right-wing parties still proceeded with their campaign. They hoped that their propaganda would undermine the combativeness of the working class, which would also be heavily preoccupied with the Two-Year Plan. In this situation, and aided by their sympathisers in the judicial apparatus, the right hoped to secure the bulk of the confiscated enterprises for the private sector.

They seriously underestimated the opposition their campaign would arouse amongst the trade unions. The central committee of the textile workers asked ÚRO to ensure that its full weight was placed behind the demand for linking confiscated firms to national enterprises.[123] The weekly journal *ÚRO* reported a fortnight later that the KORs in Ústí, Karlovy Vary, Liberec and Šumperk, all border districts where the number of confiscated enterprises was high, had requested that these enterprises be attached to the nationalised sector. They expressed concern at some press reports calling for their allocation to individuals.[124] On 10 February 1947, when workers at the Zátka flour mill in České Budějovice learned that the factory was to be returned to private owners, they immediately went on strike. They returned to work after assurances from the KOR that the matter was still under consideration and the ÚRO would insist on its return to the nationalised sector.[125] The ÚRO management committee meeting of 14 February passed a resolution which expressed concern at the uncertainty surrounding the destiny of the Zátka mills and blamed some officials and administrators for thwarting nationalisation of the enterprise even though the mill was above the requisite capacity. The resolution spoke of various manipulations on the part of these officials and pointed out that similar complaints about the bias of state organs in favour of private enterprise were coming from other factories, including several mills in the Slovak town of Piest'any.[126]

The decisive clash on this issue came in the border area of Varnsdorf. On the morning of 5 March over 10,000 workers in the 100 or so major industrial factories in the Varnsdorf area went on strike. They were protesting at the decision of the district court to hand back the confiscated Eichler factory to its former owner, Beer. When this had been announced on 4 March, workers at the factory had immediately gone on strike. The following morning the area trades council called all its members out, an action which had the full support of the local KSČ. The three other political parties, however, defended Beer and opposed the action. The strikers demonstrated outside the local town hall and their representatives went to negotiate on the question. By the end of the day it had been confirmed that the Eichler factory would remain under national management, and with their main demand fulfilled the strikers returned to work.[127]

The Varnsdorf strike was the most significant action taken by trade unionists over the question of the confiscated enterprises. Although further strike action did occur, building workers holding a one-day strike in Brno, Kladno and Ostrava on 11 March in protest at the delay in the nationalisation of former German construction firms,[128] the issue now subsided. By its quick, united action ROH had thwarted the attempt to strengthen the capitalist sector of the economy by the addition of the confiscated enterprises. The right-wing parties had been placed on the defensive on this issue, and at the National Front meeting of 15-18 March they accepted that where appropriate confiscated enterprises would be attached to the public sector.[129] At the ÚRO Plenary session on 3-4 April, Zápotocký noted satisfaction at the outcome of the conflict and considered that the government's statement would calm the situation.[130]

Whatever growing strength the Czech bourgeoisie may have had at an economic level, this controversy showed their weakness at a political level. For the right-wing forces to advance their position not only did they need to widen their economic base but (more importantly) the Communist domination of the working class movement had to be disrupted. Above all, the united left leadership of ROH had to be undermined.

Works council elections[131]

An opportunity arose over the works council elections held in spring 1947. As indicated earlier, the works council decrees of October 1945 had limited the powers of the councils in relation to management and incorporated them within the apparatus of ROH. In particular, local ROH branches had absolute control over the election of works councils. They were responsible for drafting a list of suitable candidates, which was posted in advance and open to alteration. The trade-union branches were responsible for running the elections, which were organised on the basis of individual balloting rather than at a general meeting of all employees. The number of candidates proposed equalled the number of council places available; the council was to sit for one year and contained no provision for recall. Conflict had arisen within the government over the election procedures, the decrees stating that a council was elected only if it received 80 per cent of the votes cast. The controversy on this question continued throughout 1946; only with the government order of 5 November specifying the precise details of election procedure was the matter resolved.

At stake in the controversy were a number of fundamental questions concerning the character of the trade-union movement. Learning from their pre-war experience, trade-union leaders insisted that ROH remain free of direct interference by political parties in their internal affairs. As the spokesman for Zlín KOR baldly declared at the ROH Congress, "In the trade unions, trade unionists must decide and no one else."¹³² This expressed a general ROH sentiment,¹³³ and consequently they opposed any attempts to secure election to trade-union committees and works councils on the basis of party proportional representation, a proposal put forward in various guises by representatives of the NSS, DS and LS.¹³⁴ ROH had sound reasons for rejecting such proposals, since they would have undermined some fundamental premises of trade unionism. The trade union represented all the members in a particular industry and unified them in defence of their interests as workers. This was the basis on which members were in a union, not because of their party political affiliation. While many trade unionists were members of political parties, the majority were not: to have countenanced the direct interference of political parties within the trade unions would have infringed these members' democratic rights and would also have denied the specific character of trade unionism.

Yet ROH refused to recognise the existence even of genuine political differences in the working class. ROH staunchly supported the national democratic revolution, which it viewed as a transitional stage on the road to socialism. As such it was partisan and political: it pursued a policy which aligned it very closely with the KSČ and left wing of the SDS, and it was a policy which many trade unionists unaffiliated to a political party supported. On the other hand, some ROH members opposed this overall policy, and their opposition was not restricted just to trade unionists who were members of the NSS and LS or adhered to the right-wing elements with the SDS. Undoubtedly, there were unaffiliated elements in ROH which considered their sectional, craft or professional interests as primary.

ROH refused to acknowledge publicly these political differences. In the statements of ÚRO and of trade-union leaders, they constantly referred to nominations for trade union and works council posts being made on the basis of "the best from the best".¹³⁵ In discussion about the election procedure for works councils they insisted that a united list be put forward on this basis. Given the left majority within ROH and the democratic centralist organisational structure, this method ensured that a left-wing slate of candidates was presented to the workers. Not surprisingly the KSČ vigorously supported ROH's position on the question of a united list, and the government eventually agreed to this.

In consequence those who opposed the majority's left-wing policy had no way of presenting themselves as candidates in the works council elections. Therefore during the government discussion the right-wing parties suggested electoral formulae which would guarantee effective consultation with their parties and like-minded trade unionists by indirect means. Their major stipulations were that the candidate list carry the same number of names as there were places to be elected, that the necessary majority for election of the list be 80 per cent of all votes cast, and that if this percentage was not attained, balloting would be repeated until it was achieved. The logic behind this cumbersome formula was that if an 80 per cent vote was necessary for successful election and if balloting continued *ad infinitum*, then those opposed to the left majority would have to be consulted and their co-operation ensured — at some political cost to the left.

The final agreement, reached after much negotiation, did not provide the indirect guarantees the right desired. Its three main points were that the slate offered no choice, that the necessary majority for election was 80 per cent, and that balloting would last for two rounds. If then a council failed to be elected, its place would be taken by a "substitute body" nominated by the local union branch. The right-wing formula had been accepted — except for its linchpin, the infinite ballot. Without this their proposals became meaningless, for if no works council had been elected after two rounds of balloting, the ROH-appointed substitute body, perhaps composed of the same list of candidates, would assume the role. Indeed, this made the political value of the entire works council elections somewhat obscure, though obviously the tactics of the right were to concentrate on ensuring that many councils did not receive the required majority, since this would weaken the cohesion and unity of the ROH leadership.

Yet to many workers the council elections did not appear very significant anyway. The role of these councils had been strictly limited in the decrees of October 1945, a policy which ROH supported, as Zápotocký emphasised in his main speech to the ROH Congress.[136] As Šmídmajer wrote in an official ÚRO pamphlet in 1947, "They [the works councils] do not control the factory; the control of the factory is entrusted to specialist forces; they do not publish independent economic and industrial instructions — that is a matter for the management of the factory — but they watch over all economic and industrial measures".[137] Šmídmajer further explained that it was the responsibility of the competent trade-union organ to guide and direct the entire activity of the works council, including elections.[138] The factory union branch had to be invited to every meeting of the works council. Their representatives had the responsibility not only of following the discussion but also of putting the line and position of ROH and demanding its observance by the works council. Šmídmajer, in accord with the official view, maintained that this regular contact gave both bodies the possibility of the closest co-operation on all matters.[139] Yet in reality no mutual co-operation or interaction between the two bodies occurred. The works councils were merely a transmission belt for carrying out the relevant policies of the ROH. Having opposed the development of autonomous works council organisations in 1945, ROH found itself in the position of having responsibility over bodies that fulfilled no significant function, especially in enterprises where the great majority of workers were unionised. The report to the Second ROH Congress in April 1949 acknowledged the reality of the situation: "In the factories there are now formally two organs; in fact, of course there is only one, since at the meetings of the factory branch committee all questions pertaining to the activity of the works councils are solved."[140] This was a reality which many workers, especially in the larger enterprises, recognised already in spring 1947. Having already elected their trade-union committee, the election of an impotent works council aroused little enthusiasm, especially as they were presented with a united slate of candidates anyway. Given this situation, and with the NSS, LS and often the SDS opposing acceptance of the united list, it was not surprising that the 80 per cent majority was not achieved in over a quarter of cases.[141]

These results aroused some concern in the ROH leadership, the more so since it was in the industrialised areas[142] and in the major industrial unions[143] that opposition was greatest. In the eight most industrialised districts of the country there was a 64 per cent average of councils elected in the first round, as against 77 per cent in the less industrial areas, while in the second category there was only one district with results lower than the average of the first category. It was in the main industrial unions such as mines, metals and chemicals that support for the councils was weakest. For instance, only in five pits in the Ostrava district did the candidate list secure an 80 per cent vote in the first round. In seven others the list attained over 70 per cent, in another eleven between 60-70 per cent and the remaining eleven under 60 per cent.[144] Kliment commented on the unsatisfactory position in some major metal enterprises, including Škoda and the Vítkovice Iron and Steel Works,[145] where only 53 per cent voted for the list in the first round and 64 per cent in the second.[146]

Despite these trends the significance of the results as a sign of disunity within ROH must in no way be overestimated. They did not herald the disintegration of the left leadership within the trade unions. The ÚRO management committee even overcame the problem of the "substitute body" in a classically administrative manner. The central organisational commission merely suggested that the designation "substitute body" be dropped and that it assume the same rights and functions as an elected council. Vandrovec, an NSS member, objected to this move, which went against the resolution passed at an ÚRO Plenary session. However, Zápotocký, Zupka and Šmídmajer were among those who favoured the commission's proposal, which was carried with two against.[147] The point of the elections was devalued even further.

The confidence of the ROH leadership had been shaken somewhat but its position not seriously undermined. The right, especially the NSS and right-wing SDS leaderships in Plzeň and Ostrava, had campaigned for rejection of the united slates, and in large enterprises, where they had their own factory party branches, their activity was undoubtedly influential.[148] Yet the results posed no immediate threat to the leadership of ROH, the opposition to the united lists not having been sufficiently widespread to develop this. Indeed, it would be wrong to assert that workers' opposition to the united list meant that they identified with the right on other questions. Many opposed the list as a protest against the character of the elections or because they appeared pointless. The elections were marked by considerable apathy and abstentionism.[149] In some places the right was able to channel this discontent to its advantage, but not in a manner which secured workers' allegiance to it on other questions. For example, there was to be no firmer support for the left in the February events of 1948 than that which came from the core of the industrial working class in Ostrava.

What the election results did bear witness to was the spontaneous rejection by considerable sections of industrial workers of the conception of works councils which the ROH leadership was proposing. The right was unable to capitalise on this, since it proposed no alternative and was certainly not interested in a return to the independent institutions that had flourished momentarily in summer 1945. Herein lay the long-term significance of the elections, for deprived of the possibility of creating viable, autonomous institutions of their own, the working class began to sink into passivity. The signs of this trend apparent in the election results were ignored by the left. The main concern of the ROH leadership was that though the election results were rather disappointing, its position had not been seriously weakened by the attack the right had made over the issue.

It was a sign of growing division: an expression within the working class of the increasing tensions both within the country and abroad. Another was the attempt to exclude ROH from governmental discussions. In March 1947 the Ministry of Food had set up a commission to discuss the fate of confiscated enterprises in the industry. It had been the practice to invite ROH to such discussions, on the grounds that in a popular democracy the trade union should take part in all aspects of state economic and political life. However, the ÚRO management committee meeting of 20 June noted that attempts had been made to stop ROH attending the commission. The meeting passed a resolution condemning this tendency and demanding that it be reversed.[150] The episode was a further example of how the right wing — Majer, the food minister, was a prominent member of the right in the SDS — was attempting to weaken the influence of ROH.

Despite the escalating tensions the KSČ in spring 1947 continued to adhere to its course, and ROH followed suit. In his speech to the plenary session of ÚRO on 3-4 April, Zápotocký stated:

> We shall proceed to socialism by the calm and evolutionary path, that we nationalise only a certain part of large industrial production and enterprises; we have reconciled ourselves to this, that a whole series . . . of enterprises shall remain un-nationalised. We must reckon on that. We cannot retreat from an agreement to which we have acceded.[151]

It was becoming increasingly obvious that the path to socialism could not be "calm and evolutionary" for much longer, and that when conflicts arose previous agreements would be broken. Within the country the initiative lay with the left and above all with the KSČ, its decisive component. As the storm broke on the international scene, the KSČ, its domination of the working class relatively unimpaired, was to ensure that the conflict within Czechoslovakia was resolved in its favour.

IV
The Storm

11
"Who is Master of Bohemia is Master of Europe"

The simmering antagonism between the two major world powers flared in the spring and summer of 1947. In these months the fragile equilibrium of the immediate post-war years was shattered. International developments had played the decisive role in the history of Czechoslovakia in the previous decade, and all astute contemporary politicians and observers recognised that the country's future political development was largely dependent on the course of relations between the USSR and the USA. Any analysis of the developments in Czechoslovakia culminating in the events of February 1948 must therefore be placed within the context of the onset of the Cold War.

At the end of the war the Soviet Union had two major concerns: security and reconstruction. Her military strength was such that in a series of agreements culminating in the accords at Yalta the American and British governments recognised Eastern Europe as a Soviet sphere of influence. The Soviet government's basic security needs were guaranteed by this, for the pre-war *cordon sanitaire* had been broken.

As regards her other major concern, the USSR found her Allies less conciliatory. The USSR wanted heavy war reparations exacted from Germany so that the enormously weakened Soviet economy, desperately short of labour and capital, could recover rapidly, while joint Allied control of the Ruhr would ensure that no renewed war threat from Germany could occur. At Yalta, and especially at Potsdam, the Soviet government found her Allies unresponsive on this question.

Divergent views on how to tackle the country's post-war problems existed within the Soviet leadership.[1] The majority considered that the government had to concentrate on policies which would secure the "time" and "space" the country needed to recover from the ravages of the war. Central to the success of such a policy was the continuation of the wartime coalition, for only with this could the Soviet Union secure the loan from the USA[2] or exact the reparations from Germany necessary for rapid economic renewal. Until early 1947 the Soviet government based its strategy on the assumption of continued inter-Allied co-operation; as a corollary to this it counselled caution and moderation on the part of communist parties abroad.

The onset of the cold war

The USA emerged from the war as the world's major power, dominant in a way that not even Britain had been in its Victorian heyday. Three-quarters of the world's invested capital and two-thirds of its industrial capacity were within her borders.[3] The USA was the leading military power, maintaining over 400 naval and air bases around the world.[4] In addition she was the sole possessor of the atom bomb, a weapon of unparalleled might. The deployment of this power was the key factor in the determination of international relations.

The main group of political and business leaders wanted the government to pursue a traditional Open Door policy. They were doubtful about the possibilities of post-war co-operation with the USSR, and feared the economic restrictions likely to be imposed on US capital within Eastern Europe. The use of America's power to secure this Open Door policy was advocated by Averell Harriman, US Ambassador in Moscow, as early as May 1945. His response to Stalin's request for a $6 billion loan from the USA was to advise cutting the initial amount down to a tenth and defining it as a credit over which the USA would maintain greater control. Harriman proposed to exploit Soviet weakness and thereby force them to accept American policy, declaring that the Russians "should be given to understand that our willingness to cooperate wholeheartedly with them in their vast reconstruction problems will depend upon their behaviour in international matters. . . . I would apportion that credit out piecemeal, demanding in return concessions on the political field."[5]

It was to take almost two years, however, for this position to be explicitly adopted by the American government. As Rostow, from 1947 to 1949 special assistant to the Executive Secretary of the Economic Commission for Europe, has somewhat regretfully noted, "The mood of the policy-makers in post-war Washing-

ton was then to some degree coloured by ambiguities from the past.
... To some extent American diplomacy in 1945-46 still operated under inhibitions derived from the war."⁶ These "ambiguities" and "inhibitions" were nothing less than the agreements the US government had reached with the USSR at Teheran and Yalta and which they could not immediately revoke. As Rostow himself admits, "The central fact about American diplomacy in Europe in the immediate aftermath of the second world war is that Eastern Europe was surrendered to the Soviet Union, and the split of Europe along the line of the Elbe was accepted as the more or less legitimate outcome of the second world war."⁷

It was this outcome that the American government became increasingly determined to change. As De Gaulle later stated, "The Americans and British hoped to recover in practice what they had conceded in principle (at Yalta)."⁸ Traditional Open Door expansion gradually asserted itelf as the dominant trend of US policy. This policy was seen both as a means of assuring the continued productive development of the US, averting the possibility of another domestic slump and delving into new markets abroad, and as a way of containing the advance of an alternative social system which would impinge upon those markets. As Bullitt, the new ambassador to the Soviet Union, stated in 1946: "Every time the Soviet Union extends its power over another area or state, the United States and Great Britain lose another normal market."⁹ By early 1947 the US government was prepared to enunciate boldly its Open Door policy and to "contain" Soviet influence. With the announcements of the Truman Doctrine on 12 March, followed by the Marshall Plan on 5 June, the Big Three coalition collapsed. The Truman Doctrine heralded an ideological crusade aganist the USSR and communism;¹⁰ the Marshall Plan offered large-scale American aid to help European economic recovery, and was also a political move aimed at weakening communist influence in Europe.¹¹ Succinctly and crisply George Kennan, director of the newly formed Policy Planning Staff of the State Department, expressed government thinking in a paper written in February 1946 and published anonymously in mid-1947. He concluded that "the United States has it in its power to increase enormously the strains under which Soviet policy must operate, to force upon the Kremlin a far greater degree of moderation and circumspection than it has had to observe in recent years and in this way to promote tendencies which must eventually find their outlet in either the break-up or the gradual mellowing of Soviet power."[12]

To such a direct challenge the Soviet government could not fail to respond. With the central plank of its post-war strategy broken, an alternative had to be speedily implemented. The essence of the Soviet response was to shift its strategy from an overoptimistic Popular Frontism to a rather crude, leftist sectarianism. It signified, in a somewhat milder form, a reversion from the strategies of the Seventh Comintern Congress to those of the Sixth. Western European communist parties were to resume their role as advanced bulwarks of the USSR; the parties in Eastern Europe were to take power so that the entire Soviet sphere of influence was sealed from Western penetration. This strategic shift took place during the summer, and at the conference of ten European communist parties in Poland in September the new line was confirmed and cemented. To the Soviet leadership it represented the only possibility of securing the time and space necessary for recovery.

Although the Truman Doctrine was global in scope, the decisive arena in the initial stages of the Cold War was Eastern Europe, since this was the region which had been consigned to the USSR in Yalta. The Soviet government viewed the Marshall Plan as part of the attempt to entwine East European countries within the Western trading and commercial network. In preliminary discussions in Paris, Molotov, the Soviet Foreign Minister, sharply rejected the Anglo-French proposal for European economic reconstruction fuelled by American credit. The plan was to integrate the national economies of Europe. As Molotov viewed it, this meant each country producing what it produced best; East European countries would have to jettison their national plans for industrialisation and continue their pre-war economic pattern. In 1938, 80 per cent of Eastern Europe's exports consisted of raw materials, foodstuffs and semi-finished goods, nearly three-quarters of them going to Western Europe.[13] The essentially semi-colonial economic relationship of this area to the rest of Europe had also entailed political weakness. The national plans were attempting to overcome this economic and political dependency, and Molotov objected to their being forfeited.[14]

However, his rejection of the Marshall Plan was made in such a manner as to strengthen its advocates and to influence some waverers in its favour. The shift in Soviet policy following the Truman Doctrine and consequent failure of the foreign ministers' conference in Moscow in March 1947 had been an awkward, uneasy process, and the new policy had not been fully clarified by the time of the Paris meeting. Molotov's diplomacy lacked finesse, and his hostile tirade against American imperialism surprised many who welcomed the offer of credit to finance European recovery and did not appreciate its political aspects. Molotov could have welcomed genuine initiatives to aid European recovery but insisted that they be handled by the United Nations Economic Commission for Europe, the appropriate international and therefore non-partisan organisation. Such a move would have placed the Americans on the defensive and tested the political character of their initiative. Instead, Molotov's response hardened the antagonism, and his aggressive rhetoric gave credence to the view that the Soviet Union had no interest in European recovery.

With the departure of the Soviet delegation from Paris the new policy crystallised. Stalin decided that Eastern Europe would have to be closed from the West. The previously ambiguous response to the Marshall Plan was replaced by a resoundingly negative one. Direct political pressure was placed on East European countries not to attend the forthcoming conference. Nowhere was the political pressure as direct and the political implications so apparent as in the case of Czechoslovakia.

Czechoslovakia and the Marshall Plan

The Czechoslovak government, along with the Polish and Yugoslav governments, as participants in the wartime allied coalition, had received invitations to attend the Paris conference on the Marshall Plan. The government took the view which Masaryk had expressed at a press conference in Norway on 22 June: they were for action which united Europe and against that which divided it.[15] The Cabinet met on 4 July and Masaryk proposed formal acceptance of the invitation. He argued that American credits would help refurbish the economy, although he stressed that the country would not accept any conditions incompatible with its political and economic independence. Initial participation was agreed upon unanimously.[16]

The matter was discussed again at a cabinet meeting on 7 July.

In the meantime the positive attitude of Polish ministers to the Marshall Plan had been expressed in talks between the Polish delegation in Prague and their Czechoslovak counterparts. Minc, the Polish Minister for Industry, had told Löbl, the departmental head at the Ministry of Trade, of his support for the plan,[17] while both the Polish Prime Minister and Foreign Minister indicated their interest in press interviews.[18] And Masaryk had spoken with the Soviet chargé d'affaires in Prague, Bodrov, who explained the Soviet position but declared that he had received no instructions asking the Czechoslovak government not to go to Paris.[19] These soundings bolstered the Czechoslovak government's intention to be at the conference on 12 July and then to decide its ensuing attitude towards the Marshall Plan. This position was adopted without dissent.

Two days later the Soviet position had changed.[20] A Czechoslovak delegation composed of Gottwald, Masaryk and Drtina had flown to Moscow to consult the Soviet government about the proposed Czechoslovak-French treaty and certain economic and commercial matters. However, Gottwald saw Stalin alone first of all, and an item on Czechoslovakia's participation at the Paris conference was placed at the head of the agenda. Gottwald was undoubtedly informed of Stalin's hostility to such a move; when the full delegation met Stalin, Molotov and Bodrov on the night of 9 July, they were informed in no uncertain terms that they should reverse their decision. Stalin declared that other East European states had changed their decisions on this matter, notably Poland, and if the Czechoslovak government did not, its alliance with the Soviet Union would be severely weakened. The Czechoslovak delegation sent a telegram to Prague explaining the Soviet position and demanding an immediate reversal of the decision.

The government met on the morning of the 10 July. Rightwing ministers, notably Zenkl, Stránský and Ursíny, were obviously unhappy and spoke of the harm such a reversal would do to the government's prestige abroad;[21] but as Ripka later expressed it, "we had no alternative but to give way."[22] Beneš viewed the situation similarly despite his initial strong support for the Marshall Plan.[23] In the afternoon the government issued a statement which said:

It has been decided that the states of central and eastern

Europe with which Czechoslovakia carries close economic and political relations, based upon her contractual obligations, will not participate in the conference of Paris. In these circumstances the participation of Czechoslovakia could be interpreted as a blow to the friendly relations existing between her and the Soviet Union, as well as with her other allies. For this reason the government has decided unanimously not to take part in the conference.[24]

With this incident, the link connecting Czechoslovakia with both East and West was snapped: the much-vaunted bridge had broken. Contemplating the harsh realities of international politics from within the Kremlin walls, Stalin called a halt to the "special roads to socialism" which had been spawning in Eastern Europe. Any doubtful elements had to be removed from these governments and the whole region secured firmly and quickly within the Soviet sphere. In this operation Czechoslovakia was crucially important both economically, as the most developed country in the region, and militarily, as the key to the Soviet defence system. Lying East-West in the heart of Europe, Czechoslovakia's strategic importance was overwhelming. Defence in depth was crucial to the Soviet Union because of its military weakness vis-à-vis the United States at this time. The main military threat to her was from manned nuclear bombers, and the second world war had shown that the effectiveness of a fighter defence system multiplied greatly with the depth of the defence zone. In this sense the integration of Czechoslovakia into the Soviet zone was essential: if Czechoslovakia was in the Western orbit, the Soviet military position would be severely weakened.[25]

One thing above all others stood out: in the changed international climate, all possibility of a "special road to socialism" was killed off. Such a tender, delicate plant could barely survive the first breezes of cold war. The Marshall Plan incident heralded a qualitatively new moment in the development of socialist revolution in Czechoslovakia. The sharply altered international conditions quickened the internal tempo of the revolution and polarised the forces within the country.[26] Most significantly, KSČ policy veered to the left.

The details of the discussions and contact between Moscow and the KSČ remain hidden from history. From the Soviet point of view the new international situation demanded the speedy consolidation of Communist power in Czechoslovakia. This necessity was undoubtedly impressed upon KSČ leaders in July and August, while within the KSČ leadership remnants of the old, sectarian attitudes of the "class against class" era re-emerged. Some KSČ leaders were happy to retreat from the complexities and sophistications of class alliances back to the old, tried and tested stomping-ground of "the battle against reaction" led by "the vanguard of the proletariat". These reawakened sectarian tendencies merged with the *decisive* impetus to the revolution given by the Soviet leadership.

By the end of August the policy shift was already publicly apparent. On 24 August in a speech near Brno, Gottwald analysed the political situation, and two themes emerged that were to underpin Communist strategy in the following months.[27] He called upon democratic forces within the other parties of the National Front to ensure that they did not tolerate opponents of the National Front within their ranks. This theme, which Slánský emphasised a fortnight later in a major address at České Budějovice,[28] was to constitute one of the major tactics which the KSČ adopted in the following months in their attempt to reconstruct the National Front under Communist domination. The success of this policy required a larger Communist Party, for as Gottwald declared, "Everything in the end is dependent on how strong our party is."[29] He set a target of one-and-a-half million party members by the time of the elections in May 1948. This target was reaffirmed at an important meeting of KSČ district political and organisational secretaries in Prague on 28 August. Slánský delivered the main report, emphasising the altered character of the situation and the new response it demanded.[30] The KSČ's new, political campaign had begun and at the weekend major rallies were held at Pardubice (80,000), Jihlava (35,000) and Plzeň (40,000),[31] followed by demonstrations at Ostrava (35,000), Kladno (55,000) and České Budějovice (35,000) a week later.[32] More dramatically, the start of September saw the KSČ launch a campaign in support of the millionaires' tax, in which they attacked the right-wing parties in the National Front with an unprecedented stridency and vehemence.

The complicated process of economic recovery had been seriously hampered by the severe drought which affected the

country in summer 1947. As a result only 63 per cent of the
planned amount of grain was harvested, 48 per cent of potatoes,
53 per cent of sugar beet and about one-third of fodder crops.[33]
Food rations were cut to below the 1945 level and firm measures
taken against speculation in foodstuffs. The government gave
prompt and substantial aid to the farmers, importing fodder,
raising procurement prices and granting the necessary subsidies.
These emergency measures placed a considerably added strain on
government expenditure, and the two main parties of the National
Front proposed alternative solutions as to how they should be paid
for. The KSČ considered the best solution to be a levy of the
wealthy, the so-called millionaires' tax. Included among the millionaires in 1947 were, it was estimated, 14,000 factory owners,
16,000 landowners with more than 123 acres, 6,000 major export
traders and 8,000 wholesalers and retailers.[34] The right-wing
parties were opposed to this tax, which would have penalised the
economic interests they sought to defend. The NSS proposed
that the necessary funds should come from the budget, which
would have necessitated either savings in other areas of state
expenditure or a general increase in taxation.[35]

On 2 September, KSČ ministers proposed a millionaires' tax
to provide money for the agricultural crisis at a government meeting. Their proposal was rejected.[36] In reply the KSČ resorted to
their strength outside parliament to obtain support for their
proposal and pressurise the government to reverse its decision.
The issue provided the KSČ with an opportunity to test out its
new policy and its effectiveness. The question rapidly assumed a
wider political significance and was used by the KSČ to identify
the right-wing parties with the wealthy.

A fiercely polemical propaganda campaign was launched by the
Communists. *Rudé právo* named the ministers who had voted
against the millionaires' tax[37] and then denounced *Svobodné
slovo*, the NSS daily paper.[38] Meetings were held throughout the
country, while in the factories Communist trade unionists mobilised support for the measure. Resolutions of support poured in
from major industrial enterprises to the government, KSČ headquarters and to ÚRO. Vítkovice ironworks, the ČKD engineering
plant, car plants in Mladá Boleslav, eight pits in North Bohemia
and a meeting of trade-union functionaries in Prague were just a
few of the places to register their backing for the KSČ proposal.[39]

On 5 September the ÚRO Presidium came out in favour of the tax.[40] Such was the degree of popular support that on 11 September the SDS signed a new agreement with the KSČ which included a proposal for joint action on the millionaires' tax.[41] The KSČ campaign was undoubtedly a political success. Their simple, clear propaganda spotlighted the class nature of the right-wing parties' opposition to the tax. In consequence many workers who were in the SDS or NSS supported this KSČ policy rather than follow the vacillations or hostility of their own leaderships. The struggle over the tax showed the preparedness of the non-Communist majority to support specific KSČ policy. The right-wing parties were discredited by their attitude on the issue, which was resolved in October when the National Assembly passed a luxury tax and a millionaires' levy.

For the KSČ the campaign was a "dry run" for the events to follow. They had shown that in a political conflict they possessed the support of working people and organisations outside parliament and that they could mobilise this support on their own behalf. Such pressure would shift the vacillating SDS to their side and ensure a KSČ victory on any major issue at stake in the government. The US Chargé in Czechoslovakia, Yost, accurately summarised the situation in his cable to the Secretary of State on 9 September when he noted that "sharp evolution has occurred in Czech Communist Party strategy and hence in Czech political situation during the past week. . . . It is possible that Communists may be laying groundwork for drastic action . . . in case increasing international tension should persuade Kremlin that Communist control of Czecho must be radically strengthened."[42] The groundwork had indeed been laid.

In late September Slánský, along with Bašt'ovansky, the general secretary of the KSS, attended the conference of ten communist and workers' parties in Poland at which the Communist Information Bureau was set up. In his address to the conference[43] Slánský reviewed the main political developments which had occurred in Czechoslovakia since liberation. Having discussed the national committees and nationalisation he turned to land reform and agricultural policy and discussed the new laws which the Communist Minister of Agriculture was proposing. These were especially important, since although the KSČ had gained wide support amongst the peasantry, reactionary influences remained strong in the countryside and "the strengthening of the alliance between workers and peasants is the most important basis for the further strengthening of the new régime in Czechoslovakia."[44] Slánský's report recognised that the sharpening of the international situation had and would continue to accelerate the process of differentiation within the parties of the National Front. He considered that the aim of the right-wing parties was to isolate the Communists and create a government from which the KSČ would be excluded, as had happened to the communist parties in France and Italy. The conditions for this would be created by undermining popular confidence in the existing Communist-led government's ability to deal with the country's major problems. However, Slánský was sure that such plans would be rebuffed, for the KSČ was working to unite the democratic and patriotic elements in all parties so that the reactionary elements in some of those parties could be expelled from the National Front. In this process the role of the mass organisations, especially the trade unions, was vitally important, for "in the future they must play a more active part in the National Front."[45] His report gave a clear indication to Zhdanov, the main Soviet representative at the conference, that the KSČ was on the way to consolidating its power in the way the new situation demanded. No mention of "the Czechoslovak road to socialism" was to be found in Slánský's speech. Indeed, the establishment of the Cominform signified a new era of ideological solidity in the international Communist movement, and a suppression of its nascent polycentrism.

On his return from the conference Slánský gave a wide-ranging report of its proceedings to a meeting of KSČ deputies, district secretaries and leading workers at the central secretariat. He declared that the conference had demonstrated that the most important task was to bolster the National Front, "from which, of course, exponents of domestic and foreign reaction must be expelled,"[46] an extremely clear hint to the right-wing parties of the fate that awaited them. Slánský was to repeat this theme to a meeting of Communist miners several days later.[47] Indeed, the KSČ general secretary seems to have been the key figure in this policy shift. Gottwald's standing in Moscow had been lowered as a result of the Marshall Plan incident[48] and Slánský, who had overall responsibility on party matters, had to ensure the smooth implementation of the new line. Steinhardt astutely observed the change that had occurred since the Marshall Plan incident. He cabled on 30 September:

> Moscow is now taking a greater interest in Czechoslovakian affairs than heretofore. . . . Gottwald and other moderate Communists who had hoped and expected to gain an absolute majority at elections next May . . . are now being forced to proceed more rapidly . . . to bring Czechoslovakia into line.[49]

Such a development was hardly surprising. After all, there was no politician more likely than Stalin to grasp the essence of Bismarck's Bohemian adage.

12
Approaching the Climax

Henceforth almost every sphere of state life was to be an arena of sharp political struggle. The prospects for the right-wing parties in these conflicts appeared bleak. In attempting to counter the moves of the KSČ, to isolate them and to draw Czechoslovakia into the Western orbit, they faced three major obstacles.

First, the absence of a large industrial and commercial bourgeoisie greatly weakened the right-wing forces. At a political level it deprived them of a major base of support and a source of money and propaganda. In addition, at an economic level the nationalisation decrees meant that the state sector was the primary force in the economy. The far-reaching character of the Košice programme placed the right in the position where they had to challenge and reverse the existing economic order if they were to succeed in their aim. Such a reversal was a complicated political manoeuvre, and the petty and medium urban and rural bourgeoisie which formed the main nucleus of the right possessed neither the social cohesion nor the stature necessary for the task, especially if it was to happen quickly.

This fact was of considerable importance, especially when considered in combination wth the changed character of the armed forces. In many countries the army provided a firm base which a weak bourgeoisie could rely upon to ensure control, but this was not the case in Czechoslovakia. After the war, extensive personnel and structural changes were carried out in the army, along the lines proposed in the Košice programme. The removal of all collaborationist officers from their posts altered the political character of the army, as did the structural and educational measures carried out in accord with the programme. The Czechoslovak army modelled itself on its Soviet counterpart; as the US Chargé in USSR, Durbrow, noted in August 1946, the equipping by the USSR of ten divisions of the Czechoslovak army constituted an "important step in direction of increasing dependence Czechoslovak army on Red army."[1] In November Steinhardt was reporting that steps were being taken to integrate Czechoslovakia within the military plans of the USSR and that a joint headquarters would be set up at Banska Bystrica. The importance of these developments in the Czechoslovak military forces has been insufficiently recognised in the literature on the revolution.

The Košice programme did not only bring about a purge of right-wing elements in the upper echelons of the army: binding the army to the USSR meant that its military potential and effectiveness became dependent on the Red Army, while Czechoslovak military leaders trained and educated at Soviet military academies tended to adopt a standpoint similar to that of their colleagues. This represented a key power-political element in the launching of the revolution, for the Soviets and Czechoslovak communists possessed, as Steinhardt realised, "sufficiently substantial influence in army at least to neutralise any possible action by pro-Western elements therein."[3] This realisation was not confined to Steinhardt alone, and it illustrated the weak position of the pro-Western forces in the country at large.

Futhermore, the agreements at the end of the war had placed Czechoslovakia in the Soviet sphere of influence. While the United States was prepared to give the maximum encouragement and indirect support to its allies within the country, it was extremely unlikely that the Americans would engage in direct military intervention at this time. Conventional manpower was the main missing ingredient in Washington's attempts to alter the power balance which Yalta had recognised. Truman's attempts to secure an armed force capable of backing his diplomacy proved abortive,[4] and as Harriman was later to recall, "Only by keeping our military forces in being after Germany and Japan surrendered could we have attempted to *compel* the Soviet Union to withdraw from the territory it controlled."[5] These forces had not been increased by late 1947, so direct American military help to pro-Western forces inside Czechoslovakia could be discounted. Steinhardt certainly did not expect it, for in his cable of 30 September he somewhat resignedly wrote, "We must from now on reckon with probability that within a period of months, Czechoslovakian government will became a subservient tool of Kremlin in internal as well as external affairs and that such degree of independence as government has been able to exercise up to present time will rapidly diminish."⁶ Steinhardt's implicit evaluation of the weakness of the right-wing parties was borne out in the following months. As the political clashes grew sharper and the parties jostled for the key positions and power bases, the right proved unable to overcome its objective weaknesses; the general, if not yet complete, domination of the KSČ became apparent.

Slovak crisis

Slovakia was the main right-wing stronghold and it was here that a major political crisis developed, in autumn 1947.⁷ The neofascist clerical elements in the country, former suporters of the Hlinka party, had stepped up their activity during the year They gained increasing influence among the Slovak Democrats, tried to secure a reprieve for Tiso, the former leader of the wartime Slovak puppet state who had been sentenced to death, and stepped up their separatist underground activity. The DS took on an increasingly conservative character, but as yet it was unable to align itself consistently with the Czech right-wing parties. The latter recognised Slovakia's independence as a nation "only grudgingly," as Ripka later admitted,⁸ but efforts to form a common anticommunist front were in motion by the late summer.⁹

The KSČ had recognised the potential danger to it posed by the situation in Slovakia since the elections.¹⁰ The increased activity of former collaborationists re-emphasised the threat, especially as they received encouragement from the policy of the DS. With the drought and bad harvest creating drastic food shortages by the late summer, the political situation in Slovakia had become extremely volatile.

The situation became more tense when the Slovak Minister of Interior, General Ferjenčík, announced on 14 September that an anti-state conspiracy controlled by separatist elements had been uncovered. The movement was directed from abroad by Sidor and Durčansky, two ministers in the Slovak puppet state, and its aim was to break the united republic. Implicated in the plot were three Slovak Democratic deputies and a civil servant in the office of Jan Ursíny, the DS vice-president in the government.

With these revelations the KSČ and KSS saw a chance to weaken the position of the DS in Slovakia, and the following weeks saw sharp clashes, culminating in the political crisis at the end of October. To those who considered that the conspiracy charges were a fabrication of the communist-dominated Ministry of the Interior, the remarks of anti-Communist commentators merit attention. Ripka recognised that "certain undesirable elements . . . had insinuated themselves into the [DS] ranks,"[11] and the NSS "asked the Slovak Democrats to rout out of their party all elements likely to compromise them,"[12] while on the charges themselves "it was impossible to reject all the accusations offhand."[13] Steinhardt considered there was "some proof" of them.[14]

At the same time the unwillingness of the DS to grapple with the economic situation resulted in growing criticism, especially from the Slovak working class and peasantry. The worsening food situation forced them on to the black market, where they were prey to the traders and businessmen who supported the DS, while the DS continued to oppose further land reform. Steinhardt noted "that Food and Agriculture Ministries in hands of inefficient Slovak Democrats out of sympathy with legislation they are supposed to implement."[15]

In combination, these developments created a favourable situation in which the communists could undermine the position of the DS. In the political crisis that followed they used many of the tactics they were to employ in February. After consultation with the KSČ, a meeting of the Central Committee of the KSS decided to initiate a campaign to restructure the Board of Commissioners and other state organs, thereby reducing the hold of the DS. Pressure for this was exercised by the mass organisations of workers, peasants and partisans on the government, as well as by the KSS itself.

The Communists on the Slovak Trades Union Council, and above all Zupka, were instrumental in securing the calling of a works councils conference on 30 October to discuss the whole position.[16] The conference was attended by 1,836 delegates, and it unanimously adopted a resolution demanding the reconstitution of the Board of Commissioners with representatives from the trade unions, peasant associations and resistance groups participating. Only such a political change could halt the deterioration in food supplies and the extensive black market activity.[17] It was agreed to back up these demands with "demonstrative action" by workers on 5 November. In Bratislava all-factory meetings were held, with over 150 enterprises passing resolutions in support of the conference's demands,[18] while in Žilina, Nitra, Trnava and elsewhere meetings, assemblies and even short strikes were organised.[19]

The KSS had successfully mobilised the organised working class behind its policy, while a meeting of partisan groups on 31 October had supported the works council demands. The similar resolution passed at the national delegate conference of peasant associations on 14 November added further weight to the KSS demand for a reconstruction of the government. The Slovak Democrats resisted fiercely, and when the government in Prague intervened, the NSS and LS defended their position, for all sections of the right recognised Slovakia's political importance to them.

After protracted negotiations involving the Prague government a new Board of Commissioners was formed on 18 November, in which the DS lost its overall majority; but no representatives of mass organisations were included. The agreement represented a compromise, with the KSS and KSČ holding back from a definitive confrontation. The general reaction of the right to the conclusion of the episode was that it signified a setback for the Communists.[20] Such an assessment is misleading, however. Although the KSS had failed to secure an overall majority on the Board of Commisioners, it had gained considerably augmented support for its policies among workers and the peasantry, while the DS had been forced to annul its agreement with the Catholics. The crisis had sapped the energy of the DS. The success of this Communist "dress rehearsal" was emphasised in February, for then right-wing opposition to the events in the Czech Lands was negligible.

While neutralising one potential power base for the right, the Communists were actively securing another as their own. They clearly understood the importance of the coercive organs of the state, as their policy towards the army showed. With the sharpening conflict the KSČ turned their attention to the police and security forces; using their decisive influence in the Ministry of the Interior, they gradually assumed decisive control. The political complexion of these forces was crucial to the outcome of the revolution, but the KSČ resolved to oust their opponents by entirely bureaucratic and administrative methods. Rather than place the police and security forces under the supervision of the national committees, to which they would have been answerable, the KSČ took advantage of its influence in the Interior Ministry to place its own men in the major positions in all the departments of these forces. Security and intelligence units were singled out for special attention.[21]

These developments provoked strong opposition from the right-wing parties and was one of the main planks in their conflict with the KSČ. *Svobodné slovo* accused the KSČ of attempting to bring the entire police and security apparatus under their control. Non-Communists were being removed or transferred from their posts. In Jihlava, Klatový and Olomouc, non-Communists had been transferred to criminal police work and had been replaced in the security department by Communists.[22] Drtina gave details of the extent of this KSČ domination at the Cabinet meeting on 13 February 1948. Communists headed the three branches of the Corps of National Security Police (SNB). Of the seventeen regional officers of the SNB in Bohemia, twelve were Communists, as were four of the five senior officers in the Prague headquarters of the provincial SNB. In all, sixty of the seventy senior officers in the SNB were KSČ members, while the Communists held the three chief posts at the central headquarters of the political police.[23] It was on a security matter that the right-wing parties were to resign a week later and cause the government crisis. Yet since they did not raise the issue as one of the democratic, popular control of the police but rather as a party political question, the right found themselves outmanoeuvred. They failed to generate widespread disquiet on the matter, especially among the working class, and as a result Communist domination of the SNB continued unhampered. In the February crisis, SNB support for the KSČ policies was assured.

The repercussions were enormous. The control of security forces and police was one of the clearest examples of how the political methods used before February affected and determined subsequent events. The KSČ approach was classically stalinist in its administrative, non-popular character: the way to safeguard the security apparatus was to have one's own people run the machine. By a variety of manoeuvres, potential opponents were weeded out and loyal personnel appointed. The authoritarian, centralised and hierarchical character of these apparatuses was not altered, merely the people who directed them. The KSČ made no call for the democratisation of the police and security apparatus, no move to extend the democratic rights of those working within it, nor, most important of all, any attempt to make these institutions accountable to the people (through the local national committees, for example). The KSČ policy excluded the possibility of bringing the security and police forces under popular, democratic control. This helps to explain how these forces were able to exercise unbridled power in the post-February years and to use it unjustly to harass and persecute hundreds of Communists and ordinary citizens.

In foreign affairs Czechoslovakia strengthened her ties with the countries in the Soviet orbit. These alliances, especially that with the USSR, were portrayed by the KSČ as cementing the unity of Slav peoples and they were welcomed widely. The right-wing parties were unable to detach significant sections of the population away from the policy of firm alliance with the USSR. Popular sentiment for the Soviet Union remained high, while there were strong fears of the danger of a revived Germany. This placed the right in a very difficult position, for the West's proposed federal solution aroused the suspicions of many Czechoslovaks. The NSS supported the Soviet Union's centralised, four-power solution to the German problem and they informed American and British representatives that their attitude on Germany was posing problems for the pro-Western forces in Czechoslovakia.[24] So great was popular fear of a revitalised Germany that none of the right-wing parties felt able to disavow openly the alliance with the Soviet Union. The nationalist, anti-Teutonic feelings which the right-wing parties — as well as the KSČ — had engendered limited their manoeuvrability in the field of foreign policy. The right felt unable either to attack the Soviet Union or to extend their links with the West in the way the logic of their strategy demanded. Victims of their own propaganda, they were unable to prevent the consolidation of Czechoslovakia within the Slav bloc.

Problems with the plan
The KSČ was the strongest political party in the country and the initiator of the Two-Year Plan. In order to maintain and swell its popular support, it was essential that the plan's targets should

be met and that the recovery of the economy should proceed smoothly. However, the disruption of the National Front at a political level was reflected and exacerbated by conflicts in the economic sphere. The major structural problems of the economy — a shortage of labour and capital, accentuated by the natural disaster of the summer drought — threatened the plan, while the activities of the private sector aggravated the position. As the viability of the National Front economy was increasingly called into question, the right-wing parties hoped that the KSČ would suffer a loss of popular confidence and thus could be removed from the government.

The economic problems accumulated rapidly in the latter half of 1947. Among the indications of this was the negative trend in the balance of payments. Heavy deficits in May, June and July wiped out the original surplus, while the huge August deficit of 620.9 million crowns along with the September deficit of 160.7 million showed that this was not a temporary phenomenon.[25] The imports necessary for the Two-Year Plan were primarily reponsible for this unfavourable trend.

In agriculture output, already hampered by the shortage of labour, lack of machinery and the activities of some sections of medium-size property holders, was dealt a severe blow by the summer drought. This had a disastrous effect on food production;[26] as well as further overburdening the balance of payments, it meant more stringent food rationing was introduced.[27]

With the severe shortages of food, a black market flourished and speculative tendencies grew stronger. The report of the ÚRO National Economic Commission to the ÚRO plenary session in January 1948 showed that price levels had risen since September and that real living costs were appreciably above the official index because of a flourishing black market.[28] The number of complaints received by national committees about black marketeering and overcharging rose sharply in the latter half of the year, doubling between August and December.[29] The black market was not confined just to food but involved clothing and other consumer goods, and strong inflationary pressures were being exerted as a result.

These developments heightened the class contradictions which had previously remained relatively latent within the economy. The small and medium bourgeoisie took advantage of the opportunities offered by the situation and sought to strengthen their economic position. Pešek has estimated that "entrepreneurial income" increased by 20 per cent in 1947.[30] On the other hand the working class, though the leading political force in the state, faced increasing economic hardship and began to demand further radical, socialising measures to combat these economic difficulties. Its attitude to the private sector grew increasingly hostile.

Within the National Front the different political parties put forward alternative solutions to the economic crisis. The right wing considered that the underlying disequilibria in the economy could be removed with the aid of American credits and a restoration of Czechoslovakia's natural pre-war trading patterns, which were predominantly with the West. The immediate deficits would have to be rectified by savings in public expenditure, while the overall supply situation could be improved by giving a freer hand to the private sector.

The alternative proposals of the KSČ, which attracted wide working-class support, reflected their break with a Popular Front strategy and their desire for a rapid transition to socialism. The KSČ took advantage of the sharpening class antagonisms in the economic field to put forward demands severely restricting the scope of the capitalist sector and integrating Czechoslovakia more firmly with the other planned economies. As the conflicts mounted in this arena, the KSČ's general political dominance became more apparent.

In the course of the year it was Czechoslovakia's economic ties with the planned economies that were strengthened, rather than those with the West. Her participation in the Marshall Plan was blocked, and economic agreements were concluded with Yugoslavia, Bulgaria and Poland, while negotiations were initiated for agreements with Hungary and Rumania.[31] Despite stiff right-wing opposition another trade agreement was signed with the USSR on 11 December, by which Czechoslovakia was to receive considerable imports of foodstuffs in exchange for engineering products.[32] These agreements consolidated Czechoslovakia economically within the Soviet sphere, as the KSČ desired.

KSČ strength had also been manifested in the imposition of the millionaires' tax, despite vehement right-wing oppositon. As the supply situation worsened, the KSČ responded to the burgeoning radicalism of the working class by demanding the nationalisation of the wholesale and retail trade. There was considerable working-class discontent with the situation in the distributive trades, which were entirely in private hands,[33] and deep suspicions that many of the shortages were the result of speculation and hoarding by private wholesalers and retailers. These were confirmed by spot checks which the Ministry of Internal Trade made in late 1947 on textile wholesalers; these uncovered large stocks of hoarded goods.[34] Such revelations accentuated working-class hostility to the private sector, and KSČ demands for further nationalisation evoked an enthusiastic response.

The KSČ's command of the situation was apparent by the way in which it was able to show that the existing economic difficulties could only be resolved with the further development of the revolution. Faced with severe dislocations and shortages in the economy, it proposed measures which would restrict the activities of the private sector and strengthen its socialist bases. Most significantly, it called for a Five-Year Plan to be introduced following the completion of the Two-Year Plan.[35] Contrary to the hopes of the right, the KSČ maintained the confidence of the industrial working class. It presented a coherent set of measures by which the economic difficulties could be overcome. This was exceptionally important, because if it underestimated the specifically economic and technical problems the country faced, it nevertheless showed that it was a political force capable of leading the state. As February approached, there was no doubt that the KSČ enjoyed genuinely widespread support amongst the industrial working class.

For the KSČ to consolidate its power this working-class support had to find expression in organisational form in bodies other than the KSČ itself. The political direction of the other main working-class party, the SDS, and the mass organisation of the working class, the ROH, were crucially important. Freshly imprinted on the minds of all politicians were the experiences in France and Italy, where Social Democrats had recently split from the Communists and joined right-wing blocs which excluded Communists from the government. The latter half of 1947 saw a fierce conflict within the SDS, as the right attempted to emulate its French and Italian counterparts and draw the SDS into its orbit.

A right-wing grouping had already become apparent in the SDS during the 1946 election. Basing itself on the reformist ideas and tendencies endemic to social democratic organisations, this group enhanced its position in the following months. It also attracted support from those in the centre and even some on the left of the SDS, because of their discontent with the Fierlinger policy of close alliance with the KSČ. In their message of greetings to the Twenty-First SDS Congress in November 1947, the KSČ called for further joint co-operation "on the basis of the principle of relations between equals".[36] Yet it was precisely these reciprocal relations between political partners in the National Front that appeared unequal to many SDS members and led them to oppose the current leadership. In many ways the KSČ regarded the SDS as another transmission belt: a party which would follow *the* party line. In the eyes of the KSČ leadership the SDS had no autonomous political role, as its swift fusion into the KSČ after February showed. Since one political party does not exist merely to serve the requirements of another — and this was the essence of the policy of the Fierlinger leadership — the right-wing opposition in the SDS was able to augment its support by asserting the party's independence.

After the joint agreement between the KSČ and the SDS had been signed in September, the right wing stepped up their campaign. Its main focus was the November congress, where they aimed to disclaim the agreement and change the leadership. Their influence in key sections of the party's administrative apparatus helped them secure a majority among the congress delegates,[37] and in the vote for party leader Laušman defeated Fierlinger 283 to 182.[38] This was an important advance for the right, which had backed Laušman's candidacy. The editorial in *Rudé právo* expressed dismay at the result,[39] while there was jubilation among all sections of the right. Beneš conveyed his delight at Fierlinger's defeat to Steinhardt and "readily took credit for what he described as a major victory."[40]

The jubilation was not justified. Steinhardt himself was more restrained and wisely reserved judgement as to the congress's significance.[41] The right wing had not been strong enough to put forward a candidate of their own but rather had backed Laušman, who had a left-wing reputation. The leadership of the SDS still contained a variety of political positions, and although its left-wing dominance had been broken, the right wing were not yet able to make the party adhere to an anti-Communist bloc along with the NSS, LS and DS. Laušman had unwittingly expressed the ambiguity of his party's position in his opening speech to congress, when he had stated that the SDS would not permit its policies to be influenced by foreign interests either of the left or the right.[42] The SDS's indecision in the face of two possible alternatives it could pursue condemned it to political impotence.

Although the congress had been a setback for the KSČ strategy, it was not to prove disastrous. In the factories there was no widespread opposition from SDS members to KSČ policies, and the KSČ remained confident that in the event of a crisis the SDS would eventually follow their line (this had happened with the millionaires' tax). But fundamentally this setback was not disastrous for the KSČ because the decisive arena of working-class politics lay in the ROH, not the SDS, and there the KSČ remained dominant despite a right-wing challenge.

If the right were to succeed in ousting the KSČ from the government it was essential that they break the Communists' dominance in the working class and in ROH. The most likely way of achieving this was by fostering sectional divisions within the working class and championing the cause of one grouping. This would detach one sector of the working class away from KSČ influence and simultaneously cast doubt on the overall capability of the Communist-dominated trade-union leadership to conduct the affairs of ROH. This was what lay behind the complicated affair of the pay of public and state employees. They were a sector in which the NSS, LS and SDS retained wide support and which the right-wing parties considered most likely to agree to policies opposed by the ÚRO leadership.

In the late summer and autumn of 1947 ÚRO had held extensive discussions with the relevant unions over what kind of proposal ÚRO should submit to the government on the matter. The NSS, which had raised the issue in its 1946 election programme, wanted a 30 per cent increase, but the compromise package ÚRO submitted to the government was less inflationary and, following the proposal of the transport workers and teachers, gave preferential treatment to the lower-paid categories.[43] A complex series of negotiations with the government ensued, and by the New Year no final agreement for 1948 salaries had been reached. The ÚRO management committee meeting of 19 December, realising the position, declared that all wage increases should be backdated to 1 January 1948, and stated that prompt final discussions would take place with the Minister of Finance.⁴⁴ These were held on 9 January, when a twelve-strong union delegation headed by Zápotocký met Gottwald, Nosek and Dolanský and submitted a proposal that all public employees receive a 900 crowns taxfree quarterly supplement to their income.⁴⁵ The resolution of the ÚRO management committee the same day noted with satisfaction the meeting with representatives of the government and the assurances that the proposal would be discussed by the government.⁴⁶

Before making their proposal ÚRO had consulted Dolanský, the Minister of Finance, and had been informed that three million crowns was the maximum available in the state budget for the rearrangement of public and state employees' pay. Cognisant of the inflationary danger, ÚRO had contained their proposal within these limits and the KSČ supported them.⁴⁷ The SDS and NSS did not, however. At their management committee meeting on 15 January the SDS declared that the ÚRO proposal was unsatisfactory,⁴⁸ while at its meeting the NSS proposed a 25 per cent increase in public employees' salaries.⁴⁹ When the government discussed the matter on 21 January, only the KSČ supported the ÚRO proposal. Drtina withdrew the NSS proposal in favour of Majer's, which suggested that the public and state employees receive an increase of 800 crowns a month. Although Dolanský declared that this was well in excess of budgetary constraints, the measure was passed against KSČ opposition.⁵⁰

Whether such an obviously opportunistic move would achieve its intended political purpose was uncertain, yet ÚRO moved swiftly to meet the threat. At the ÚRO plenary session on 22 and 23 January the pay topic featured prominently in the discussion. Vandrovec, a leading National Socialist, defended the government decision to support the higher of the two proposals submitted to it. Somewhat disingenuously he remarked, "There is nothing tragic in that, especially when the government wants to give more than we suggested."⁵¹ But Vandrovec found himself almost completely isolated on the council and subject to fierce attack.⁵² In the discussion the council members displayed an awareness of the politics behind the issue. As Malík, the Communist miners' leader, declared, it was part of the right-wing attempt to undermine the confidence of trade unionists in ÚRO.[53] Jura took up a similar theme and maintained that as long as the trade unions remained united, all efforts to alter the political direction of the republic would fail. "We are not France," he pointedly remarked.[54] He said that the unions should continue to press for the ÚRO proposal on public and state employees' pay, and that calm but decisive action was necessary. The ÚRO resolution gave reaffirmed support for its pay proposal and asked its representatives to approach the government once again, so that the matter could be reviewed and a salary adjustment speedily carried out which did not threaten the process of economic consolidation. Significantly the resolution went on to give the ÚRO management committee full powers to prepare and organise any action necessary to mobilise the full strength of the trade-union movement behind this demand.[55]

The Communist-dominated ÚRO was not to permit the confidence of ROH members in its leadership to be weakened by decisions of the National Front. The previous ÚRO plenary session on 16 and 17 October had firmly restated the attitude of ROH towards the parties forming the government. Its resolution declared:

> The relationship of the trade-union movement to the political parties of the National Front is in principle positive and friendly. This friendly relationship, of course, can be broken if the activity of some of the political parties of the National Front is in conflict with the principal, programmatic mission of our national revolution to support a popular democratic development to socialism, and rather wants to strengthen the return to old, private capitalist exploitation. All conflicts which have arisen up until now between the trade-union movement and individual political parties have had their origin in this fundamental question.[56]

In support of this position, Zápotocký had referred the council to the declaration passed at the founding conference of ROH in January 1946 which stated, "We [ROH] shall support every government which aims at socialism, but we could not support a government which would want to check and sabotage the path to socialism."[57] The First ROH Congress had reaffirmed this basic position, and the ÚRO resolution of 17 October was completely in accord with this attitude.

Inextricably linked with the relationship of ROH to political parties was the matter of political differences within ROH itself. These had become more apparent in the autumn as the right made a more concerted challenge against the leadership and policies of ROH, with the NSS press being especially forthright in its opposition. The respective theoretical positions became clear during the extensive discussion on the question which took place at the ÚRO plenary session in October.

Two main right-wing tendencies can be discerned. Cigler and Peřina, both Social Democrats, considered that ROH should not be involved in party political conflicts. ROH had to be impartial in controversies such as the millionaires' tax, and should pursue a purely trade-union policy.[58] Kubát, a Social Democrat with long experience in the pre-war trade-union movement, considered that trade-union unity in a free, democratic state was not possible, for with the growing competition between political parties, whose members were in ROH and who followed the principles and tactics of their party, unity was already crumbling and would continue to do so. His response was to suggest that trade unions restrict their role to the defence of the sectional interests of their membership. In this way trade-union branches would avoid being the instruments of political parties' factory organisations.[59]

Neither of these positions was in accord with congress policy, nor were they shared by the majority of trade-union members. However, the ÚRO leadership presumed to counter these positions in a demagogic, non-political fashion, reiterating constantly the theme of unity. A typical example was Zápotocký's reply to Kubát:

> Whoever wants to maintain trade-union unity cannot just dream about it. He must struggle for the maintenance of the unity of the trade-union movement. He must defend unity and link the maintenance of that unity with the entire struggle of the trade-union movement for the enforcement of the legitimate demands of the working class.[60]

In such speeches "unity" acquired an almost mystical quality, devoid of a political content. This approach begged the question of how to handle opposition from sections of the membership to ROH policy. For the ÚRO leadership the rhetoric on unity was a substitute for handling the concrete problems posed by those trade unionists who were not socialists or who opposed left-wing policies.

This flaw in the leadership's position was shown in its plenary resolution. This stated:

> ROH is for the broadest internal democracy, freedom of expression and right of criticism. Every member and functionary of the trade-union movement has the right in his own organisational group, at membership and committee meetings, at conferences, at the management committee, etc. to discuss freely, to criticise, to give proposals and to defend them. For the utilisation of these rights nobody in ROH shall be persecuted.[61]

However, these rights were entirely negated by the next sentence:

> Of course we shall defend ourselves against internal organisational discussion being abused in the party political press ... for the organisation of a campaign of incitement against ROH.[62]

Under the banner of unity, administrative methods were being used by ÚRO to crush any right-wing opposition within ROH, for such opposition was declared to be disruptive and an incitement against the unity of ROH, i.e. against its left-wing character. ROH's democratic centralist structure suppressed the political opposition within the trade unions to the policies of the leadership. Although such opposition was of a limited scope at this time, the way it was combated had a damaging effect on the level of political debate within the working class. It bred quiescence. Neither was this quiescence overcome by any debate within the left over its own understanding of socialism. To the ÚRO leadership, with their implicitly monolithic conception of socialism, this was not an issue.

However, these serious weaknesses within ROH were not of immediate significance. In order to show the level of support for ROH and its policies among the working class, the October plenary session initiated a special recruitment campaign to draw into ROH the remaining non-unionised sections. During November 52,507 new members were gained[63] and in December another 70,852 members were recruited, the highest monthly increase in the year,[64] leaving ROH with 2,249,976 members.[65] This was but one indication that the attempt by the right to undermine ROH and the structure it had established was doomed. The right had neither the base nor the position in the leadership to pose any sustained challenge to the left. As the conflict in the country approached its resolution, Communist dominance over the trade-union movement was assured.

The exceedingly powerful position of the KSČ stands out as the major political development in the months preceding February. The KSČ considered that the right was trying to provoke a government crisis in which, with the situation deadlocked, the President would intervene and form a "government of officials", after which a new government could be constituted with the KSČ either excluded or in a minority.[66]

In the eventuality of a government crisis the KSČ was in a position to counter the stratagems of the right. After Gottwald's call in late August, the KSČ's membership increased rapidly, exceeding one and a quarter million by the end of the year.[67] The KSČ had by far the largest membership of any political party in the country. It also had considerable support among the mass organisations, especially the trade unions, and in the event of any deadlock in the government it would not hesitate to mobilise that support. As Zápotocký declared in the National Assembly in December, the KSČ would not countenance the formation of a "government of officials" but would rather take the issue to the people, that being "the only correct, democratic way."[68] The practicality and effectiveness of this approach had already been manifested in the events over the millionaires' tax and Slovakia. It also bolstered those elements in other parties, especially the SDS, which were sympathetic to Communist policy. Special attention was focused on this matter by Gottwald in his address to the Central Committee meeting in November 1947,[69] and the KSČ was confident that the right-wing elements in these parties could be isolated. In addition, the KSČ knew that the main "power" organs of the state would remain neutral or tend to be sympathetic towards it in any major confrontation. With these strengths the KSČ was confident of combating any move by the right. As the main force in the country, the KSČ occupied the centre of the political arena and was able to determine the character of political developments. Gottwald concluded his New Year speech with the slogan, "Forward, not a step back,"[70] and as the conflict approached its climax, the KSČ held all the keys to its outcome. In February it was to drive the revolution onward.

13
The February Events

On Friday 20 February the National Socialist, Popular Party and Slovak Democrat ministers resigned from the government and the political conflict entered its decisive phase. The National Socialists considered that the issue of the composition of the police and security forces was the one most likely to attract popular support and gain the SDS to their side. The NSS leadership feared that the forthcoming Works Councils congress, followed by that of the peasant commissions, would propose radical socialisation measures which the SDS would be unable to oppose and which would ensure that the KSČ retained its initiative. This possibility the NSS intended to counter by provoking a government crisis on the security issue before the congress.[1]

Security and police matters had formed a major part of the right wing's campaign against the KSČ, with fierce opposition to the growing Communist domination of the SNB being voiced. At the meeting of the parliamentary security committee on 29 January both NSS and SDS deputies opposed changes within the main command of the SNB and the apparatus of the Ministry of the Interior which had resulted in non-Communists being transferred and replaced by Communists. *Svobodné slovo* hoped that as a result of their joint opposition the SDS would link up with the NSS in a united struggle for a purge of the SNB.[2]

At the Cabinet meeting on Friday, 13 February Drtina illustrated and objected to the degree of Communist control of the SNB. During the course of the meeting it became known that eight non-Communist divisional police commissioners in Prague had been replaced by Communists. Nosek, the Minister of the Interior, was absent from the meeting owing to illness, but the Cabinet passed a resolution annulling those changes, calling for an investigation and barring further appointments until this had been completed.[3]

On 16 February the NSS ministers Zenkl, Drtina, Stránský

and Ripka, together with the deputies Krajina and Firt, met and decided to transform "the latent crisis into open crisis,"[4] by resigning from the government if the KSČ did not yield on the security question. Communist intentions on this were made clear at the Cabinet meeting on 17 February when, in Nosek's continued absence, they refused to place the matter on the agenda and confirm whether the 13 February decision had been carried out. Gottwald declared that Nosek would report on police and security matters at the next Cabinet meeting on 20 February. He then adjourned the meeting.[5]

This settled the NSS in its decision to initiate an open crisis. They informed Popular Party and Slovak Democrat ministers of their plan and received their backing as well as that of Majer, representing the right wing of the SDS.[6] On 18 February Ripka and Zenkl went to visit Beneš to inform him of their intentions and ascertain his attitude.[7] Beneš fully supported them and declared, "You are right; it is absolutely necessary that the decree of 13 February should be carried out. . . . Remain firm, as you have been up to now. Do not let yourselves be intimidated. As for me, I won't give way. You can count on me."[8]

Assured of presidential support, the NSS felt confident enough to bring the crisis to a head. Their press continued to emphasise the security issue, and a party statement declared that security was the responsibility of the whole government, not of just one party.[9] On Friday 20 February, *Svobodné slovo* appeared with the headline "We shall not permit a police régime", and charged that the Ministry of the Interior was employing illegal methods in its work.[10]

The NSS, LS and DS ministers did not appear at the Cabinet meeting due to commence at 10 a.m. that morning. Gottwald was informed that they would only attend the meeting if they were given an assurance that the Cabinet's decision on police and security of 13 February had been carried out. Gottwald gave no indication on this in his letter of reply, but announced that Nosek would give a report to the meeting. With the situation deadlocked and the SDS willing to attend the Cabinet only with all parties represented, no meeting could be held.[11] During the course of the afternoon twelve ministers resigned from the government. They were Zenkl, Drtina, Stránský and Ripka of the NSS; Šrámek, Hála, Kopecký and Procházka of the LS; and Kočvara, Pietor,

Franek and Lichner of the DS.[12] The SDS convened an executive committee meeting to discuss their attitude, but did not resign. Neither did the two non-party ministers, Masaryk and Svoboda. Thus with a majority remaining in the government it was able to continue functioning legally, according to the 1920 constitution. This fact was rapidly to assume considerable tactical significance.

The urgency of the right's moves was necessitated by the acceleration in the pace of political developments initiated by the KSČ. Throughout the events of February the most significant factor was the command and control of the situation which the KSČ exercised. Their strategic perspectives had been determined by the altered international situation and by the reorientation of strategy this had generated in Moscow.

Indeed, the Soviet government took a very close interest in the events inside Czechoslovakia, yet it would be incorrect to suggest that they engineered the crisis. Although Zorin, Soviet Deputy Foreign Minister, arrived in Prague for an official visit on 19 February, he played no significant part in the proceedings. Along with Steinhardt, who returned to Prague from Washington also on 19 February, Zorin symbolised the interest of the major powers in the Czechoslovak events, but suggestions of his direct involvement appear unfounded. The specific tactics of February were the work of the KSČ leadership.[13] Their tactical approach was flexible, as they realised that the conflict could be resolved in several ways, but that its actual resolution depended in part on the policy adopted by the right.[14]

Within this flexible outlook there were three definite features. First, the KSČ was determined to retain the initiative it held as the strongest party in the government. It continued to call for the fulfilment of all the measures contained in the government programme, including a new national insurance law, tax relief for farmers and small tradesmen and a new land reform, as well as completion of the Two-Year Plan. By standing firmly by the government programme the KSČ appeared as a responsible, constructive political force; by occupying the centre of the political stage, it made its opponents appear as disruptive elements on the fringe. Secondly, in the event of any crisis the KSČ would immediately invoke the support of the mass organisations of working people, above all the trade unions, thereby ensuring that the crisis would not be resolved purely at the parliamentary and presidential level. Thirdly, in a time of crisis, as well as standing by the government programme, the KSČ would suggest new measures appropriate to the changed situation.

The KSČ felt confident that such an approach would guarantee them victory in the forthcoming elections. An opinion poll survey conducted by the district organisations of the KSČ estimated that the KSČ would gain an outright majority,[15] but within the leadership growing doubts developed as to the likelihood of this.[16] One of the most prominent themes of subsequent emigré historiography has been that the Communist coup occurred because the KSČ feared electoral defeat,[17] although Ripka, for example, accepted that it would remain the strongest party.[18] Yet psephological speculation is no alternative to analysing the realities of the situation and the possibilities it offered. At that time there were only two feasible choices of government, and both involved the dissolution of the existing National Front: either the Communists were to be excluded from government, or the right-wing parties were to be barred. Each side played to its strengths and tried to expose the other's weaknesses, with the right emphasising public employees' pay and the security question and the KSČ stressing land reform and further nationalisation. With the government decision of 21 January on public employees' pay, the friction between the contending elements of the National Front increased considerably, and along with it the probability that the conflict would be resolved before the election.

Assessing the exacerbation of tension at the end of January, the KSČ Politburo resolved to retain their position as the determinant force and drive the conflict to its conclusion. Tactically the situaton demanded the intervention of the mass organisations and a new series of proposals. At its Politburo meetings on 9 and 11 February the KSČ leadership discussed these points.[19] They resolved that the national conference of works councils which ÚRO had agreed upon should be held as soon as possible, while the peasant associations should also call an early conference. At these two conferences, proposals for further nationalisation and land reform would form a focal point of the discussion. The Politburo formulated detailed proposals on these two measures and intended to have resolutions passed at the conference incorporating them. In this manner two elements in the KSČ's tactical armoury were to be fused, the intention being to increase popular support for KSČ policy and to isolate their opponents.

Throughout the KSČ realised the fundamental necessity of mobilising the support of the working class and especially its industrial core. They paid close attention to the question of holding a works councils conference in connection with the public employees' pay issue, and were eager to broaden its scope. As Zápotocký explained in his political report to the ÚRO management committee on 6 February, a whole series of questions required rapid resolution. This was threatened by the sharpening pre-electoral activity which was undermining the government's capacity to act. If a situation developed in which legislative activity was further jeopardised, ÚRO would call an all-state conference of works councils and trade-union branches to discuss their attitude and course of action. The committee agreed to this, and the organisation department was entrusted with the necessary preparations.[20]

The decisions of the Politburo meeting on 9 February had a crucial influence on the timing and character of events. The government was expected to reject ÚRO's pay proposal for state and public employees again on the following day, and the KSČ prepared its response in anticipation. When the rejection occurred, Zápotocký issued a long statement which said:

> We cannot be satisfied with the solution which the majority of the government has suggested and carried. Therefore we are submitting the whole question, in association with questions which are related to it, for solution by our national congress of representatives of works councils and trade-union branches, which we shall call in the immediate future.[21]

The 9 February Politburo meeting had been critical in altering the urgency of the congress. The indefinite timing of the 6 February decision had been replaced by the immediacy of the statement on the 10th. At the meeting of the ÚRO Presidium on 12 February,[22] Zápotocký forcefully proceeded with his — and the Politburo's — proposals. The Presidium agreed on the congress date, Sunday 22 February, with the Industrial Palace in Prague as the venue and a "discussion and decision on the further progress of the Revolutionary Trade Union Movement to the solution of contemporary questions and problems" as the main theme. Zápotocký had stated that as well as discussion on public employees' pay and on how to find a solution which would not strengthen inflationary trends, the further nationalisation of industry and trade needed urgent consideration. Along with the national insurance law and land reform, these were the related questions he had in mind in his statement of 10 February. Zápotocký and his Communist colleagues were meticulously implementing the decisions of the Politburo. They easily carried the ÚRO Presidium with them. Only Šplíchalová, an NSS member, objected. She attempted to delay the congress by asking for a meeting of the ÚRO management committee to approve the congress date. Her request received no support. Kolský informed the meeting of the organisational and technical arrangements necessary to cope with the expected 8,000 delegates, while trade-union organisations in factories, offices and districts were asked to send in resolution on the issues involved to the ÚRO Secretariat. Swiftly and smoothly the KSČ leadership had set up the platform from which it could launch a mass mobilisation of the working class.

In a similar way the KSČ had laid the base for garnering the support of small and medium peasants. At a meeting on 16 February the chairman of the district peasant commissions had issued a statement expressing dissatisfaction with the delay of the new land reform and other agrarian measures. They had resolved to call a national congress of peasant commissions to discuss these and related topics. The congress was to be held in Prague on 28 and 29 February.[23]

The impetus for both these conferences sprang directly from the KSČ Politburo, and they illustrate the overwhelming influence which the KSČ exerted in these organisations. At times of revolutionary crisis the political process inevitably becomes concentrated and centralised, but the degree of control which the KSČ displayed here revealed these organisations as being entirely one-way transmission belts for the execution of KSČ policy. Their importance was emphasised in the Politburo statement of 17 February. The KSČ charged that some parties in the government were attempting to provoke an open crisis, as a result of which "a government of officials" would be installed. The forthcoming congresses had a vital role in forestalling such manoeuvres and resolving the present problems "in the spirit of popular democracy and socialism."[24] The statement provided further clear evidence to the right-wing parties that in the eventuality of a government crisis the KSČ would not permit its solution to be restricted to the parliamentary and presidential sphere.

The KSČ also carefully prepared its own membership, issuing clear directives for action. With the announcement of the Works Councils Congress and the request for resolutions, a major task of KSČ factory branches was to obtain the support of workers in their enterprises for the proposals agreed upon at the Politburo meetings of 9 and 11 February. Communists in the peasant associations had a similar task. Organisational preparations were made. The central secretariat called a meeting of Communist activists and organisers in all the major Prague factories on 17 February. Over 2,000 attended this meeting, which was addressed by Slánský. As well as being informed of the precise situation in the government and the possibility of an attempted repeat of the events of December 1920, all the KSČ factory branches were asked to form watch patrols of their most reliable members to reinforce the Works Guard.[25] Similar meetings were held in other major regions, an important one being held in Bratislava on 18 February,[26] while over 700 people attended a meeting in Ostrava the next day.[27] The entire party was poised to deal with the crisis.

When the resignations of the NSS, LS and DS ministers came on Friday, 20 February, the KSČ response was swift. All districts were instructed to hold demonstrations the following day in support of the Gottwald government.[28] The Politburo statement that evening called for the immediate mobilisation of the entire strength of the working people, and appealed to workers, peasants, artisans, intelligentsia and all patriotic Czechs and Slovaks to stand firm in their support of the National Front.[29] During that night the KSČ leadership decided on its tactical response to the new situation. Following the guidelines of Gottwald's seminal speech of 24 August and Slánský's address to the Cominform, the KSČ proposed to transform the National Front. Taking astute tactical advantage of the fact that a majority still remained in the government the KSČ demanded the exclusion of the resigning ministers and their followers from a reconstituted government. In his speech on 21 February at the Old Town Square in Prague, Gottwald explained the formula:

> We propose that the ministers who have resigned should be replaced by new men who have remained true to the spirit of the National Front. . . . We believe that there are enough such good Czech and Slovak men and women in all the political parties and in all the national organisations. . . . The completed government of the National Front, relying on the confidence of progressive force in all political parties and national organisations, could take on the task of carrying out the government programme.[30]

This was the demand contained in the Politburo's letter to Beneš on 21 February,[31] and it was a constant theme of all KSČ activity. It was a shrewd move which strengthened the KSČ's control of the situation and placed the right-wing parties on the defensive.

The inherent weaknesses of the right became rapidly evident after 9 February when the KSČ decided on its offensive. The uncertainty and hesitancy of the right was displayed in its handling of the Works Councils Congress. The initial response of *Svobodné slovo* was one of easy confidence. It declared that nobody had any objections to the congress, since it would turn against the Communists.[32] Two days later the attitude was less certain, while by the 18th the paper was forthrightly condemning the congress, declaring it to be in disregard of ÚRO's own rules.[33] *Právo lidu*, which was controlled by the right wing of the SDS, declared that the congress was inspired by those who wished to use the trade unions for their own party political purposes, but neither the paper nor the SDS management committee gave any clear guidance to their supporters as to what action to take.[34]

This inability to respond in any effective manner to new political developments was matched by the ineptitude of the right's main tactical gambit. In deciding to resign they placed great reliance on Beneš, and expected the President to be the crucial factor in the determination of a new government. They presumed that the government would automatically fall with their resignations, and were extremely concerned when this did not occur. Despite their protestations to the contrary,[35] the resignations were a move by the right to weaken the position of the KSČ in the government with a view to their ultimate exclusion. After the resignations, any kind of future harmony with the KSČ was obviously impossible. The leading right-wing politicians must have appreciated this, and that the KSČ would resist such a move, but they organised no major events to lend weight to their action. They hoped to restrict the resolution of the crisis to presidential and parliamentary circles, yet the KSČ had made it abundantly clear that in the event of a crisis it would "go to the people". In their complete inability to counter the KSČ's mobilisation lay the right's fundamental weakness.

The right wing of the SDS declared their adherence to parliamentary democracy. In response to the statements that the Works Councils Congress would be "a parliament of the working people" Majer told SDS functionaries that there was only one parliament in the country, the Constituent National Assembly.[36] On 21 February *Právo lidu* similarly declared, "We have but one parliament in Czechoslovakia and that is neither in the Industrial Palace nor Perštýn but opposite the National Museum, where the Constituent National Assembly meets and where the laws of the republic are created."[37] However, this rhetoric was merely a shield for impotence.

A resolution of the NSS management committee on 18 February declared its opposition to any attempts to set up a dictatorship of one political party, objected to the forthcoming Works Councils and Peasant Commissions Congresses, and claimed that the KSČ's new nationalisation proposals were contrary to the government programme.[38] Neither then nor in the subsequent days did the NSS suggest any specific measures for action which their supporters could take. At the height of the crisis *Svobodné slovo* issued a call to all National Socialists. They were asked to remain calm and disciplined: the solution to the crisis lay in the hands of the constitutional representatives and executive committees of the National Front parties. The NSS would adhere to its programme and traditions and ensure that the crisis was resolved in a parliamentary way.[39] The incapacity of the main right-wing force was plainly revealed. The NSS, along with the LS and DS, proved incapable of initiating organised opposition to the KSČ among the population. One of the most prominent features of the February events was the absence of any significant opposition to the KSČ. Already, before the resignations, the right had lost the ability to evaluate realistically its situation. Naïvely, it assumed that the government crisis would be resolved in a pre-war fashion, the outcome entirely dependent on presidential and party political negotiations. As the KSČ went beyond these confines and garnered huge popular support for its policies, the right became isolated and dispirited. Their atrophy prevented more than a minimal display of support by their followers. During February the working class were the only actors on the political stage, with the KSČ directing the production.

The relationship between the KSČ and the working class represents one of the more complex features of February. A close rapport existed between them, the KSČ policies undoubtedly corresponded to working-class aspirations. The high degree of class consciousness amongst the Czechoslovak working class meant that it displayed considerable hostility towards both the right-wing parties and private industry and trade. However, autonomous working class initiatives were largely absent in February. The entire course of events was orchestrated by the KSČ, the relationship of the working class to its main political party being of an essentially passive character.

When the expected government deadlock materialised on 20 February, the central KSČ secretariat immediately issued instructions to all districts for demonstrations in support of the Gottwald government to be held the following morning. The entire party apparatus was prepared. For example, in Ostrava the thirty-five full-time party workers directed their efforts towards the large factories, industrial works and mines. They secured fleets of cars from the national committee, SNB and nationalised enterprises — showing the partisan character of these bodies — and this quickly enabled the Ostrava party leadership to inform their branches and leading members of the immediate tasks required of them. Local KSČ leaders addressed workshop meetings at Vítkovice Iron Works at 6.00 a.m. on 21 February during the shift changeover, and urged the workers to attend the KSČ demonstration that morning. Other KSČ leaders addressed similar meetings in steelworks, chemical plants and at pitheads. The KSČ utilised its strength within the trade unions, and ROH functionaries recommended their members at factory meetings to attend the KSČ rally. That morning nearly 40,000 people demonstrated their support for the Gottwald government in the centre of Ostrava.[40] Events followed a similar course elsewhere, as the KSČ mobilised the working class in support of its demands. Demonstrations were held in all the major towns of the republic,[41] with over 20,000 present at Plzeň and more than 50,000 at Brno.[42]

Most significant was the large rally which the KSČ organised in the capital. On the evening of the 20th the KSČ gathered 2,500 of its factory activists at the People's House in Vysočany, a working-class district of North Prague. Among the matters discussed was the rally planned for the following morning.[43] On the morning of the 21st, at the commencement of the morning shift, factory meetings were held in all major Prague enterprises. They were called by the trade-union organisation at the instigation of the KSČ factory branch in the enterprise. At the meetings the chairman of the works council or trade-union committee gave a report of the previous day's events and called on the workers to participate in the KSČ rally in the Old Town Square that morning. There was an overwhelmingly favourable response to this call, with many factories passing resolutions calling for the exclusion of the resigning ministers from a new government and sending deputations to the President informing him of their views. Workers from all parts of Prague left their factories and marched to the Old Town Square, where a crowd of 80,000 was joined by large delegations from factories in Kladno and Plzeň.[44]

The rally heard Klement Gottwald's proposals for resolving the crisis. The radio network carried this speech, which was relayed direct to the demonstrations in the rest of the country. The rally then agreed to a resolution which declared:

> We all stand unitedly behind the government of Klement Gottwald. . . . We most decisively demand that the President of the Republic should accept the resignation of the Ministers of the National Socialist, the People's and the Slovak Democratic parties, who by their irresponsible actions have betrayed the National Front and have placed themselves in opposition to the government.
>
> We demand a government led by Klement Gottwald without the reactionary ministers. We demand that Prime Minister Klement Gottwald should, in accordance with the constitution and in the spirit of democratic practices, complete the government with new members who are faithful to the programme of the National Front and who are resolved to serve the interests of the people. . . .

We will work unitedly and resolutely for the people's will to be achieved.[45]

The rally's message was clear and the display of Prague working-class support for KSČ policy impressive. The impact of the event was increased by the decision of the KSČ leadership to send a deputation to Beneš to present the demands of the demonstration. The selection of the delegation was the responsibility of the Prague district leadership, and they chose a 55-strong delegation composed of workers from the largest factories in Prague, Kladno and Plzeň.[46] At its head was Bedřich Kozelka, chairman of the Enterprise Council at the ČKD engineering works and a member of the KSČ district committee. He has recalled how the delegation was refused access to the President, and that only after determined negotiation with Beneš' aides did the President agree to meet a three-man delegation. The workers chose five from their ranks and Kozelka presented the rally's demands to Beneš.[47] Every resolution agreed upon at the KSČ demonstrations that morning incorporated these demands, and telegrams urging Beneš to pursue this course of action flowed into the Presidential palace. Under the tight direction of the KSČ leadership the waves of extra-parliamentary pressure surged in on the President.

The Works Councils Congress and its impact

With the National Congress of Works Councils and Trade Union branches the following day, the volume and depth of this pressure swelled. In ten days ÚRO's organisational department had prepared a congress with 8,000 delegates representing every significant sector of the Czechoslovak working class, and the congress was to express its overwhelming support for KSČ policies.

With the decision of the ÚRO Presidium on 12 February to call the congress for the 22nd, the ÚRO organisational department had to move swiftly. At the meeting of trade-union secretaries on 13 February Kolský, who had overall responsibility for its organisation, outlined the preparatory details. The congress would last a day and be held at the Industrial Palace on the Old Exhibition Ground in Prague. Room was available for 8,000 delegates. Each factory was to send one delegate for every 350 employees, with a maximum of ten delegates from any one enterprise being permitted. Smaller factories were to be grouped together and allowed to send a joint delegate. If an enterprise sent only one delegate, it had to be the chairman of the works council, and if it sent two, the second had to be the chairman of the trade-union branch. In larger enterprises the further delegates were to be decided by a joint meeting of the works council and trade-union branch. Delegates' credentials were to be issued via the District Trades Council structure.[48]

In all 8,030 credentials were issued for delegates to attend the conference. Table 5 gives a comprehensive survey of all the delegates from Bohemia and Moravia by union and district.[49] There were another 2,030 in addition to these 6,000; 864 represented unions in Slovakia; 841 came from central committees; a further 96 from ÚRO; 214 represented district and area trades councils and 15 were on the supervisory council.[50] This breakdown illustrates the scope of the congress and its extensive, representative character.

Its rapid arrangement was a tribute to the efficiency of ROH's organisation. However, the congress preparations confirmed that the works councils were merely levers for the implementation of ÚRO policy. The autonomous role which they had enjoyed in the summer of 1945 had been completely extinguished. In an attempt to weaken the congress, the right raised this point and declared that the congress contravened ÚRO's own rules by extending beyond their legitimate jurisdiction.[51] An SDS statement said that since works councils included non-unionised workers they could not decide on trade-union policy.[52] In the abstract such points were valid, but ÚRO countered them with the rules relating to works council activity which had been incorporated in the government decrees and agreed upon by all parties. As Zápotocký declared correctly at the congress, the decrees gave ÚRO the overall responsibility for the direction of works council activity.[53]

Criticisms of this kind by the right lacked credibility in the light of their earlier disregard for autonomous works councils. As has been already noted, restrictions placed on these institutions severely handicapped the self-activity and initiative of the working class both during and after February. All the working-class organisations were excessively centralised and controlled from above. Two examples in relation to the congress illustrate this point. First, the congress was held at the behest of the central trade-unon bodies, not as a result of pressure from below by

Table 5
Delegates from Bohemia and Moravia at the Works Councils Congress 22 February 1948

	Brno	České Budějovice	Hradec Králové	Jihlava	Karlovy Vary	Kladno	Klatovy	Kolín	Liberec	Mladá Boleslav	Most	Olomouc	Ostrava	Pardubice	Plzeň	Praha	Šumperk	Tábor	Ústí n. L.	Zlín	Znojmo	Union Total
Miners	14	2	4	—	15	25	—	1	1	—	88	—	156	1	12	7	—	1	3	—	—	330
Transport	63	24	25	17	20	40	15	34	25	25	34	49	60	30	60	200	10	18	30	15	6	800
Metal	115	20	30	10	15	50	10	30	60	40	40	50	160	40	83	299	11	33	40	55	4	1,195
Agriculture	24	12	6	8	5	15	12	11	6	8	5	11	22	7	16	22	5	8	4	17	6	230
Foodstuffs	17	7	13	8	2	15	4	17	6	13	6	30	17	16	14	74	5	3	24	10	4	300
Chemicals	14	10	18	5	3	8	2	12	2	13	20	5	18	18	9	54	7	1	22	12	—	250
Print	14	2	4	2	2	2	1	3	4	3	2	5	5	3	5	68	—	—	4	3	—	130
Building	40	4	10	1	6	10	7	12	4	1	10	9	30	10	16	55	5	8	8	16	5	280
Wood	23	7	6	7	3	7	5	6	4	8	2	14	8	8	13	22	2	9	7	25	1	190
Textiles	70	10	130	12	30	7	25	23	100	58	10	45	41	41	11	44	21	9	8	57	—	780
Glass	9	3	3	34	21	7	2	8	19	5	2	—	2	—	4	9	—	2	6	6	3	130
Distribution	21	3	8	4	3	7	1	8	9	5	15	10	20	7	26	143	2	5	6	5	3	300
Banking	8	1	—	2	—	8	1	1	2	1	5	—	1	—	2	30	—	1	1	1	1	60
Health	16	3	6	1	1	—	2	—	5	4	—	2	—	5	6	55	5	3	4	5	4	160
Int. External	29	7	12	6	6	4	7	5	7	8	5	8	11	13	18	143	3	13	6	17	—	350
Finance	8	4	4	3	5	9	3	11	4	2	2	10	15	—	2	21	4	2	2	2	3	80
Justice	3	1	4	1	2	1	1	3	2	2	2	2	5	1	1	10	—	1	1	2	—	35
Education	22	6	11	5	4	7	3	2	4	8	5	10	12	8	—	40	3	6	6	16	4	190
SNB	7	5	5	3	6	5	2	9	2	2	5	3	6	3	8	13	2	4	3	8	3	100
Various	8	1	3	1	2	5	6	4	5	8	5	6	6	2	7	21	1	4	2	5	1	70
Art; Culture	2	—	1	1	1	2	1	2	4	3	—	1	1	1	4	28	—	3	2	1	—	40
District Total	527	132	301	125	153	224	110	200	275	213	270	267	597	217	318	1,358	85	133	183	263	49	6,000

220

works councils or trade-union branches. Secondly, the ÚRO organisational department instructed workers as to who their delegates were to be, rather than leaving that decision to factory meetings. The suspicion within the KSČ of independent working-class action has already been analysed. This meant that the party was unable to blend the efficiency and effectiveness of centralised apparatuses with local working-class initiatives. The latter element was strictly dependent on the former. The KSČ was the hegemonic force in the working class. Yet it had stifled the working class's spontaneous activity and moulded its organisations in accord with the KSČ's essentially administrative and organisational conceptions of working-class politics. These conceptions proved adequate to the requirements demanded by the February events, but their overall viability as a model of working-class politics remained doubtful.

These comments notwithstanding, the Czechoslovak working class made its attitude to the political conflicts very clear in the week before the congress. Workers' meetings were held in all major enterprises to decide their viewpoint on the important questions due for discussion at the congress. The central issues were those of public employees' pay and further nationalisation. The KSČ factory branches played a decisive role in the outcome of these meetings and the resolutions they passed. These branches had been informed by their districts of the decisions of the Politburo at its meetings on 9 and 11 February and they had to persuade workers in their workplace that these Communist policies were the way to resolve the situation.[54] In this task they achieved overwhelming success, above all in the core of the industrial working class concentrated in the large-scale heavy industrial enterprises.

On 17 February *Práce* was reporting that ten major factories in České Budějovice had agreed to the ÚRO proposal on public employees' pay, as had the joint works committee at the Vítkovice Ironworks.[55] The following day *Práce* stated that workers representing 50,000 miners in Ostrava-Karvina had also backed ÚRO's proposals.[56] Support for ÚRO's position built up during the week, and on Friday 2 February, Kolský announced that resolutions approving of ÚRO's policy had been received from over a thousand of the largest enterprises in the republic.[57]

Demands for further nationalisation became incessant. In

Prague the KSČ resolution contained three demands: the acceptance of ÚRO's pay proposal, completion of the measures contained in the government programme, and the extension of the nationalised sector of the economy to cover domestic and foreign trade and all enterprises with over 50 employees. This resolution was discussed at meetings of all the workers in a factory and often received unanimous support. All the major industrial plants in Prague passed the resolution.[58] Throughout the country workers called for similar nationalisation measures. Workers at the Vítkovice and Kladno ironworks, at the Zbrojovka arms factory, at the Škoda car plant, at the pits in Northern Bohemia and at the Bat'a shoe factory in Zlín were just a few of the major industrial enterprises that demanded an extension of the public sector to all enterprises with more than 50 employees.[59]

The situation among white-collar workers was less clearcut. *Svobodné slovo* and *Právo lidu* reported trade-union branches in the public employees' sector which had agreed with the proposal put forward by the SDS and backed by the NSS.[60] ÚRO received ninety-six resolutions from branches in the public employees' sector which opposed ÚRO policy and favoured Majer's proposal, while 137 agreed with ÚRO's suggestion.[61]

Within the trade-union leadership a similar pattern was apparent. The key industrial unions, notably the metalworkers, miners, builders, transport, chemical, wood and textile workers, came out solidly in favour of both the congress and the Communists' demands. These were the unions which carried the weight and influence in the trade-union movement, and the right found no support here or in the District Trades Councils, which all approved of the congress.[62] Only among some white-collar unions, including those in justice, finance and distribution, were doubts raised about the congress. A meeting of the Presidium of the Union of Workers in Internal and Foreign Trade passed a resolution regretting the calling of the congress.[63] But on the whole, effective opposition from the right to the congress was negligible. There was a similar situation in ÚRO. On 20 February the ÚRO management committee met to make final preparations for the congress and to consider the resolution it would present. Vandrovec was opposed to the resolution, and was supported by Kubát who said, "We have ways other than demonstrations."[64] An extensive discussion followed, in which most speakers expressed clear support for the resolution, which was passed with three votes against.[65]

On 22 February at 9.10 a.m., with almost 8,000 delegates crammed into the Industrial Palace, Zápotocký opened the congress. Gottwald was the first main speaker; in his speech[66] he expressed confidence "that our disciplined and conscious working class" would foil the attempt by the right to revert to a pre-Munich social order. He reiterated the KSČ demand for a reconstructed National Front, and then said:

> There is only one — and I repeat and underline it three times — only one way to prevent the disorder and chaos which reaction wishes to provoke, and that is to secure further advance. This is the way proposed by the Communists, interpreting the will of the working people, which has been displayed, among other things, by the large demonstrations of the past few days, especially those of yesterday.
> I am convinced that your historic meeting today will declare itself in favour of these proposals.[67]

The enthusiastic response to his speech suggested it would. What the congress was being asked to endorse were Communist proposals, not those of the trade unions or works councils. The KSČ was intent on maintaining its hold on the trade-union movement. Following Gottwald, Zápotocký outlined these demands in detail and called for a one-hour token strike on 24 February, throughout the country, as part of the campaign for their implementation.[68] A resolution to this effect was to be presented at the end of the congress. With assurance Zápotocký concluded, "Today it is time to decide whether there will be a popular democratic development towards socialism or a return to the past. . . . Our goal is given; our demands are known. We shall press them and we shall win."[69]

In the face of such strength the right offered meagre resistance. On the eve of the congress both the NSS and the SDS had held meetings for their members who were delegates, 400 attending the former and 500 the latter.[70] Yet they were unable to organise effective opposition to the resolution put before the congress. Neither Vandrovec nor Šplíchalová, the two most prominent NSS trade unionists, spoke directly against the resolution.[71] Vandrovec made some oblique reference to the question of internal trade-union democracy and wanted the resolution taken in parts, but neither made the forceful statement that was required if the right was to succeed in splitting the congress. Bílý, a railwayman from Ostrava and a member of ÚRO, did make a direct attack later in the discussion. He warned of the trade unions becoming the preserve of one political party and declared his support for the government decision on public employees' pay. Shouts of opposition from the floor prevented him completing his speech.[72]

Altogether twenty-three delegates spoke in the discussion, and the general mood of the congress was clear from the reception the delegates accorded the speakers. At the end of the discussion Zápotocký read out the detailed resolution and in the vote is was overwhelmingly carried.[73] The resolution did not mention the government crisis but incorporated all the main Communist proposals, which were unacceptable to the right-wing parties. It demanded:

1. The immediate promulgation of National Insurance. . . .
2. The promulgation of the Constitution. . . .
3. . . . that all proposals submitted by ÚRO regarding state employees should be put into practice. . . .
4. In view of the fact that the remaining capitalist sector of our economy has become the centre of economic and political intrigues against the public, the congress demands further nationalisation. This includes the nationalisation of all wholesale home trade, of all capitalist enterprises with more than 50 employees.
5. . . . that small and medium enterprises with up to 50 employees should be safeguarded by the Constitution.

We decisively support the peasants' demand for the enactment of the new land reform in accordance with the new government bill. . . . We empower ÚRO to submit these demands to the government and to all political parties. It is up to the parties to proclaim whether they are willing not only to recognise these demands, but also to fulfil them. To emphasise our firm and united will to do everything necessary for the realisation of our demands we are calling for a one-hour token strike in all factories on Tuesday 24 February 1948, during which all workers should be informed about the discussion and resolution of the national congress. . . . We grant responsibility to ÚRO and its organs for the implementation of the resolution passed and indeed we empower them to organise all the necessary actions, mass demonstrations and a general strike if these demands of ours should meet with opposition.[74]

These demands would only be acceded to by a government reconstituted along the lines proposed by Gottwald. The strike on 24 February would directly influence the outcome of the government crisis. The KSČ had succeeded in utilising the congress as a platform from which to generate working-class support for their policy. Such was the power and influence exerted by the congress that the strike was agreed to by almost every unionised factory, workshop and office in the country. Even those who were hesitant or hostile to the resolution felt obliged to accept the congress decision. The degree of strike-breaking was negligible. Reports from the districts indicated that up to $2\frac{1}{2}$ million workers took part in the strike.[75] This united demonstration of working-class support for KSČ policy settled the crisis: the carefully controlled intervention by the working class proved decisive in sealing the fate of the right and ensuring political victory for the KSČ.

It was also the determining factor in the resolution of the internal conflicts within the SDS. Its policy at the beginning of the crisis was marked by the vacillations and hesitations which had characterised it for many months. The statement of the SDS management committee on the evening of 20 February criticised both the resigning ministers and the KSČ. It proclaimed that the current National Front government still provided a basis for the further co-operation of all political parties. The SDS ministers did not resign, and the statement illustrated their attempt to preserve a neutral position in the conflict.[76]

Internal conflicts sharpened as both the right and left wings tried to turn the party in their direction. Majer wanted the SDS ministers to resign and so align the party with the NSS, LS and DS.[77] On the other hand Fierlinger wanted the SDS to agree to Gottwald's proposals. During the weekend rank-and-file pressure by left-wing Social Democrats on their party leadership grew.[78] The failure of the SDS eve-of-congress meeting to sway noticeably SDS members at the Works Councils Congress from voting for the ÚRO resolution further strengthened the left wing. Their

225

ascendancy became increasingly apparent at a long, bitter meeting of the SDS executive committee on Monday, 23 February, as the Laušman grouping shifted to the left. The committee decided that the SDS ministers would not resign and that the SDS would be willing to co-operate with the KSČ and continue negotiations with them.[70] Laušman's uncertainty persisted, however. In a discussion with Gottwald on the morning of the 24th he urged the maintenance of the National Front and Majer's inclusion in any new cabinet. The size and unanimity of the one-hour strike provided further impetus to the left's pressure. That night the SDS leadership agreed on a proclamation in favour of a reconstituted National Front. They also decided to expel leading right-wing politicians from their ranks, notably Majer and Vilím, the general secretary.[80] With SDS backing assured, the KSČ leadership intended to settle the crisis the following day.

The Politburo meeting during the night of 24-25 February decided that Gottwald, Nosek and Zápotocký should see Beneš in the morning. They would demand the immediate acceptance of the tendered resignations and presidential approval for Gottwald's reconstructed government.[81] At this stage no other outcome to the crisis was conceivable. The KSČ's command of the situation was complete.

It had recognised the need to combat right-wing elements not only within the government but in all spheres of economic and social activity. To this end it called for the establishment of Action Committees of the National Front. The KSČ visualised these Action Committees as the organisational machinery which would remove all significant right-wing influence in the country. As early as 20 February Dolanský, in his speech to KSČ activists at Vysočany, had called for Action Committees to be set up in factories, offices, localities and villages, throughout the country.[82] In his Prague speech on the 21st Gottwald had issued an instruction to "form Action Committees of the National Front composed of democratic and progressive representatives of all parties and all national organisations in the communities, districts and regions."[83] On Monday 23 February, a meeting was held under the auspices of ÚRO which set up a preparatory body charged with the responsibility of establishing a Central Action Committee.[84] Already throughout the republic local Action Committees had been set up in response to the KSČ call.[85] Although many non-

Communists were members of these Action Committees, they were controlled by the KSČ. The committees formed the machinery by which the KSČ was to consolidate its political victory at all levels of Czechoslovak society.

The likelihood of armed opposition by the right had been minimised by the measures which the KSČ had undertaken. First, the party secretariat called upon its factory branches to form watch patrols to reinforce the Works Guard. These patrols were to take responsibility for the internal security of the enterprise. Some of their members were armed, using the reserve weapons of the Works Guard. At the KSČ meeting in Vysočany on 20 February branches were instructed to transform these patrols into emergency units, which would guard not only the enterprise but also the surrounding locality and if necessary strategic points in the town centre. These units were to form the basis of the people's militia which the central party secretariat decided to set up on 22 February.[86] KSČ district secretariats ensured that their branches in large factories also established militia,[87] with the weapons for some militia groups coming from the Zbrojovka Arms works in Brno.[88] Although the militia were not drawn into armed action, they symbolised the strength of the KSČ and its following among the working class.

The subjective impact of the militia must not be underrated. Undoubtedly, it provided considerable inspiration to the participants in the events and bred confidence about their eventual victory. The Politburo meeting on the night of 24 February decided to arm the militia which they had organised in the factories, since the following day promised to be crucial to the outcome of the crisis. Smrkovský, the architect of the May Rising, was placed in charge of the operation. 5,960 rifles were issued to the militia in the Prague factories, and armed columns of workers marched to strategic points in the town or joined the demonstration in Wenceslas Square.[89] The militia's presence in Prague and other major towns undoubtedly cowed the opposition, but their military value was primarily symbolic: the KSČ's control of the police and army were the decisive factors in hampering the possibility of armed right-wing resistance.

The KSČ used its control of the Ministry of the Interior and SNB to foil any attempt by the opposition to resort to arms. Security at strategic buildings in Prague was strengthened, arms were issued to SNB patrols, and reserves were brought into Prague from surrounding districts.[90] A division of the SNB escorted the lorries which delivered the weapons from the Zbrojovka arms factory to the militia in Prague,[91] while the police viewed with equanimity the rallies and demonstrations which the KSČ organised during these days.

The predominance of Communists in the key positions of the SNB apparatus guaranteed SNB support for the Gottwald government. Neither within the SNB nor the army were those who supported the right strong enough to mount an armed rising. Army backing for the Gottwald government came on 23 February when General Svoboda attended the inauguration meeting of the Central Action Committee. Svoboda, who was accompanied by General Klapálek and General Boček, the Chief of the General Staff, declared that the government had to remove disruptive elements and fulfil its programme.[92]

As well as exerting control over the "physical" elements of the state apparatus, the KSČ exercised dominance in the main ideological sphere, the radio network. Kopecký at the Ministry of Information ensured that KSČ policy received favourable and prominent coverage. KSČ statements and proposals were widely broadcast.

Thus the KSČ dominated all the crucial organs of power within the state as well as enjoying widespread support from the working class.[93] In addition, potential opposition from other social classes or groupings was effectively countered. Most important in this respect were the peasantry. The KSČ took considerable care to link working-class demands with those of the peasantry as, for example, in the resolution at the Works Councils Congress. Every KSČ statement reiterated its firm commitment to the new land reform and other agrarian reform measures. This was exceptionally important, because it assured the KSČ of continued support from wide sectors of the agrarian population.

Undoubtedly considerable sections of the rural population were uneasy at the course of events. Medium and large property holders feared the new land reform, while many peasants were wary of further socialist development. However, the widespread support which the KSČ received, especially from small property holders, prevented a cohesive oppositional bloc forming in the countryside.[94] Neither the LS nor the NSS was able to mobilise the countryside against the towns; during the crisis the villages remained quiet.

Similarly, potential opposition from artisans, small-scale producers and traders was partly neutralised by KSČ economic policies, while the KSČ's declared adherence to the government programme and its patriotism won it a certain degree of support from the intelligentsia. As we have already seen, the right lacked a powerful base, either economic or military, around which it could cohere its disparate forces. With the KSČ splitting or weakening the main social groups it hoped to draw upon, the paralysis of the right during the crisis is not surprising. The only public display of support for the right came from Prague high-school and university students on 24 and 25 February. Their demonstrations were swiftly dispersed, and no more right-wing actions occurred.[95]

In this situation President Beneš had no option open to him other than acquiescence to Gottwald's demands. That Beneš objected to these was clear from his letter of reply to the KSČ letter of 21 February. In his reply, Beneš wrote: "The present crisis of our democracy can only be solved in a democratic and parliamentary manner." He appealed "to all to find agreement and successful co-operation in a parliamentary manner and through the National Front. . . . Let us all again begin jointly to agree on further permanent co-operation and let us not prolong the division of the nation into two conflicting camps. I believe that reasonable agreement is possible."[96]

The KSČ reply was firm:

> The Politburo of the KSČ . . . states again that it cannot enter into negotiations with the present leadership of the National Socialist, People's and Slovak Democratic parties because it would be in conflict with the interets of unity and harmony of our nation, as well as with the interests of the further peaceful development of this country. . . .
> The KSČ Politburo has endorsed the proposals of Prime Minister Gottwald according to which the vacancies in the government are to be filled by representatives of all parties and vital national organisations. . . . (It) expresses the firm hope that after careful consideration you will recognise the correctness of our proposals and agree with them.[97]

At its meeting during the night of 24-25 February the Politburo decided to hold a mass rally in Wenceslas Square for the following afternoon and, if the President refused to accept Gottwald's demands, to call for a general strike. Gottwald, Nosek and Zápotocký met Beneš for two hours the next morning, but no new government was announced when the meeting ended. The determination of the Communists to enforce their demands had been made clear to Beneš, however, and the President quickly realised that continued resistance was impossible. In mid-afternoon Beneš saw Gottwald again. He accepted the resignations of the twelve ministers, along with those of Majer and Tymeš, of the SDS, and the replacements which Gottwald had suggested.[98]

Gottwald hurried from the presidential palace to Wenceslas Square, where he triumphantly announced to the waiting crowd of over 200,000 that the President had accepted the Communists' proposals.[99] He then reminded the crowd that with the crisis resolved "we return again to our work, to our construction work for the completion of the Two-Year Plan."[100] The revolution was over.

14
The Passive Revolution

Tactically the KSČ leadership had executed their plan brilliantly. The Politburo retained its mastery of the situation throughout, while the party's smooth and swift organisation bore witness to its efficiency. The KSČ dominated the reconstructed National Front government, and after February was the only real political force in the country. The events also guaranteed Czechoslovakia's firm adhesion to the Soviet bloc.

The transformation of the National Front had been carried out within the terms of the 1920 constitution, a point which Communist politicians and historians have constantly emphasised.[1] This only affected the form by which the crisis was resolved. There were three dominant elements in its determination: the popular pressure exerted on the President by the KSČ through mass organisations and demonstrations, the KSČ's control of the main organs of the state, and the less obvious but nevertheless most crucial consideration that Czechoslovakia came within the Soviet sphere of influence.

On 10 March Gottwald announced the programme of the new government to the Constituent National Assembly.[2] He promised the speedy enactment of the main parts of the previous government programme which had not been carried out, along with the measures on land reform and nationalisation which the Works Councils and Peasant Commissions Congresses had demanded.[3] These measures were rapidly passed.[4] By 1 May 1948, only 5.1 per cent of those working in industry were engaged in the private sector.[5]

The KSČ saw the socialisation of the means of production, distribution and exchange in the economic sphere as a complement to the assertion of its exclusive control in the political sphere. Before February the Czechoslovak state had been of a transitional character, containing within it contradictory political elements, though with the left predominant. After February the KSČ, pursuing the Soviet model of socialism, assumed a monopolistic role. As the report to the Ninth KSČ congress explained:

> February 1948 changed and broadened the tasks and methods of cadre policy. *The party assumed responsibility for all events in the state* and for its further development. With that the duties and tasks of Communists in all sections of political and economic life in the republic increased.[6]

The socialist state was seen as a monolithic social formation, with the party in sole charge. As the Action Programme of the Czechoslovak Communist Party expressly described it twenty years later, the party assumed the role of "universal caretaker".[7] This model of socialism was an identikit picture of that which had evolved in the Soviet Union in the Stalin period. The previous talk of a Czechoslovak road to socialism was all forgotten as the kind of administration, planning and political system already existing in the USSR was introduced into the country.

Effectively this meant that all political parties aside from the KSČ were banned. As early as 10 March Gottwald was saying that "the component parts of the regenerated National Front can only be regenerated political parties and non-party organisations. The agents of reaction must be unconditionally removed from these parties and organisations."[8] The phrase "agents of reaction" hid a multitude of sins. It was the rhetoric employed to prevent the promulgation of any political viewpoint which differed from that of the party leadership. No alternative political voice was permitted in the country. The SDS was merged with the KSČ. The other "regenerated political parties" were empty shells with no existence of their own. Majority support among the people was not to be won by countering and defeating the policies and ideas of other parties. Force and coercion were the weapons employed by the Gottwald leadership to quell opposition views and any disagreements. It was similar in the working-class movement. The resolutions which had been sent to ÚRO showed that a substantial number of public employees disagreed with the ÚRO pay policy, and it was in these strata that the non-Communist parties had most influence. Rather than tackle these problems politically and ideologically, the KSČ sought to resolve them in an exclusively organisational manner. As Šmídmajer admitted to the ÚRO management committee, action committees had been set up in many public and state employees' offices to carry out a purge, since "there was no guarantee that the trade-union bodies would adopt a positive attitude to the people's democratic order."[9] In this situation the KSČ had resorted to a body external to the trade-union movement and directed it to intervene in trade-union affairs. This intervention was effective in removing the public expression of disagreement, and these infringements of trade-union rights highlighted the fragility of the trade unions as autonomous working-class institutions.

The administrative consequences of ROH's democratic centralist structure also became apparent after February. For example, those members of ÚRO and its management committee who had opposed ÚRO policy during February lost their posts. This was not a decision made by the membership of their own unions but by the ÚRO management committee.[10] Within the democratic centralist structure, union members had forfeited the right to elect their own union leadership. This was not all, for a directive to all ROH organs stated:

> From membership of ROH shall be expelled only those individuals whose political and public activity up till now is in absolute contradiction to the principles and mission of ROH. No other member shall be expelled. Those who have offended against the interests of the united trade-union movement (have organised petitions against ROH, were initiators of various resolutions, voted against the resolution of the Works Councils Congress, did not take part in the strike, etc.) shall only be relieved of their functions, but otherwise membership shall not be taken from them.[11]

This directly violated two basic democratic rights of trade-union members. The first was the right of every trade unionist to express and maintain publicly a political view that was not that of the leadership. Since trade unions are voluntary mass organisations with membership not dependent on political outlook, they contain a wide range of political viewpoints within their ranks. If they are to remain democratic institutions these views have to be permitted expression. Secondly, the base unit of the union, the factory or area branch, has the right to decide its policies and its own functionaries. The ROH directive declared that those who opposed the leadership in February had to relinquish any trade-union position held, even if they were supported by the branch. The relentless logic of ROH's democratic centralist structure asserted itself here, to the detriment of basic democratic trade-union rights.

These failures of internal trade-union democracy were paralleled by the denial of an autonomous role for the trade unions in society at large. With all power in the hands of the party leadership, the role of the trade unions was to carry out faithfully their directives. The logic of organising the trade-union movement on democratic centralist lines was now remorselessly driven home. The works councils movement had already suffered from this logic, culminating in their disbanding in 1949. The acceptance of the stalinist thesis of trade unions as one-way transmission belts reduced the movement to an entirely passive role, carrying out decisions and targets made elsewhere.

The monolithic conception of socialism had further implications. In the major coercive spheres of the state — army, police, security, judiciary — the process of removing those hostile to the new government was accelerated and completed. The state machinery was transformed by replacing personnel rather than undertaking a thorough process of democratisation, which would have entailed personnel changes only as a part of the process. These apparatuses remained as unaccountable to the people as previously, and indeed, with the centralisation in all spheres of society, were to become effectively removed from any popular control in the 1950s.

In the ideological arena the assertion of exclusive party control also heralded an end to debate and discussion. In the press and media only the marxist-leninist line of the party was to be found. Its ubiquitous influence was to permeate education, culture, and historical and scientific research.

This monolithic system inevitably produced serious tensions. While considerable rates of economic growth were achieved for a decade, particularly in underdeveloped Slovakia, the imposition of the Soviet model of extensive economic development was inappropriate to the relatively advanced industrial character of the country. As well as creating economic and technical difficulties, this system of directive and centralised management prevented participation by workers in decision-making and fostered inefficiency and complacency in management.

Relations between Czechs and Slovaks also suffered from centralisation. Proposals to equalise relations between the two nations by making the country a federal state were shelved. The subordinate political, national and cultural position occupied by Slovakia within the country was a source of friction and resentment among the Slovak people.

The effect on culture and ideology was also serious, especially as a strict censorship operated. This atmosphere hampered cultural developments. It had a destructive effect on marxism, with set phrases and slogans being substituted for analysis.

The key to this entire system lay in the concentration of political power in the hands of a narrow section of the party leadership and the state security apparatus. The bulk of the party, the trade unions and the other mass organisations of the people had no autonomous role to play. They had to carry out the decisions made by the leadership: there was no representative method by which they could take part in decision-making or oppose policies they considered harmful. The undemocratic practices in the party, trade unions and works councils during 1945-1948 now took their toll. Ironically and cruelly they affected the KSČ most heavily. While thousands of innocent citizens were imprisoned or lost their jobs, in the early 1950s it was on the supposed "enemy within" that the party leadership and security forces focused most of their attention. Thousands of party members were harassed, persecuted or imprisoned, while the notorious rigged trial of 1951-2 resulted in the execution of eleven communist leaders, including Rudolf Slánský and Otto Šling.

Stalinism and passive revolution

These events were not the necessarily inevitable results of the revolution. However, the seeds of this monolithic system were well-sown in the stalinist practices that characterised the KSČ's politics during 1945-1948. Limiting the role, activity and organisational effectiveness of the people before February obviously restricted their participation afterwards. The manner of winning state power directly affected the manner in which it was exercised. The achievement of unity primarily by organisational and administrative methods encouraged the use of such methods to much more damaging effect when state power was gained.

Furthermore, it altered the character of politics. Primary emphasis was placed on imposing unity rather than winning it. This had the most serious consequences of all, especially after February, when the impulses behind this approach became more explicit. The party as the vanguard of the working class naturally knew what was best for the people. Therefore it had no need to win majority support for its policies. Conversely, those who opposed the party were viewed as enemies of the people. As Gottwald had said as early as 10 March, they were "agents of reaction". It was not long before Communists who had held or were believed to hold a different point of view from the dominant leadership were similarly treated. Imposing policy rather than winning agreement for it meant that force decided political matters. It was fundamental to stalinist politics that it operated primarily on the terrain of coercion, not consent.

These features were sharpened by the international situation. The escalation of the Cold War placed the USSR on the defensive as it tried to prevent the US policy of "roll-back" in Eastern Europe. Its response was to close ranks and exercise tight domination over the socialist countries of the region. Soviet economic and political systems were imposed regardless of specific, national conditions. When Yugoslavia objected, she was removed from the Cominform and denounced. Thus the precise features of Czechoslovak socialism cannot be ascribed solely to the way in which the revolution was achieved. Centralist and monolithic tendencies were aggravated by the position Czechoslovakia occupied internationally, particularly as the conflict between the two major powers sharpened.

A much broader question is raised here concerning the actual degree of national sovereignty and genuine independence that Czechoslovakia had ever enjoyed. This issue always represents a real problem for any small country, especially when it is as strategically located as Czechoslovakia. The country was conceived at Versailles by the Western powers as a bastion of peace and order in central Europe, only to be sacrificed by the same powers at Munich twenty years later. While the ensuing alliance with the Soviet Union differed, in that it was based on genuine popular friendship and wartime solidarity, it nevertheless placed the country firmly within the Soviet orbit. The pervasive influence of this diplomatic and military reality on the course of events after 1945 has been explained in the rest of this book. It facilitated the imposition of a Soviet model after February, and two decades later enabled the Soviet Union to intervene militarily to halt the attempt by the KSČ to develop a different kind of socialism. Nevertheless, the experience of Yugoslavia since the war suggests that these limitations are not insuperable, provided they are fully understood and can be resisted militarily as well as politically.

From the foregoing it should be clear why I have entitled this book "Passive Revolution". The working class was a largely willing accomplice to the revolution but not its driving force. The impetus lay in Moscow and in the KSČ leadership's belief that Soviet policy and strategy was necessarily best for its own working class. This meant that a Popular Front policy was pursued from 1941 until mid-1947, when with the altered international situation there came a shift to a leftist, sectarian policy reminiscent of the "class against class" period. The role of the mass of the party and the organised working class was the execution of a predetermined policy and never its strategic formulation. This being the case, the KSČ modelled its own party and the mass organisations of the working class on lines appropriate to its role. The KSČ was highly centralised, with its districts and branches able to carry out swiftly the leadership's directives; the Communists secured a similar structure in ROH. Also, by incorporating the works councils within ROH, the KSČ guaranteed that they were subject to the central instructions of ÚRO and had no autonomous existence. The democratic element of democratic centralism was minimised within the KSČ, while its application to the trade-union movement undermined democratic practices in ROH. KSČ branches, trade unions and works councils became levers for the execution of KSČ policy.

At the end of this chain came the working class. Its actions during the resistance, in the conflict over nationalisation, for the fulfilment of the Two-Year Plan and finally during February, bore witness to its class consciousness and combativity. It was no weak link in the process, yet its role in the post-war period was primarily passive: it responded when activated by the KSČ. After the summer of 1945 it possessed neither the organisational nor the ideological equipment to generate its own self-activity. The KSČ's stalinist practices, both in relation to its own party and to the mass organisations of the working class had a dual effect:

they deprived the working class of the development of its own autonomous institutions, while the monolithic conceptions they embodied resulted in an absence of political debate on the left. The decisive impetus to the revolution came from above and abroad. Between 1945 and 1948 Czechoslovakia underwent a two-stage revolution which transformed the country's economic, social and political system. Yet the determining political elements in this process limited the role of the working class in the making of the revolution and consequently restricted its capacity to act in the post-February period. It was to be fully two decades before the working class re-entered the political arena. Therein lay the tragedy of the passive revolution.

From passive revolution to Euro-Communism

To the present party leaders in Czechoslovakia, February and its aftermath "convincingly confirm anew the validity of the general laws of transition from capitalism to socialism".[12] Interestingly, most of their polemic on the thirtieth anniversary of February was directed at Euro-Communism and the events of 1968. Their argument that these general laws apply to all advanced industrial countries as well as to underdeveloped peasant ones, and that "the party is guided by the *general* laws of socialist construction,"[13] precludes any different models. Their assertions seek to justify Czechoslovak experience (excluding 1968, of course) and present policy as expressing universal socialist principles, thereby excluding any alternative roads to revolution or models of socialism. Therefore it is not surprising that so much of their polemic is directed at Euro-Communism, which offers viable alternatives in both areas.

Whether space for the Euro-Communist type of option existed in 1945 is clearly open to question. Yet one cannot conclude that it was impossible just because of the developing cold war which excluded Communists from government in Western Europe and right-wing parties from government in the East. The domination of stalinist methods and ideology within the communist movement, and the subordination of each working-class movement to the needs of the Soviet Union, prevented the elucidation of coherent strategies for socialism in each country. The "Czechoslovak Road to Socialism" was never seen as a strategic programme which related present policy to the future character of socialism, because the latter issue was never properly discussed. If it had been, and a monolithic model had been outlined, enormous strains would have been placed on the National Front government and the KSČ's relation with other parties. As it was, it saw the "Czechoslovak Road to Socialism" effectively as a tactical route to power and not at the same time a new way of exercising it. In reality the strategy still subordinated the "national road" to the international needs of the Soviet Union and encased the strategy in the straitjacket of stalinist thought.

While this situation remained, no alternative strategy was to emerge from within the mainstream of the socialist movement. Existing perspectives were only viable when countries were in the Soviet sphere of influence, and even then containd many negative features. They offered no model for elsewhere. If there was no neighbouring sympathetic country exercising political and military influences, then the key to socialist revolution had to be the active participation and conscious determination of the people. This required a commitment to alliance with other political forces, support for the autonomy and freedom of action of trade unions and other mass organisations, and recognition that success depended on winning the agreement of the mass of the people. The involvement of a plurality of forces during the transition to socialism had to continue after the achievement of power, and the primary feature in gaining and retaining state power had to be consent rather than coercion. These features were the antithesis of stalinism: they represented active, not passive, revolution.

For those charting new ways forward now in the West and for those seeking to understand "existing socialism", this period offers a rich heritage. The wartime resistance and the Košice programme show the feasibility of Popular Front strategies welding a broad range of forces in alliance for progressive change. The implementation of the programme also illustrated some of the complexities of this strategy and how it provides no automatic panacea for those seeking fundamental social transformation. For example, the balance between retaining maximum unity and encouraging the most advanced forces to press ahead always needs fine judgement. In 1945 the KSČ's caution undoubtedly led it to emphasise the former.

Yet this caution was a reflection of the dilemma of Popular

Front strategy when it had no organic connection with the socialist future. The unity of forces in the National Front governments and in the country at large was most effective when the KSČ rarely spoke of socialism. As soon as it did, the KSČ ceased to think in terms of Popular Fronts. The diversity of forces present in the transition from capitalism had no place in a monolithic conception of socialism. The absence of any dialectical relation between the two phases weakened and restricted the Popular Front period, while it meant that socialism could only be won in a sectarian, exclusive manner.

Thirty years later the paradoxical character of the "passive revolution" is more clearly visible and more rewarding options are open to the socialist movement. In these options socialism and democracy are not antipodes but twins. Variously termed "Euro-Communism", "socialism with a human face", "socialism in national colours", they have all evolved out of the experiences of stalinism and as alternatives to it. In place of "passive revolution" they seek to reassert the marxist principle that it is the masses who make history.

Notes

Chapter 1

1. B. Laštovička, V. Londýne za války ("During the War in London"), Prague, 1961, pp. 494-5.
2. See C. A. MacCartney and A. W. Palmer, *Independent Eastern Europe: A History*, London & New York, 1962, chapters 3-4.
   R. J. Kerner (ed.), *Czechoslovakia: Twenty Years of Independence*, Berkeley & Los Angeles, 1940, chapter 4.
   H. Hanak, "The Government, the Foreign Office and Austria-Hungary 1914-1918", in *Slav. Review*, 1969, pp. 188-97.
3. V. Olivová, *The Doomed Democracy: Czechoslovakia in a Disrupted Europe 1914-1938*, London, 1972, pp. 130-34.
4. See A. Teichová, *An Economic Background to Munich*, Cambridge, 1974.
5. B. Glos, *The Mobilisation of Labour in Czechoslovakia*, Prague, 1948, p. 21.
6. A. Zápotocký, *Nová odborová politika* ("New Trade Union Politics"), Prague, 1948, p. 191.
7. H. G. Skilling, "The Comintern and Czechoslovak Communism 1921-1929", in *American Slavic and East European Review*, vol. 19, 1960, pp. 234-45.
   P. E. Zinner, *Communist Strategy and Tactics in Czechoslovakia 1918-1948*, London and Dunmow, 1963, pp. 43-5.
8. Skilling, op. cit., p. 245.
9. K. Gottwald, *Spisy* ("Works"), vol. 1, Prague, 1953, p. 322.
10. Skilling, op. cit., pp. 244-5.
11. J. Degras (ed.), *The Communist International 1919-1943: Documents*, London, 1965, vol. 3, p. 362.
12. This congress had exceptional significance for the international communist movement both as regards its strategic response to fascism and in laying the groundwork for the later formulation of independent national strategies for socialist revolution.
13. K. Gottwald, *Spisy VII*, Prague, 1953, p. 96.
14. See E. L. Woodward and R. Butler, *Documents on British Foreign Policy 1919-1939*, Third Series, London, 1949, vol. I, esp. pp. 55-6, 91, 149, 360-61, 501, 573; vol. II, esp. pp. 34, 50, 112,

195, 248, 307, 373, 425, 615. See also Sir A. Cadogan, *The Diaries of Sir Alexander Cadogan 1938-1945* (ed. D. Dilks, London, 1971, esp. 25 April 1938, p. 71., M. Gilbert and R. Gott, *The Appeasers*, London, 1967, 2nd edn., esp. chapters 2-3.
15. R. Luža, *The Transfer of the Sudeten Germans*, London, 1964, pp. 150-64.

Chapter 2

1. L. Chmela, *Hospodářská okupace Československa; její methody a důsledsky* ("The Economic Occupation of Czechoslovakia; Its Methods and Consequences"), Prague, 1946, p. 92. R. Olšovský et al., *Přehled hospodářského vývoje Československa v letech 1918-1945* ("A Survey of the Economic Development of Czechoslovakia 1918-1945"), Prague, 1961, pp. 540-50.
2. V. Král, *Otázky hospodárského a socialního vývoje v českých zemích v letech 1938-1945* ("Questions of Economic and Social Development in the Czech Lands from 1938-1945"), 3 volumes, Prague, 1957-9, volume 1, pp. 54-5.
3. Ibid., p. 210; Olšovský et al., op. cit., p. 537.
4. Král, op. cit., vol. 1, pp. 212-21; Olšovský et al., op. cit., pp. 537-9.
5. Olšovský et al., op. cit., pp. 532-5.
6. E. Beneš, *Memoirs: From Munich to New War and New Victory*, London, 1954, p. 256.
7. The estimated loss of Party members in the period was 24,920, with another 60,000 thrown into concentration camps or prison. See *Sněm budovatelů. Protokol VIII řadného sjezdu KSČ ve dnech 28-31 března 1946* ("An Assembly of Construction. The Proceedings of the Eighth Congress of the KSČ, 28-31 March 1946"), pp. 50-51.
8. Ibid., p. 85: the speech of Josef Smrkovský.
9. O. Janaček (ed.), *Odboj a revoluce 1938-1945* ("Resistance and Revolution 1938-1945"), Prague, 1965, p. 345.
10. ÚRO, 13 September 1945, p. 5. This comment was made by Kubát, an SDS trade unionist, at the founding meeting of ÚRO on 1 May 1945. Verbatim report contained in this first edition of ÚRO.
11. *Sněm*, op. cit., p. 50. In all, including members of the central committee elected at the Seventh KSČ Congress, 42 members of five central committees were lost during six years of Nazi occupation.
12. S. Zámečník, "ÚRO a české květnové povstani v roce 1945" ("ÚRO and the Czech May Rising in 1945"), in *Odbory a naše*

revoluce, Prague, 1968, pp. 9-47.
13. J. Doležal, *Jediná cesta. Cesta ozbrojeného boje v českých zemích* ("The Only Way. The Way of Armed Struggle in the Czech Lands"), Prague, 1966, p. 179.
14. A detailed account is contained in G. Husák, *Svedectvo o Slovenskom národnom povstaní* ("Testimony about the Slovak National Uprising"), Bratislava, 1969. Husák himself was one of the leading figures in the rising.
15. Doležal, op. cit., p. 191.
16. All were prominent members of the trade-union movement after the war.
17. As stated in a private conversation with the author in Prague, June 1973.
18. ÚRO, 13 September 1945. ÚRO stood for Ústřední rada odborů ("Central Trades Union Council").
19. Zámečník, op. cit., p. 18.
20. ÚRO, 13 September 1945.
21. M. Klimeš et al. (eds.), *Cesta ke květnu. Vznik lidové demokracie v Československu* ("On the Way to May. The Origins of People's Democracy in Czechoslovakia"), 2 volumes, Prague, 1965, pp. 330-32.
22. Ibid., p. 335.
23. *Budování jednotných odborů 1944-1946: sborník dokumentů* ("The Construction of the United Trade Unions 1944-1946. A Collection of Documents"), Prague, 1965, p. 30.
24. Ibid., p. 31.
25. Klimeš *et al.*, op. cit., p. 335.
26. Ibid., pp. 366-9.
27. Ibid., p. 376.
28. See ibid., pp. 134-5; 272-3; and Doležal, op. cit., p. 210.
29. For the case of Yugoslavia see F. W. D. Deakin, *The Embattled Mountain*, London, 1971, and for Greece see D. Eudes, *The Kapetanios*, London, 1972.
30. For example, see Janaček, op. cit., pp. 371, 396.
31. *Budování*, p. 31.
32. Klimeš *et al.*, op. cit., p. 330. This was the phrase contained in resolution of the fourth illegal ÚV KSČ in January 1945.

Chapter 3

1. R. Medvedev, *Let History Judge*, London, 1972, p. 469.
2. According to official Soviet estimates between 15 and 20 million Soviet citizens had been killed during the war. The Germans had destroyed completely or partly 15 large cities,

1,710 towns and 70,000 villages, while 31,850 industrial enterprises and 65,000 kilometres of railway track had been demolished. An estimated 7 million horses, 17 million cattle, 27 million sheep and goats and 110 million poultry had been slaughtered or taken. See D. Horowitz, *The Free World Colossus: A Critique of American Foreign Policy in the Cold War*, London, 1965, pp. 51-2.

3. J. V. Stalin, *War Speeches, 3 July 1941-22 June 1945*, London, 1946, p. 112.
4. W. A. Williams *The Tragedy of American Diplomacy*, New York, 1972, pp. 213-28.
5. See especially US Department of State, *Foreign Relations of the United States: The Conferences at Malta and Yalta 1945*, Washington, 1955. (Henceforth this series is indicated as FRUS, volume and year.)
   J. V. Stalin, *Stalin's Correspondence with Churchill, Attlee, Roosevelt and Truman 1941-1945*, London, 1958, 2 volumes.
6. D. Horowitz, *Imperialism and Revolution*, London, 1969, p. 190.
   H. L. Stimson and McGeorge Bundy, *On Active Service in Peace and War*, New York, 1948, p. 639.
7. Klimeš *et al.*, op. cit., p. 55. Gottwald, Šverma, Slánský and Kopecký represented the KSČ at these discussions.
8. Ibid., pp. 35-40.
9. A. Gramsci, *Selection from the Prison Notebooks of Antonio Gramsci*, eds. Hoare and Nowell Smith, London, 1971, p. 53.
10. Klimeš *et al.*, op. cit., p. 182.
11. Ibid., p. 186.
12. R. Slánský, *Za vítězství socialismu: Stati a projevy* ("For the Victory of Socialism. Articles and Speeches"), 2 volumes, Prague, 1951, vol. 1, pp. 381-2.
13. Beneš, op. cit., pp. 263, 272.
14. L. K. Feierabend, *Ve vládě v exilu* ("In the Government in Exile"), 2 volumes, Washington, 1965, vol. 1, p. 114.
15. Klimeš *et al.*, op. cit., pp. 340-41.
16. Ibid., pp. 358-66.
17. Laštovička, op. cit., pp. 498-9.
18. Klimeš *et al.*, op. cit., p. 358.
19. Laštovička, op. cit., p. 505.
20. Ibid., pp. 503-5; 510-17.
21. Ibid., pp. 517-22; 532-45.
    Kopecký, V. *ČSR a KSČ* ("The Czechoslovak Republic and the Communist Party of Czechoslovakia"), Prague, 1960, p. 580.
    Opat, J. *O novou demokracii 1945-1948* ("For a New

Democracy"), Prague, 1966, pp. 44-8.
22. Kopecký, op. cit., pp. 373-4.
23. Klimeš et al., op. cit., p. 420. Emphasis added.
24. K. Gottwald, Spisy XII 1945-1946 ("Works", volume 12), Prague, 1955, pp. 77-8.
25. Ibid., p. 13.
26. Ibid., p. 21.
27. Ibid., p. 80.
28. Ibid., p. 98. See also Spisy XI, p. 374.
29. Ibid., p. 32.

Chapter 4

1. K. Bartošek, Pražské povstaní 1945 ("The Prague Uprising 1945"), Prague, 1960, p. 114.
   V. Koucký, Ilegální KSČ a pražské povstaní ("The Illegal KSČ and the Prague Rising"), Prague, 1946, pp. 14-15.
2. Janaček, op. cit., pp. 378-9.
3. Doležal, op. cit., p. 190.
4. Benčík and Kural, op. cit., pp. 341-6.
5. Doležal, op. cit., p. 188.
6. See J. Šverma, Vybrané spisy ("Collected Works"), Prague, 1955, pp. 399-408.
   Gottwald, Spisy XI, pp. 372-6; XII, pp. 17, 26-8.
7. Zámečník, op. cit., pp. 35-6.
8. Koucký, op. cit., p. 21.
   Bartošek, op. cit., pp. 20-21.
9. Ibid., pp. 140-45.
10. Some Russian prisoners of war held in Germany joined Vlasov units. At the end of the war those units in Northern Bohemia fought against German troops, but the left majority on the Czech National Council refused to have official dealings with them.
11. Bartošek, op. cit., p. 175.
12. Ibid., pp. 202-3.
13. D. D. Eisenhower, The Papers of Dwight D. Eisenhower: The War Years, 5 volumes, ed. A. D. Chandler, Baltimore and London, 1970, volume 4, 15 and 23 April, pp. 2613, 2640-41.
14. FRUS 1945 (IV), pp. 444-5.
15. Ibid., p. 446.
16. Eisenhower, op. cit., vol. 4, 4 May, pp. 2679-80.
17. Ibid., p. 2680, 5 May.
18. Ibid, 6 May, p. 2680.
19. Kolko, op. cit., p. 372.

20. *FRUS 1945* (IV), p. 447.
21. Bartošek, op. cit., pp. 203-8.
22. *FRUS 1945* (IV), p. 447.
23. Kolko, op. cit., p. 410-14.
24. Kopecký, op. cit., pp. 384-5.

Chapter 5

1. Klimeš *et al.*, op. cit., p. 727.
2. Ibid., p. 55.
3. L. Svoboda, *Výbor z projevů a článků 1942-1945* ("Selection of Speeches and Articles 1942-1945"), vol. 1, Praue, 1970, p. 137.
4. *Mladá fronta*, 12 June 1945.
5. Klimeš *et al.*, op. cit., pp. 384-5.
6. Luža, op. cit., p. 279.
7. Ibid., p. 283.
8. See V. Peša, "Brněnský ilegálni časopis 'Boj o zítřek' březenduben 1945" ("The Illegal Brno Journal 'Boj o zítřek' March-April 1945") *Brno v minulosti a dnes*, vol. 5, 1963, pp. 197-228.
9. L. Bednařík, "Z dějin brněnské Zbrojovky od osvobození do znárodnění" ("From the history of the Brno Zbrojovka Enterprise from Liberation until Nationalisation") in *Brno v minulosti a dnes*, vol. 7, 1965, p. 13.
10. *Práce*, 4 August 1945.
11. *Rudé právo*, 2 August 1945.
12. This information was confirmed by several anti-fascist Czech Germans in conversation with the author in Prague, June/July 1973.
13. *Rudé právo*, 6 June 1945.
14. *Sněm budovatelů*, op. cit., pp. 114-15.
15. K. Kaplan, "Odbory v mechanismu lidově demokratické moci v letech 1945-1948" ("Trade Unions in the Mechanism of Popular Democratic Power 1945-1948"), in *Odbory a naše revoluce*, p. 98.
16. See Gottwald, *Spisy* XI, p. 376, XII p. 17.
17. For one example, see V. Peša, "Ústavení a činnost národního výboru v Brně v dubnu až květnu 1945" ("The Establishment and Activity of the Brno National Committee from April to May 1945"), in *Brno v minulosti a dnes*, vol. 2, 1960, pp. 23-44.
18. Klimeš *et al.*, op. cit., pp. 381-2.
19. G. Beuer, *New Czechoslovakia and her Historical Background*, London, 1947, pp. 111-12.

20. V. Pachman, "Boj o odborovou jednotu v letech 1945-1948" ("The Struggle for Trade Union Unity 1945-1948"), ČsČh, vol. 8, 1960, pp. 793-813.
21. L. Lehár, "Závodní milice v letech 1945-1948" ("The Works Militia from 1945-1948"), in *Odbory a naše revoluce*, pp. 253-9.
22. Klimeš *et al.*, op. cit., pp. 386-7.
23. K. Jech (ed.), "The Czechoslovak Economy 1945-1968", *Collected Papers*, pp. 20-21, Prague 1968.

Chapter 6

1. For two examples see Jukl, op. cit., pp. 531-40; Bednařík, op. cit., pp. 11-14.
2. L. Bajger, "Znárodnění ostravsko-karvinských dolů ("the Nationalisation of the Ostrava-Karvina Mines"), in *Slezský sborník*, no. 63, 1965, p. 148.
3. V. Vrabec, "ROH a znárodnění 1945" ("ROH and Nationalisation in 1945"), in *Odbory a naše revoluce*, p. 141.
4. Gottwald, *Spisy* XII, p. 17.
5. Reported in Bajger, op. cit., pp. 145-6. Speech not included in Gottwald's works.
6. Archív ÚRO *Plenum*, 7 June 1945, p. 8. Zápotocký had been the leading pre-war Communist trade-union figure.
7. *Práce*, 22 June 1945.
8. Gottwald, *Spisy* XII, pp. 13-21, 54-5.
9. *Právo lidu*, 13 June 1945.
10. Ibid., 15 May 1945.
    Věstník závodních rad ("Bulletin of Works Councils"), May 1945, p. 8. Henceforth VZR.
11. *Právo lidu*, 12 June 1945.
12. Ibid., 28 June 1945.
13. Ibid., 19 June 1945.
14. Archív ÚRO — *ÚRO Plenum*, 16 May 1945, pp. 1-3.
15. *Práce*, 14 May 1945.
16. Bajger, op. cit., pp. 151-4.
17. Vrabec, op. cit., p. 143.
18. Zápotocký, op. cit., p. 14.
19. *Práce*, 16 June 1945.
20. *Zprávy tiskové komise ÚRO 1945* ("Reports of the ÚRO Press Commission 1945"), 26 June 1945. (The story did not appear in *Práce*.) Henceforth ZTK.
21. *Práce*, 4 July 1945; *Rudé právo*, 5 July 1945.
22. Vrabec, op. cit., p. 144.
23. Ibid., p. 147.

K. Kaplan, *Znárodnění a socialismus* ("Nationalisation and Socialism"), Prague, 1968, quoted p. 22.
24. Kaplan, *Znárodnění* . . ., op. cit., p. 22.
25. *Rudé právo*, 5 July 1945, 10 July 1945.
26. Ibid., 15 July 1945.
27. Zápotocký, op. cit., p. 24.
28. Gottwald, *Spisy* XII, p. 82.
29. Ibid., p. 92.
30. Ibid., pp. 92-3.
31. Vrabec, op. cit., p. 149.
32. *Práce*, 12 July 1945.
33. Vrabec, op. cit., p. 144.
34. *Rudé právo*, 25 July 1945.
35. Ibid., 17 July 1945.
36. *Práce*, 25 July 1945.
37. Ibid., 26 July 1945.
38. Ibid., 7 August 1945.
39. *Rudé právo*, 12 August 1945.
40. *Práce*, 24 August 1945.
41. Ibid, 29 August 1945.
42. Ibid., 15 August 1945, and *Rudé právo*, 15 August 1945.
43. *Práce*, 23 August 1945.
44. Ibid., 25 August 1945.
45. Vrabec, op. cit., p. 163.
46. K. Kaplan, "Poznámky ke znárodnění průmyslu v Československu 1945" ("Notes on the Nationalisation of Industry in Czechoslovakia in 1945"), in *Pkd KSČ*, no. 6, 1966, p. 4
47. Ibid., p. 4.
48. Gottwald, *Spisy* XII, p. 121.
49. Ibid., pp. 120-21.
50. *Právo lidu*, 2 September 1945; 7 September 1945.
Rudé právo, 8 September 1945; 11 September 1945.
51. *Svobodné slovo*, 25 September 1945.
52. *Právo lidu*, 2 September 1945.
53. Ibid., 20 September 1945.
Práce, 26 September 1945.
54. *Právo lidu*, 15 September 1945.
55. *Rudé právo*, 21 September 1945.
56. Ibid., 26 September 1945.
57. *Právo lidu*, 27 September 1945.
58. Ibid., 3 October 1945.
59. *Rudé právo*, 4 October 1945.
60. Ibid., 26 September 1945.

61. "Přehled o složení nejvyšších orgánů KSČ v letech 1945-1966" ("A Survey of the Composition of the Highest Organs of the KSČ between 1945 and 1966"), in *Pkd KSČ*, no. 6, 1966, p. 393. He was probably co-opted at the meeting on 2 July. The exact date is uncertain.
62. Archiv ÚRO — *ÚRO Plenum*, 7 June 1945.
63. See Kaplan, "Znárodnění...", op. cit., p. 26.
64. O. Mrázek, *Lidovláda v hospodářství* ("Popular government in the Economy"), Prague, 1945, p. 3.
65. Archív ÚRO — *ÚRO Představenstvo*, 22 August 1945, p. 4.
66. Vrabec, op. cit., p. 164.
67. *Práce*, 4 October 1945.
68. *Právo lidu*, 8 September 1945.
 Rudé právo, 8 September 1945.
69. *Právo lidu*, 2 September 1945, 15 September 1945, 20 September 1945, 27 September 1945.
70. Vrabec, op. cit., p. 162.
71. *Svobodné slovo*, 25 September 1945.
72. *Právo lidu*, 22 September 1945.
 Práce, 22 September 1945.
73. *Svobodné slovo*, 19 September 1945.
74. Ibid., 16 October 1945.
75. Ibid., 4 October 1945.
76. *Právo lidu*, 30 September 1945.
 Rudé právo, 30 September 1945.
77. *Právo lidu*, 19 October 1945.
78. Ibid., 20 September 1945.
79. Ibid., 23 September 1945.
80. *Práce*, 29 August 1945.
81. *Právo lidu*, 2 September 1945; 7 September 1945.
82. *Práce*, 30 August 1945.
 Rudé právo, 8 September 1945, 16 September 1945.
83. Ibid., 16 September 1945, 19 September 1945, 22 September 1945, 26 September 1945.
 Práce, 22 September 1945, 23 September 1945, 26 September 1945.
 Právo lidu, 18 September 1945, 19 September 1945.
84. Jukl, op. cit., p. 550.
85. *Právo lidu*, 2 October 1945.
86. Ibid., 2 October 1945.
87. Bednařík, op. cit., p. 22.
88. Kaplan, "Znárodnění...", op. cit., pp. 50-51.
89. O. Mrázek, *Patnáct let rozvoje znárodněného průmylsu ČSSR*

("Fifteen Years of the Development of Nationalised Industry in ČSSR"), Prague, 1960, p. 53.
90. Decrees of the President of the Republic of 24 October 1945. *Nationalisation in Czechoslovakia*, Prague, 1946, p. 44.
91. Ibid., p. 55.
92. ROH — *Zpráva . . . potravin*, op. cit., p. 82.
93. Kaplan, "Znárodnění . . .", op. cit., p. 26.
94. *Decrees*, pp. 19-20.
95. Ibid., pp. 21-2.
96. F. J. Kolár, *Zestátněni průmyslu a peněžnictví* ("The Nationalisation of Industry and Finance"), Prague, 1945, p. 23.
97. *Decrees*, p. 16.
98. Ibid., p. 26.
99. Ibid., p. 27.
100. *Právo lidu*, 26 October 1945.
 Práce, 26 October 1945.
101. *Svobodné slovo*, 26 October 1945.
102. *ÚRO*, 31 October 1945.
103. Kaplan, "Znárodnění . . .", op. cit., p. 53.
104. In a speech to NSS factory branches reported in ÚRO, 22 November 1945.
105. *Decrees*, pp. 5-8. Emphasis added.
106. E. Beneš, *The Opening of the Prague Parliament*, Prague, 1946, p. 36. Emphasis added.
107. Feierabend, op. cit., p. 114. See Chapter 3.
108. Gottwald, *Spisy* XII, p. 172.
109. Ibid., p. 122.
110. Mrázek, *Lidovláda*, op. cit., p. 24.
111. Quoted in Kaplan, "Znárodnění . . .", op. cit., p. 56.

Chapter 7

1. Quoted in *ÚRO*, 13 September 1945.
2. Degras, op. cit., vol. 3, p. 365.
2. Šverma, op. cit., pp. 385-8.
4. Ibid., pp. 388-9.
5. Gottwald, *Spisy* XI, p. 373.
6. Klimeš et al., op. cit., p. 389.
7. Ibid., p. 389.
8. *Práce*, 12 May 1945.
9. Ibid., 9 June 1945.
10. *Právo lidu*, 13 June 1945.
11. Jukl, op. cit., p. 533.
12. Bednařík, op. cit., pp. 11-14.

13. Vrabec, op. cit., pp. 140-41. More detailed information on the character and scope of the works councils movement in this period is not available at present. Contemporary papers and journals contain only fragmentary material and a historical study of the movement is still awaited.
14. Quoted in *ÚRO*, 13 September 1945.
15. *ÚRO — Budování*, pp. 37-9.
16. J. V. Stalin, *Works*, vol. 6, Moscow, 1953, pp. 184-6. See Chapter 9 for a detailed discussion of this question.
17. J. Kolský, *Pod revolučním praporem* ("Under the Revolutionary Banner"), Prague, 1963, p. 159.
18. *ÚRO — Budování*, p. 45.
19. *Práce*, 9 May 1945.
20. *VZR*, May 1945, p. 8.
21. Ibid., p. 7.
22. Archív ÚRO — *ÚRO Plenum*, 16 May 1945, p. 2.
23. Ibid., 16 May 1945, p. 4.
24. ZTK ÚRO, 6 June 1945.
25. Archiv ÚRO — *ÚRO Plenum*, 7 June 1945, p. 4.
26. Ibid., p. 2.
27. Ibid., p. 8.
28. Zápotocký, op. cit., pp. 9-10.
29. *VZR*, June 1945, p. 2.
30. Zápotocký, op. cit., p. 18.
31. *VZR*, June 1945, p. 3.
32. *Práce*, 24 June 1945.
33. Zápotocký, op. cit., p. 52.
34. *Práce*, 1 August 1945.
35. *Rudé právo*, 10 August 1945.
36. Zápotocký, op. cit., p. 41.
37. Ibid., p. 41, see also pp. 72, 91 for similar arguments.
38. Ibid., p. 46.
39. Ibid., p. 46.
40. *Práce*, 26 August 1945. The extent to which works councils successfully managed production in this period is impossible to gauge, this being an area where historical research has yet to be undertaken.
41. Slánský, op. cit., vol. 2, p. 26.
42. Kolský, op. cit., p. 158.
    Rudé právo, 17 July 1945.
43. Kolský, op. cit., p. 159.
44. See Archív ÚRO — *ÚRO Představenstvo*, 19 September 1945, pp. 1-2.

45. Beuer, op. cit., pp. 139-40. Emphasis added.
46. *VZR*, December 1945, p. 5. For a fuller discussion on this procedure see Chapter 10.
47. *Decrees*, pp. 26-7.
48. *VZR*, January 1946, p. 4.
49. *Práce*, 10 June 1945.
50. *VZR*, May 1945, p. 2.
51. *Práce*, 10 June 1945.
52. Zápotocký, op. cit., pp. 21-2.
53. *Práce*, 18 August 1945; 29 August 1945. For further discussion of these points see Chapter 9.
54. ROH — *Zpráva o činnosti* ..., op. cit., p. 34.
55. *ZTK ÚRO*, 30 May 1945.
56. Archív ÚRO — *ÚRO Plenum*, 7 June 1945, p. 4.
57. *Rudé právo*, 17 July 1945.
58. ROH — *Zpráva o činnosti* ..., op. cit., pp. 247-51.
59. Ibid., pp. 258-61.
60. Ibid., pp. 275-7.
61. Ibid., pp. 272-4.
62. Ibid., p. 34.
63. Ibid., pp. 32-3.
64. Ibid., p. 32.
65. Zápotocký, op. cit., p. 150.

Chapter 8

1. KSČ—*Sněm budovatelů* ..., op. cit., p. 5.
2. L. Lehár, "První všeodborový sjezd" ("The All Trade Union Congress of ROH"), in *Odbory a společnost*, no. 1, 1966, p. 42.
3. J. Kozák, "O hlavních problemech dějin KSČ v období 1945-1948" ("Concerning the Main Problems of KSČ History in the period 1945-1948"), *in Pkd KSČ*, no. 2, 1962, p. 749. For a Western view see Z. Eliáš and J. Netík, "Czechoslovakia", article in *Communism in Europe*, ed. W. E. Griffith, vol. 2, p. 189.
4. Stalin, *War Speeches*, op. cit., p. 112.
5. On this point see, among others, J. R. Storabin, "Origins of the Cold War: The Communist Dimension", *Foreign Affairs*, vol. 47 (July 1969), pp. 681-96.
   Horowitz, Imperialism, op. cit., chapter 10, especially pp. 190-201.
   Deutscher, Stalin, op cit., chapters 13 and 14.
6. See Kolko, op. cit., especially chapters 14 and 23.
7. *Rudé právo*, 7 August 1945.
8. Material on this topic is very elusive. Some indirect light is

cast on Italy by M. A. Macciocchi, *Letters from inside the Italian Communist Party to Louis Althusser*, London, 1973, pp. 114-39.
9. *Rudé právo*, 29 July 1945, 31 July 1945, 8 August 1945, 4 September 1945.
10. Data compiled from Opat, op. cit., p. 69; J. Kašpar, "Členská základna komunistické strany Československa v letech 1945-1949" ("The Membership Base of the KSČ from 1945-1949"), in *ČsČH*, vol. 19, 1971, pp. 4-7.
11. Bednařík, op. cit., p. 15.
12. Jukl, op. cit., p. 534.
13. KSČ — *Sněm budovatelů* . . ., op. cit., pp. 37, 57.
14. Kaplan, "Znárodnění . . .", op. cit., p. 111.
15. J. Moravec, "Nástup komunistů ostravského kraje za získaní většiny národa" ("The Drive by the Communists of the Ostrava District for the Gaining of the Majority of the Nation"), in *Slezský sborník*, no. 61, 1963, p. 18.
16. Kaplan, "Znárodnění . . .", op. cit., p. 111.
Opat, op. cit., pp. 69-70.
Kašpar, op. cit., p. 6.
17. Kaplan, "Znárodnění . . .", op. cit., p. 110.
Opat, op. cit., pp. 72-6.
If membership of a political party is taken as a guide these figures illustrate the exceptionally high degree of politicisation amongst the Czechoslovak population at this time.
18. Kaplan, "Znárodnění . . .", op. cit., p. 110.
Opat, op. cit., pp. 75-6.
19. KSČ — *Sněm budovatelů* . . ., op. cit., p. 68.
20. Ibid., p. 70. Emphasis added.
21. Ibid., pp. 23-5.
22. Ibid., pp. 21-2.
23. Ibid., p. 9.
24. Ibid., p. 65.
25. Ibid., p. 67.
26. Ibid., p. 70.
27. Ibid., p. 103. For other examples see pp. 57, 58, 75, 78, 79.
28. Ibid., p. 95.
29. Ibid., p. 115.
30. Ibid., p. 17. Four major historical personalities and patriotic figures in Czech history.
31. Ibid., p. 119.
32. Ibid., p. 38-51.
33. Ibid., see pp. 18, 105, 114, 127.
34. Ibid., p. 71.

35. Gottwald, *Spisy* XV, pp. 123-61.
36. Kozák, op. cit., p. 753.
37. KSČ — Ústav dějin — *Dějiny KSČ* ("The History of the KSČ"), Prague, 1967, 3rd edition, p. 204.
38. G. Bolton, *Czech Tragedy*, London, 1955, p. 216.
39. J. Korbel, *The Communist Subversion of Czechoslovakia 1938-1948. The Failure of Co-existence*, Princeton, 1959, pp. 135, 142.
40. KSČ — *Sněm budovatelů*, op. cit., p. 147. Emphasis added.
41. For an important Czechoslovak contributon to this discussion see J. Opat, "K metodě studia a výkladu některých problémů 1945-1948" ("On the Methods and Explanation of Some Problems of the Period 1945-1948"), *Pkd KSČ*, no. 5, 1965, pp. 65-84.
42. *Daily Herald*, 22 August 1946.
43. *The Times*, 18 November 1946.
44. Gottwald, *Spisy* XIII, pp. 230-31.
45. For an example see Kozák, op. cit., p. 750.
46. KSČ — *Sněm budovatelů* . . ., op. cit., pp. 9-13.
47. Ibid., p. 192.
48. This was confirmed by several leading KSČ members of the period in personal conversations with the author in Prague during May to July 1973.
49. KSČ — *Sněm budovatelů* . . ., op. cit., p. 197.
50. Ibid., p. 197.
51. Ibid., pp. 190-91.
52. At their trials in the 1950s accusations were levelled against Smrkovský, Husák and others because of the independent initiatives they had taken during the domestic resistance.
53. This was again confirmed by leading KSČ members of the period in personal conversations with the author in Prague, May-July 1973.
54. KSČ — *Sněm budovatelů* . . ., op. cit., p. 197.
55. KSČ — Ústav dějin, Přehled, Pkd KSČ, 1965, op. cit., pp. 757-84.
56. This was after the initial huge decline in membership in 1929.

Chapter 9

1. *Práce*, 12 January 1946, 13 January 1946, 15 January 1946.
2. Archív ÚRO — *ÚRO Plenum*, 30 January 1946, 2/4, pp. 13-14.
3. ROH — *Bojem a prací k vítězství socialismu. Zápis I celostátního všeodborového sjezdu ROH* ("By Struggle and Work to the Victory of Socialism. Record of the 1st All-State Trade Union Congress of ROH"), Prague, 1946, p. 230.

4. Ibid., pp. 22-72.
5. Quoted in *Práce*, 29 August 1945.
6. ROH — *Bojem* . . ., op. cit., p. 237.
7. Ibid., p. 84.
8. Ibid., p. 236 (emphasis added). See also Zápotocký, op. cit., p. 134.
9. Contrast this with Togliatti's dictum that "Organisation is the daughter of politics".
10. ÚRO — *Kupředu k socialismu. Zpráva o činnosti ROH od I-II všeodborového sjezdu* ("Forward to Socialism. Report of the Activity of ROH from the 1st to the 2nd All Trade Union Congress"), Prague, 1949, p. 144.
11. See Chapter 7.
12. Pachman, in *ČsČH*, 1960, op. cit., p. 802. Cites one example.
13. Ibid., p. 802.
   K. Růžička, *ROH v boji or rozšířeni moci dělnické třídy, 1945-1948* ("ROH in the Struggle for the Spreading of the Power of the Working Class, 1945-1948"), Prague, 1963, p. 98.
14. ROH — *Bojem* . . ., op. cit., pp. 184-5, 194-7, 207-8.
15. Ibid., pp. 233-41.
16. The KORs were centred in: Brno, České Budějovice; Hradec Králové; Jihlava; Karlovy Vary; Kladno; Klatovy; Kolín; Liberec; Mladá Boleslav; Moravská Ostrava; Most; Olomouc; Pardubice; Plzeň; Praha; Šumperk; Tábor; Ústí; Zlín; and Znojmo.
17. ROH — *Zpráva o činnosti* . . ., op. cit., pp. 400-401.
18. Ibid., pp. 394-9.
19. Ibid., p. 425.
20. Ibid., p. 399.
21. Ibid., pp. 415-16.
22. Ibid., pp. 422-3.
23. Ibid., p. 391.
24. ROH — *Zpráva o činnosti svazu zaměstnanců v kovoprůmyslu* ("Report of the Activity of the Metalworkers' Union"), Prague, 1947, p. 113.
25. Ibid., p. 131.
   ROH — *Výroční zpráva KOR v Ostrave za rok 1946* ("Annual Report of Ostrava KOR for 1946"), Ostrava 1947, p. 25.
26. Table compiled from data contained in ROH — *Zpráva o činnosti* . . ., op. cit., pp. 343-422.
27. ROH — *Bojem* . . ., op. cit., p. 136.
28. Opat, *O novou demokracii*, op. cit., p. 84.
29. Ibid., pp. 84-5.
30. Lehár, in *Odbory o společnost*, 1966, op. cit., p. 51.

31. *Práce*, 24 July 1945.
32. Archív ÚRO — *ÚRO Představenstvo*, 7 August 1945, 1/2, p. 1, *ÚRO*, 13 September 1945.
33. For the report of the Chairman of the Slovak trade unions and the resolution which the conference passed see *ÚRO — Budování*, op. cit., pp. 76-86.
34. *Práce*, 12 January 1946.
35. Ibid., 3 April 1946.
36. These ideas were expounded in Zápotocký, op. cit., pp. 136-7. See also ROH — *Bojem* . . ., op. cit., p. 257 for similar views contained in the congress resolution.
37. Zápotocký, op. cit., p. 147.
38. Růžička, op. cit., pp. 93-5.
39. Zápotocký, op. cit., p. 196. Emphasis in text.
40. Ibid., p. 214.
41. Ibid., p. 199. Emphasis in text.
42. Ibid., pp. 199-212.
43. Ibid., p. 216.
44. ROH — *Bojem* . . ., op. cit., p. 257.
45. Zápotocký, op. cit., p. 215.
46. ROH — *Bojem* . . ., op. cit., p. 257.
47. Zápotocký, op. cit., pp. 135-7, 217.
48. *Práce*, 13 January 1946.
49. Archív ÚRO — *ÚRO Plenum*, 14 March 1946, 2/5.
50. Zápotocký, op. cit., p. 197.
51. Ibid., p. 232.
52. ROH — *Zpráva o činnosti* . . ., op. cit., p. 135.
53. Zinner, op. cit., p. 162.
54. Zápotocký, op. cit., p. 42.
55. KSČ — Ústav dějin. *Příruční slovník k dějinám KSČ* ("A Pocket Dictionary of the History of the KSČ"), Prague, 1964, pp. 303-4, 316, 999-1000, 1026.
56. For example the nominations of the electoral commission were accepted "by acclamation". See ROH — *Bojem* . . ., op. cit., p. 252.
57. Lehár, in *Odbory a společnost*, 1966, op. cit., p. 58.
58. Stalin, *Works*, op. cit., vol. 6, pp. 184-6.
59. Klimeš et al., op. cit., p. 606.
60. Ibid., p. 608.
61. V. I. Lenin, *On Trade Unions. A Collection of Articles and Speeches*, Moscow, 1970, p. 456. This was written before the introduction of the New Economic Policy.
62. I. Deutscher, *The Prophet Unarmed: Trotsky 1921-1929*, London,

1970, pp. 507-10.
63. An analysis as to why the Bolsheviks failed to adhere to this framework cannot be attempted here.
64. Zápotocký, op. cit., p. 11.

Chapter 10

1. *Statistical Bulletin of Czechoslovakia*, Prague, 1946-1948, nos. 2/3, p. 10.
2. *Koho volit? Programy k prvním svobodným volbám r. 1946. Program politiých stran* ("Who to vote for? The programmes of the Political Parties in the First Free elections of 1946"), Prague, 1946, pp. 111-53.
3. Ibid., p. 137.
4. Ibid., pp. 126-7.
5. Ibid., p. 133.
6. Ibid., pp. 130-31.
7. Ibid., pp. 112-20.
8. Ibid., p. 136.
9. Specific references were made in the programme about the church, freedom of worship and religion being proclaimed, and about T. G. Masaryk, whose great historical role was recognised; ibid., pp. 138-40.
10. Ibid., pp. 5-66.
11. Ibid., p. 12.
12. Ibid., pp. 13-19.
13. Ibid., pp. 27-37.
14. Belda *et al.*, Na rozhraní, op. cit., p. 65.
15. Opat, *O novou . . .*, op. cit., chapter 7, pp. 148-67 for a discussion on this question.
16. *FRUS*, 1946 (VI), p. 240.
17. H. Ripka, *Czechoslovakia Enslaved: The Story of the Communist Coup d'Etat*, London, 1950, p. 80.
18. Opat, *O novou . . .*, op. cit., p. 126.
19. *Koho volit . . .*, op. cit., pp. 87-110.
20. Ibid., pp. 87-9.
21. Ibid., p. 92.
22. Ibid., p. 98.
23. Ibid., p. 94.
24. *FRUS*, 1946, (VI), pp. 189-90.
25. *Koho volit . . .*, op. cit., pp. 104-5.
26. Ibid., p. 75. Emphasis in text.
27. Ibid., p. 72.
28. Ibid., p. 74. Emphasis in text.

29. Ibid., p. 72.
30. Ibid., p. 78.
31. Ibid., pp. 79-80.
32. Ibid., p. 83.
33. Opat, *O novou* . . ., op. cit., pp. 169-72.
34. *Rudé právo*, 5 May 1946.
35. *Statistical Bulletin* op. cit., 1946, nos. 2/3, p. 10.
36. *FRUS* 1946 (VI), p. 199.
37. Ibid., p. 199.
38. Gottwald, *Spisy* XIII, pp. 75-89.
39. The average KSČ vote in Bohemia was 43.3 per cent. High votes were recorded in Karlovy Vary, 52.2 per cent; Ústí, 56.5 per cent; and Liberec, 48.3 per cent, all districts from which Germans were expelled and into which there had been intensive Czech immigration. The other high vote was recorded in Kladno, a strong industrial working-class district where the KSČ received 53.6 per cent of the vote.
    Figures from *Statistical Bulletin* . . ., op. cit., 1946, nos. 2/3, pp. 8-10.
40. Opat, *O novou* . . ., op. cit., pp. 184-5.
41. Gottwald, *Spisy* XIII, p. 82. Gottwald referred to the split in his post-election analysis.
    So did Steinhardt, who wrote "Perhaps the most interesting, while at the same time most important result of the election, will be the struggle for control of the Social Democratic Party, in which there is a strong difference of opinion between the left wing and the right wing." *FRUS* 1946 (VI), pp. 199-200.
42. Gottwald, *Spisy* XIII, pp. 80-81.
43. Opat, *O novou* . . ., op. cit., pp. 185-7.
    Belda et al., *Na rozhraní* . . ., op. cit., p. 74.
44. Opat, *O novou* . . ., op. cit., pp. 187-90.
    Belda et al., *Na rozhraní*, op. cit., p. 76.
45. *FRUS* 1946 (VI), p. 204.
46. Out of a total of 4,417 members of area national committees there were 1,927 KSČ members. Of the 162 Chairmen of these area committees 127 were Communists.
    Opat, *O novou* . . ., op. cit., p. 181.
47. Gottwald, *Spisy* XIII, pp. 83-4.
48. Ibid., pp. 84-5.
49. Ibid., pp. 120-56. For these matters see especially pp. 121-3, 144-55.
50. Z. Deyl and Z. Snítil, "K některým problémům hospodářské politiky KSČ v letech 1945-1948" ("Concerning some Problems

of KSČ Economic Policy from 1945-1948"), *Pkd KSČ*, no. 5, 1965, p. 695.
51. Z. Snítil, "O dvouletce a jejím místě v politice KSČ v roce 1946" ("On the Two-Year Plan and its Place in KSČ Policy in 1946"), in *Pkd KSČ*, no. 7, 1967, pp. 676-8.
52. D. W. Douglas, *Transitional Economic Systems: The Polish-Czech Example*, New York, 1972, p. 103.
53. Gottwald, *Spisy* XIII, pp. 124-5. See also, *The First Czechoslovak Economic Plan*, Prague, 1947, p. 107.
54. Gottwald, *Spisy* XIII, p. 138.
55. Z. Deyl, *Pkd KSČ*, 1965, p. 693.
56. Gottwald, *Spisy* XIII, pp. 142-3.
57. Ibid., p. 219.
58. Ibid., p. 231.
59. Zápotocký, op. cit., p. 284.
60. Ibid., p. 284.
61. For examples see ibid., pp. 292, 297, 323.
62. Ibid., p. 284; see also pp. 274, 322.
63. Ibid., pp. 313-21.
64. In October conferences were held in Prague; Moravská Ostrava; Brno; Pardubice; Plzeň; Kolín; Liberec; Bratislava and České Budějovice. In November conferences were organised in Jihlava; Mladá Boleslav; Most; Ústí nad Labem; Karlovy Vary; Hradec Králové; Banská Bystrica; Košice and Žilina. Růžička, op. cit., p. 120.
See also Snítil, Z. "Uloha jednotných odborů při přípravě dvouletky a organizaci našeho hospodářství" ("The Role of the United Trade Unions in the Preparation of the Two-Year Plan and the Organisation of Our Economy"), in *Odbory a naše revoluce*, op. cit., pp. 196-7.
65. Jech, op. cit., pp. 30-32.
66. Douglas, op. cit., p. 105.
67. On 1 January 1946 Germans still constituted 45 per cent of the work force in the glass industry, 40 per cent in textiles and 38 per cent in paper. L. Kalinová and V. Brabec, "K některým stránkám vývoje struktury a postavení čs. dělnické třídy v letech 1945-1948" ("Concerning Some Aspects of the Development of the Structure and Position of the Czechoslovak working class from 1945-1948"), in *Odbory a naše revoluce*, op. cit., p. 54.
68. Ibid., pp. 53-9 for further discussion.
69. Glos, op. cit., p. 25.
70. Gottwald, *Spisy* XIII, p. 136.

Zápotocký, op. cit., pp. 274, 276.
71. Ibid., pp. 205-13.
72. Glos, op. cit., p. 108.
Kalinová et al., op. cit., pp. 64-7.
73. Ibid., p. 60.
74. Ibid., p. 60.
75. Zápotocký, op. cit., p. 214.
76. Gottwald, *Spisy* XIII, p. 138.
77. Klimeš et al., op. cit., p. 383.
78. ROH — *Zpráva o činnosti* . . ., op. cit., p. 44.
79. For the example of the metalworkers see ROH — Zpráva v kovoprůmyslu, op. cit., p. 64.
80. ROH — *Zpráva o činnosti* . . ., op. cit., p. 46.
81. Ibid., p. 45.
82. ROH — *Bojem* . . ., op. cit., p. 237.
83. ÚRO — Kupředu . . ., op. cit., p. 159.
84. ROH — *KOR v Ostrave*, op. cit., pp. 10, 66.
85. ROH — *Zpráva . . . v kovoprůmyslu*, op. cit., pp. 60, 64.
86. Information contained in ROH — *Zpráva o činnosti* . . ., op. cit., p. 45.
For Erban's speech to the congress see ROH — *Bojem* . . ., op. cit., p. 87.
87. Glos, op. cit., p. 107.
88. Material contained in *Statistical Bulletin*, 1946, no. 4, p. 26, and 1948, no. 5, pp. 85-6.
89. Zápotocký, op. cit., pp. 274, 298.
90. ROH — *Zpráva . . . v kovoprůmyslu*, op. cit., p. 30.
Růžička, op. cit., pp. 38-40, 127-8.
ROH — *Zpráva o činnosti* . . ., op. cit., pp. 251-2, for details of the coal industry and mining production.
91. Růžička, op. cit., p. 126.
92. Quoted in ibid., p. 94.
93. ROH — *Zpráva . . . v kovoprůmyslu*, op. cit., pp. 37-8.
94. Ibid., p. 38.
For details of the origins of the Stakhanovite movement in Czechoslovakia see Z. Snítil, article in *Odbory a naše revoluce*, op. cit., p. 202.
95. ROH — *Zpráva . . . v kovoprůmyslu*, op. cit., pp. 41-2.
96. Ibid., p. 39.
97. Snítil, in *Odbory a naše revoluce*, op. cit., p. 178.
98. Zápotocký, op. cit., p. 321; see also p. 349.
99. ROH — *Jdeme správnou cestou* ("We are going along the Right Road"), Prague, 1947, p. 15.

100. Kaplan, "Znárodnění ...", op. cit., p. 54.
101. See ROH — *Zpráva o činnosti* ..., op. cit., p. 54.
102. Kaplan, "Znárodnění ...", op. cit., pp. 75, 93-7.
103. ÚRO — *Kupředu* ..., op. cit., 58-9.
104. Ibid., pp. 61-4.
105. *Věstnik ROH* ("Bulletin of ROH"), 24 January 1947, p. 20.
106. ROH — *Jdeme* ..., op. cit., p. 29.
107. Z. Deyl, *Pkd KSČ* 1965, p. 704. The chief target of the plan in industry was met. In the last quarter of 1948 the volume of industrial production was 10 per cent ahead of the 1937 level.
108. Jech, op. cit., p. 78.
109. Růžička, op. cit., pp. 128-33.
110. *FRUS* 1946 (VI), p. 220.
    J. F. Byrnes, *Speaking Frankly*, London, 1947, pp. 143-4.
111. *FRUS* 1946 (VI) Cables on 25 January 1946; 26 February 1946; and 6 September 1946 to be found on pp. 180, 187, 217-18.
112. Ibid., p. 229.
113. p. 225.
114. Z. Deyl, "The Development of Trade Production", in *The Czechoslovak Economy 1945-1948*, ed. K. Jech, op. cit., p. 139.
115. Ibid., pp. 148-9.
116. Ibid., pp. 133-7.
117. *FRUS* 1946 (VI), p. 201.
118. Růžička, op. cit., p. 141.
119. Ibid., pp. 143-6.
120. ROH — *Bojem* ..., op. cit., p. 257.
121. Růžička, op. cit., pp. 148-9.
122. *Rudé právo*, 5 January 1947.
123. ÚRO, 2 January 1947.
124. Ibid., 16 January 1947.
125. Růžička, op. cit., pp. 151-3.
126. *Věstnik ROH*, 21 February 1947, p. 52.
127. For this paragraph see V. Dědek, *Varnsdorfští šli v předních řadách* ("The People of Varnsdorf Enter the Front Ranks"), Liberec, 1962.
    KSČ — *Padesat let práce, bojů a vitězství KSČ na severu Čech* ("50 Years of Work, Struggle and Victory for the KSČ in Northern Bohemia"), Ustí nad Labem, 1971, p. 172.
    Růžička, op. cit., pp. 158-65.
128. Růžička, op. cit., p. 165.
    Moravec, in *Slezký sbornik*, op. cit., p. 16.
129. Růžička, op. cit., pp. 166-8.
130. *Věstnik ROH*, 11 April 1947, pp. 92-3.

131. Much of the material in this section is based on Růžička, op. cit., pp. 171-94, and K. Kovanda, "The Works Councils in Czechoslovakia 1945-1947", in *Soviet Studies*, April 1977, pp. 255-69.
132. ROH — *Bojem* . . ., op. cit., p. 181.
133. Ibid., p. 88 for Erban's speech.
134. Růžička, op. cit., p. 171.
135. J. Šmídmajer, *Závodní rady a odborové hnutí* ("Works Councils and the Trade Union Movement"), Prague, 1947, p. 12.
    Věstník ROH, 11 April 1947, p. 93. For the resolution passed at the ÚRO Plenary session on 3/4 April.
136. ROH — *Bojem* . . ., op. cit., p. 132.
137. Šmídmajer, op. cit., p. 9.
138. Ibid., pp. 10-11.
139. Ibid., p. 18.
140. ÚRO — *Kupředu* . . ., op. cit., p. 156.
141. Ibid., p. 157.
142. Růžička, op. cit., pp. 188-9.
143. *Věstník ROH*, 16 April 1947, p. 98.
144. Moravec, *Slezský sborník*, 1963, op. cit., p. 10.
145. ROH — *Jdeme* . . ., op. cit., p. 17.
146. Moravec, in *Slezský sborník*, 1963, op. cit., p. 10.
147. Archív ÚRO, ÚRO Představenstvo, 20 June 1947, 3/36, p. 3.
148. For examples see: ROH — *Jdeme*, op. cit., p. 17, and Moravec in *Slezský sborník*, 1963, op. cit., p. 10.
149. Růžička, op. cit., p. 190.
150. Archív ÚRO, ÚRO Představenstvo, 20 June 1947, 3/36, p. 4.
151. *Věstník ROH*, 11 April 1947, p. 90.

Chapter 11

1. Williams, op. cit., pp. 214-17, 225-8.
2. Horowitz, Colossus, op. cit., p. 250.
3. Ibid., p. 69.
4. H. K. Smith, *The State of Europe*, London, 1950, p. 67.
5. Quoted in Williams, op. cit., p. 221.
6. W. W. Rostow, *The United States in the World Arena*, New York, 1960, p. 179.
7. Ibid., p. 177.
8. C. de Gaulle, *War Memoirs: Salvation 1944-1946*, London, 1960, p. 199.
9. Horowitz, *Imperialism*, op. cit., quoted p. 84.
10. H. S. Truman, *Memoirs*, New York, 1955, 1956, vol. 2, p. 111. Truman describes the speech as being ". . . America's answer

to the surge of expansion of Communist tyranny." For the contents of the speech see pp. 111-12.
11. Ibid., p. 121. For the following judgement, "History, rightly will always associate his (Marshall's) name with this programme which helped save Europe from economic disaster and lifted it from the shadow of enslavement by Russian Communism."
12. G. F. Kennan, "The Sources of Soviet Conduct", in *Foreign Affairs*, vol. 25, July 1947, p. 582.
13. Kolko, op. cit., pp. 170-71.
14. *Rudé právo*, 3 July 1947.
    K. Smith, op. cit., p. 95.
15. Belda et al., *Na rozhraní* . . ., op. cit., p. 121.
16. Ripka, op cit., p. 54.
17. Ibid., pp. 52-3; see also
    E. Löbl, *Sentenced and Tried*, London, 1969, pp. 24-5.
18. *Rudé právo*, 5 July 1947.
19. Ripka, op. cit., p. 54.
    J. Belda et al., "K otázce účasti Československa na Marshallově plánu" ("On the Question of Czechoslovakia's Participation in the Marshall Plan"), in *Revue dějin socialismu*, no. 8, 1968, p. 96.
20. For the following discussion see: Löbl, op. cit., pp. 25-6; Ripka, op. cit., pp. 56-7, 64-71; and FRUS (III) 1947, pp. 318-20.
21. Belda et al., in *Revue dějin socialismu*, 1968, op. cit., pp. 98-9.
22. Ripka, op. cit., p. 60.
23. Ibid., p. 60; also
    Belda et al., in *Revue dějin socialismu*, 1968, op. cit., p. 97.
24. Ripka, op. cit., pp. 61-2.
    Rudé právo, 11 July 1947.
25. P. M. S. Blackett, *Studies of War*, Edinburgh 1962, pp. 151-2.
26. Opat, *Pkd KSČ*, 1965, op. cit., pp. 74-5.
27. *Rudé právo*, 26 August 1947.
28. Ibid., 9 September 1947.
29. Ibid., 26 August 1947.
30. Ibid., 29 August 1947.
31. Ibid., 2 September 1947.
32. Ibid., 9 September 1947.
33. Jech, op. cit., p. 57.
34. *Rudé právo*, 5 September 1947.
35. Belda et al., *Na rozhraní* . . ., op. cit., p. 153.
36. *Rudé právo*, 3 September 1947.
37. Ibid., 4 September 1947.

38. Ibid., 6 September 1947.
39. Ibid., 5 September 1947, 7 September 1947, 11 September 1947.
40. Belda *et al.*, *Na rozhraní* . . ., op. cit., p. 154.
41. *Rudé právo*, 12 September 1947.
42. *FRUS* (IV), 1947, pp. 229-30.
43. Slánský, op. cit., pp. 120-36.
44. Ibid., p. 129.
45. Ibid., p. 131.
46. *Rudé právo*, 7 October 1947.
47. Ibid., 12 October 1947.
48. For indirect confirmation, see D. Hyde, *I Believed*, London 1950, p. 234.
49. *FRUS* (IV), 1947, p. 234.

Chapter 12

1. *FRUS* (VI) 1946, p. 211.
2. Ibid., p. 237.
3. Ibid., p. 222.
4. Horowitz, *Imperialism*, op. cit., p. 90.
5. G. Alperovitz, *Atomic Diplomacy: Hiroshima and Potsdam*, London 1965, p. 224. Emphasis added.
6. *FRUS* (IV) 1947, p. 235.
7. The discussion that follows is based on material contained in: Růžička, op. cit., pp. 214-25;
Belda *et al.*, *Na rozhraní* . . ., op. cit., pp. 172-81;
Ripka, op. cit., pp. 105-19;
V. Jarošová *et al.*, *Odbory na ceste k februáru* ("Trade Unions on the Road to February"), Bratislava, 1967, pp. 199-217;
J. Lettrich, *History of Modern Slovakia*, London, 1956, pp. 243-55;
FRUS (IV) 1947, pp. 233-41, 244-5.
8. Ripka, op. cit., p. 109.
9. Ibid., pp. 110-12.
10. See Gottwald's post-election analysis *Spisy* XIII, pp. 85, 89. That the Slovak situation concerned the KSČ leadership was confirmed in conversations which the author had with leading KSČ members in Prague, May-July 1973.
11. Ripka, op. cit., p. 110.
12. Ibid., p. 112.
13. Ibid., p. 113.
14. *FRUS* (IV), 1947, p. 235.
15. Ibid., p. 240.
16. Jarošová *et al.*, op. cit., p. 202-4.

17. KSČ — *Rozhodující střetnutí* ("The Deciding Blows"), Prague, 1973, pp. 34-41, contains the entire resolution. See also Archív ÚRO — *ÚRO Představenstvo*, 31 October 1947, 3/45, p. 5.
18. Růžička, op. cit., p. 218.
19. Jarošová *et al.*, op. cit., p. 210.
20. For example see Ripka, op. cit., p. 119; *FRUS* (IV) 1947, p. 245.
21. This point was confirmed in private conversations the author had in Prague with leading KSČ members of the period, June-July 1973.
22. *Svobodné slovo*, 18 January 1948.
23. Ripka, op. cit., p. 195.
24. Belda *et al.*, *Na rozhraní* . . ., op. cit., p. 120.
25. Ibid., pp. 143-4
26. A. Václavů, "The Postwar Problems of Czechoslovak Agricultural Production", in *The Czechoslovak Economy*, K. Jech (ed.), pp. 186-8.
27. S. Novy, *Economic Developments in Czechoslovakia from 1945-1948*, unpublished paper in the author's possession.
28. Archív ÚRO — *ÚRO Plenum*, 22/3 January 1948, 5/14, p. 23.
29. Belda *et al.*, *Na rozhraní* . . ., op. cit., p. 148.
30. B. P. Pešek, *Gross National Product of Czechoslovakia in Monetary and Real Terms 1946-1958*, Chicago 1965, p. 18.
31. Belda *et al.*, *Na rozhraní* . . ., op. cit., p. 143.
32. Ibid., p. 189.
33. Archív ÚRO — *ÚRO Plenum*, 22/3 January 1948, 5/14, p. 23.
34. Jech, op. cit., p. 65.
35. Gottwald, *Spisy* XIV, pp. 137-47.
36. *Právo lidu*, 14 November 1947.
37. Gottwald, *Spisy* XIV, p. 183.
    KSČ — *Zpráva o činnosti* . . ., op. cit., p. 19.
38. *Právo lidu*, 18 November 1947.
39. *Rudé právo*, 18 November 1947.
40. *FRUS* (IV), 1947, p. 249.
41. Ibid., p. 245.
42. *Právo lidu*, 15 November 1947.
43. ÚRO, 4 September 1947, 11 September 1947.
    Belda *et al.*, *Na rozhraní* . . ., op. cit., pp. 155-7.
44. ÚRO, 1 January 1948, p. 2.
45. Ibid, 15 January 1948, p. 5.
46. Archív ÚRO — *ÚRO Představenstvo*, 9 January 1948, 4/51, pp. 3-4.
47. Belda *et al.*, *Na rozhraní* . . ., op. cit., p. 213.
48. *Právo lidu*, 17 January 1948.

49. *Svobodné slovo*, 16 January 1948.
50. *Rudé právo*, 22 January 1948.
    Belda et al., *Na Rozhraní* . . ., op. cit., p. 213.
51. Archív ÚRO — *ÚRO Plenum*, 22/3 January 1948, 5/14, p. 85.
52. Ibid., see especially pp. 100-101, 111-12.
53. Ibid., p. 79.
54. Ibid., p. 98.
55. Ibid., p. 151.
56. *Věstník ROH*, 24 October 1947, p. 320.
57. A. Zápotocký, *Jednota odborů oporou bojů za socialisaci* ("Trade Union Unity — A Source of Strength in the Struggle for Socialisation"), Prague, 1951, p. 358.
58. Archív ÚRO — *ÚRO Plenum*, 16/17 October 1947, 4/13, pp. 6/4-6/5, 17/6-17/7.
59. Ibid., pp. 4/6-5/4.
60. Zápotocký, *Jednota* . . ., op. cit., p. 387.
61. *Věstník ROH*, 24 October 1947, p. 320.
62. Ibid., p. 320.
63. Archív ÚRO — *ÚRO Představenstvo*, 19 December 1947, 3/50, p. 2.
64. *Věstník ROH*, 23 January 1948, p. 18. A breakdown of membership by district is also given.
65. ÚRO — Kupředu, op. cit., pp. 148, 150.
66. Gottwald, *Spisy* XIV, p. 190.
    Zápotocký, *Jednota* . . ., op. cit., pp. 136-7.
67. Material in Kašpar, ČsČH 1971, op. cit., p. 10. See also KSČ — Zpráva o činnosti, p. 83.
68. Zápotocký,*Jednota* . . ., op. cit., pp. 136-7.
69. Gottwald, *Spisy* XIV, pp. 184-8.
70. Ibid., p. 230.

Chapter 13

1. Ripka, op. cit., pp. 216, 218-19.
2. *Svobodné slovo*, 30 January 1948, 31 January 1948.
   See also *Právo lidu*, 13 February 1948.
3. Ripka, op. cit., pp. 194-8.
   H. G. Skilling, "The Prague Overturn in 1948", in *Canadian Slavonic Papers*, vol. 4 (1959), pp. 89-90.
   W. Storm, *The Crisis in Czechoslovakia*, Prague, 1948, p. 11.
4. Ripka, op. cit., p. 202.
5. Ibid., pp. 204-5.
   V. Král, *Cestou k únoru; dokumenty* ("On the Way to February: Documents"), Prague, 1963, pp. 329-32.

6. Ripka, op. cit., p. 204.
7. Ibid., pp. 208-20.
8. Ibid., p. 214.
9. *Svobodné slovo*, 19 February 1948.
10. Ibid., 20 February 1948.
11. Ripka, op. cit., pp. 225-6.
12. Ibid., p. 227.
    Storm, op. cit., p. 23.
13. This point was confirmed in conversations which the author had in Prague with leading KSČ members of the period, Prague, June-July 1973.
14. L. Lehár, "Úloha revolučního odborového hnutí v únoru 1948", ("The Role of the Trade Union Movement in February 1948"), in *ROH při výstavbě socialismu*, p. 108.
15. Details given in Belda et al., *Na rozhraní* . . ., op. cit., pp. 204-5.
16. This point is based on information acquired in conversation.
17. For example see Ripka, op. cit., pp. 182-3.
    D. A. Schmidt, *Anatomy of a Satellite*, London, 1953, p. 106.
    J. Brown, *Who's Next. The Lesson of Czechoslovakia*, London, 1951, p. 141.
18. Ripka, op. cit., p. 185.
19. Lehár, in *ROH při výstavbě socialismu*, op. cit., p. 114.
20. Archív ÚRO — ÚRO Představenstvo, 6 February 1948, 4/53, p. 3.
21. *Práce*, 11 February 1948.
22. Archív ÚRO — ÚRO Představenstvo, 20 February 1948, 4/54, p. 3. The minutes of the meeting of 12 February 1948 are contained in this section, pp. 1-3.
23. KSČ — *Rozhodující střetnutí*, op. cit., pp. 136-8.
24. Ibid., pp. 139-40.
25. For information contained in this paragraph see:
    Skilling, *Canadian Slavonic Papers*, 1959, op. cit., pp. 91-2.
    B. Kozelka, *Vzpomínky* ("Recollections"), Prague, 1968, p. 179.
    M. Bouček, "On the Rise of the Czechoslovak People's Militia in February 1948", in *Historica*, vol. 9 (1964), pp. 213-14. Works Guards were the successors to the Revolutionary Guards of May 1945. The Works Guards protected enterprises against sabotage, but their significance declined after the transfer of the Germans so that they comprised only a few people prior to February.
26. KSČ — *Únor 1948: sborník dokumentů* ("February 1948: A Collection of Documents"), Prague, 1958, p. 233.
27. *Vítězný únor 1948. Vzpomínky* ("Victorious February 1948.

Reminiscences"), Prague, 1959, p. 292.
28. KSČ — Únor 1948 . . ., op. cit., p. 235.
29. Král, Cestou . . ., op. cit., pp. 341-2.
30. Gottwald, Spisy XIV, pp. 252-3.
31. Král, Cestou . . ., op. cit., pp. 361-2.
32. Svobodné slovo, 12 February 1948.
33. Ibid., 18 February 1948.
34. Právo lidu, 14 February 1948, 15 February 1948.
35. In a letter to Beneš on 23 February 1948 the NSS management committee makes such a protestation. See Král, Cestou . . ., op. cit., p. 383.
36. Právo lidu, 15 February 1948.
37. Právo lidu, 21 February 1948. The Industrial Palace was the site of the Works Councils Congress. Perštýn was the headquarters of ROH.
38. Svobodné slovo, 19 February 1948.
39. Ibid., 24 February 1948.
40. Vítězný, op. cit., pp. 140-51, 285-96 for accounts. See also Práce, 22 February 1948.
41. KSČ — Unor 1948, op. cit., p. 236.
42. Práce, 22 February 1948.
43. Kozelka, op. cit., pp. 179-80.
    M. Bouček, Praha v únoru 1948 ("Prague in February 1948"), Prague, 1963, pp. 153-4.
44. For accounts of factory meetings see Vítězný, op. cit., p. 88; Kozelka, op. cit., p. 180.
    See also Bouček, Praha, op. cit., pp. 160-62.
45. KSČ — Únor 1948, op. cit., pp. 40-41.
46. Kozelka, op. cit., p. 180.
47. Ibid., pp. 180-81.
48. Information on the Congress procedure contained in:
    Práce, 14 February 1948;
    Věstnik ROH, 20 February 1948, p. 50.
    Kabinet dějin odborů, sjezd velkého rozhodováni. I celostáni sjezd delegátů závodnich rad a skupin ROH ("The Congress of Great Decision. 1st National Congress of Delegates of Works Councils and ROH Branches"), Prague, 1968, p. 124-5.
49. Kabinet dějin odborů, Sjezd, op. cit., pp. 128-9.
50. Ibid., p. 130.
51. Svobodné slovo, 14 February 1948, 19 February 1948.
    Právo lidu, 15 February 1948.
52. Ibid., 15 February 1948.
53. Kabinet dějin odborů, Sjezd, op. cit., pp. 37-8.

54. Bouček, *Praha* ..., op. cit., p. 134.
55. *Práce*, 17 February 1948.
56. Ibid., 18 February 1948.
57. Ibid., 21 February 1948.
58. Ibid., 19 February 1948.
    Bouček, *Praha* ..., op. cit., pp. 134-9.
59. *Rudé právo*, 18 February 1948, 19 February 1948.
    Práce, 19 February 1948, 20 February 1948.
    Both papers gave these and other examples of enterprises calling for further nationalisation.
60. *Svobodné slovo*, 13 February 1948, 15 February 1948, 20 February 1948.
    Právo lidu, 20 February 1948, 21 February 1948.
61. Archív ÚRO — ÚRO *Představenstvo*, 20 February 1948, 4/54, p. 6.
62. Lehár, in *ROH při výstavbě socialismu*, op. cit., p. 117.
63. Ibid., p. 117.
64. Archív ÚRO — ÚRO *Představenstvo*, 20 February 1948, 4/54.2, p. 7.
65. Ibid., p. 11.
66. Kabinet dějin odborů, Sjezd., op. cit., pp. 32-5.
67. Ibid., p. 35.
68. Ibid., pp. 37-56.
69. Ibid., p. 56.
70. Kolský, *op. cit.*, p. 165. This was confirmed by a trade unionist present at the congress, during a conversation with the author, Prague, June 1973.
71. Kabinet dějin odborů, Sjezd, op. cit., pp. 71-3, 81-3.
72. Ibid., pp. 92-3.
73. The official figures give only 10 votes against the resolution. Kabinet dějin odborů, Sjezd, op. cit., p. 108. This overwhelming degree of support was confirmed in conversations the author had with two trade unionists who were present at the congress. Emigré writers dispute this. Ripka claims that 700 voted against the resolution, op. cit., pp. 239-40, but *Svobodné slovo* gave no exact figure in its congress report, 24 February 1948.
    The official figures suggest the remaining 7,900 delegates voted in favour of the resolution. However, since this was not counted and there was no call for abstentions, this figure is probably inflated as it takes no account of those who did not vote.
74. Kabinet dějin odborů, Sjezd, op. cit., pp. 104-7.
75. Archív ÚRO — ÚRO *Představenstvo*, 4 March 1948, 4/55, p. 1.
76. *Právo lidu*, 21 February 1948.

77. Skilling, *Canadian Slavonic Papers*, 1959, op. cit., p. 95.
78. For two examples see Vitězný, op. cit., pp. 49-50.
79. *Právo lidu*, 24 February 1948.
    Skilling, in *Canadian Slavonic Papers*, 1959, op. cit., p. 101.
    B. Rohan (ed.), *What Happened in Czechoslovakia*, Prague, 1948, pp. 49-50.
80. Skilling, in *Canadian Slavonic Papers*, 1959, op. cit., p. 105.
    Ripka, op. cit., p. 276.
81. KSČ — *Únor 1948* . . ., op. cit., p. 239.
82. Kozelka, op. cit., p. 179.
83. Gottwald, *Spisy* XIV, p. 254.
84. *Rudé právo*, 24 February 1948.
85. Ibid., 23 February 1948.
    For example of Ostrava see Vitězný, op. cit., p. 294.
86. Bouček, M. *Historica*, 1964, pp. 205-31. For a detailed study of developments in Prague.
87. For two examples see Vítězný, op. cit., pp. 48, 149.
88. Bouček, Historica, 1964, op. cit., p. 222.
89. Ibid., pp. 223-8. See Vítězný, op. cit., p. 90, for an eye-witness account of the involvement of one Prague factory. See also Smrkovský's own recollections in an anniversary article in *Práce*, 24 February 1965.
90. Bouček, *Historica*, 1964, op. cit., p. 221.
91. Ibid., p. 222.
92. *Rudé právo*, 24 February 1948.
93. A significant strengthening of this support came on 22/23 February when workers in the paper industry decided to black certain right-wing papers and journals. Employees at the North Bohemian paper mill in České Kamenice decided not to supply *Svobodné slovo* or *Lidové demokracie* with rotary paper and similar resolutions were passed by workers at the S. Bohemian mills in Vetřu and the W. Bohemian mills in Plzeň. See *Práce*, 24 February 1948.
94. Some of the economic reasons for this failure to effect an alliance between different sections of the agrarian population are given in A. Václavů, in *The Czechoslovak Economy*, ed. K. Jech. See especially pp. 188-92.
95. Bouček, Historica, op. cit., pp. 225-9. The numbers involved are disputed, yet the claims of emigré writers appear wildly extravagant. The *New York Times* correspondent estimated 1,500. For details of the differing figures see Skilling, in *Canadian Slavonic Papers*, 1959, op. cit., p. 106.
96. Rohan, op. cit., p. 44, quoted.

97. KSČ — *Rozhodující střetnutí*, op. cit., pp. 233-4.
98. Ibid., p. 235.
99. *Rudé právo*, 26 February 1948.
100. Gottwald, *Spisy* XIV, pp. 274-5.

Chapter 14

1. For example Gottwald, *Spisy* XIV, pp. 308-9. In speech to the Constituent National Assembly on 10 March.
2. Ibid., pp. 309-14.
3. The Congress of Peasant Commissions held on 28 and 29 February passed a resolution welcoming the events of the previous week as a guarantee that peasant demands would be carried out. On 29 Febuary 130,000 peasants assembled in Prague and demonstrated their approval of the congress and its resolution. KSČ — *Únor 1948* . . ., op. cit., pp. 158-61, 241.
4. Jech, op. cit., pp. 68-70, 116-17.
5. See *Statistical Bulletin*, Vol III (1948), no. 7, for data for the following:

    Industrial Enterprises and Persons Employed in Czechoslovak Industry. 1 May 1948

Legal Status	No. of Enterprises	%	No. of Employees	%
Nationalised	3,329	17.2	907,700	64.3
Confiscated	8,410	43.3	392,400	28.0
State-owned	306	1.6	18,400	1.3
Run by Local Authorities	375	1.9	6,200	0.4
Co-operative	862	4.4	13,200	0.9
Private	6,108	1.6	72,300	5.1

6. KSČ — *Zpráva o činnosti komunistické strany Československa od VIII do IX sjezdu* ("Report on the Activity of the KSČ from the 8th to the 9th Congress"), Prague, 1949, p. 90. Emphasis added.
7. cf. KSČ — The Action Programme, 5 April 1968, op. cit., p. 7.
8. Gottwald, *Spisy* XIV, p. 314.
9. Archív ÚRO — *ÚRO Představenstvo*, 4 March 1948, 4/55, p. 4.
10. Ibid., 31 March 1948, 4/57, p. 3.
11. *Věstník ROH*, 12 March 1948, p. 76.
12. V. Bíľak, "February 1948—Historical Turning Point in the History of Our People", in *February Opened the Path to Socialism*, Prague, 1978, p. 8.
13. Ibid., p. 9.

Glossary of Names

The following is a glossary of the main Czech and Slovak political figures who feature in the book. Generally, the contents of the glossary are restricted to the period covered by the book.

BENEŠ. Foreign Minister 1918-35. President of the Republic 1935-48.

CIPRO. Worked in the illegal trade unions during the Resistance. Member of ÚRO Presidium.

CLEMENTIS. A Communist politician. State Secretary in the Ministry of Foreign Affairs, 1945-8.

ČIVRNÝ. Member of illegal Fourth ÚV KSČ. Member of the Czech National Council.

DAVID, J. A National Socialist politician. Deputy Prime Minister, 1945.

DAVID, V. Member of illegal Fourth ÚV KSČ and part of the leadership of the May Rising.

DOLANSKÝ. Member of KSČ Politburo. Minister of Finance, 1946-8.

DRTINA. A National Socialist politician. Minister of Justice 1945-8.

ĎURIS. A Communist politician. Minister of Agriculture, 1945-8.

ERBAN. Worked in the illegal trade unions in the Resistance. General Secretary of ROH. Left-wing member of SDS.

FEIERABEND. Former Agrarian politician. After the war became an NSS functionary.

FIERLINGER. Left-wing Social Democrat. Czechoslovak Ambassador in Moscow 1941-5. Prime Minister 1945-6. Deputy Prime Minister 1946-8. Chairman of SDS 1945-7 (November).

FRANEK. A Slovak Democrat politician. Minister for the Unification of Laws, 1946-8.

FREJKA. Chairman of the KSČ National Economic Committee.

GOTTWALD. General Secretary KSČ 1929-45. Chairman KSČ 1945-8. Deputy Prime Minister 1945-6. Prime Minister 1946-8.

HÁLA. A leading Popular Party politician. Minister of Post, 1945-8.

HUSÁK. A leader of the illegal KSS. Prominent role in the Slovak Rising. Chairman of the Board of Commissioners 1946-8.

JUNGMANN. Worked in the illegal trade unions during the Resistance. Member of ÚRO Presidium. Member of KSČ.

JURA. Leader of the Transport Workers Union. Member of ÚRO Presidium. Member of KSČ.

KLIMENT. Chairman of the Metalworkers' Union. Member of ÚRO Presidium. Member of KSČ.
KOLSKÝ. Deputy General Secretary ROH. Head of the Organisation Department. Member of KSČ.
KOPECKÝ, J. A Popular Party politician. Minister of Technique, 1946-8.
KOPECKÝ, V. Member of KSČ Politburo, with responsibility for ideological questions. Minister of Information 1945-8.
KOPŘIVA. Member of KSČ Politburo.
KOZELKA. Chairman of Works Council in ČKD engineering works. Member of KSČ Prague District Committee.
KROSNÁŘ. Member of KSČ Politburo. Chairman of Prague District KSČ.
KUBÁT. Worked in illegal trade unions during the Resistance. Member of ÚRO management committee. Member of SDS.
LAUŠMAN. A Social Democratic politician. Minister of Industry, 1945-8. Elected Chairman of SDS in November 1947.
LICHNER. A Slovak Democratic politician. State Secretary in Ministry of National Defence, 1946-8.
MACURA. Chairman of Food Employees Union. Member of ÚRO management committee. Member of KSČ.
MAJER, Right-wing Social Democrat. Minister of Food, 1945-8.
MALÍK. General Secretary of Mineworkers' Union. Member of ÚRO Presidium. Member of KSČ.
MASARYK, J. Minister of Foreign Affairs, 1945-8. Non-party.
MASARYK, T. G. President of the 1st Czechoslovak Republic, 1918-35.
MRÁZEK. Member of ÚRO National Economic Committee. Author.
NEJEDLÝ. Minister of Education 1945-6. Minister of Labour and Social Welfare 1946-8. Member of KSČ Politburo from 1946.
NOSEK. Member of KSČ Politburo. Minister of the Interior, 1945-8.
PETR. A Popular Party politician. Minister of Transport, 1948.
PIETOR. A Slovak Democratic politician. Minister of Internal Trade 1945-6. Minister of Transport, 1946-8.
PROCHÁZKA. A leading Popular Party politician. Minister of Health 1945-8.
RIPKA. A leading National Socialist politician. Minister of Foreign Trade, 1945-8.
SLÁNSKÝ. General Secretary KSČ, 1945-8.
SMRKOVSKÝ. Member of illegal Fourth ÚV KSČ. Vice-President of Czech National Council. Responsible for Works Militia in February 1948.
STRÁNSKÝ. A leading National Socialist Politician. Minister of Justice, 1945. Deputy Prime Minister, 1945-6. Minister of Education, 1946-8.

SVOBODA. Gen. Minister of National Defence, 1945-8. Non-party.

ŠIROKÝ. Elected Chairman KSS, August 1945. Deputy Prime Minister, 1945-8.

ŠMIDKE. Chairman KSS, September 1944-August 1945. Deputy President Slovak National Council.

ŠMÍDMAJER. Member of ÚRO management committee. Member of KSČ.

ŠOLTÉSZ. A Communist politician. Minister of Welfare and Social Security, 1945-6.

ŠPIC. Leader of Chemical Workers Union. Member of ÚRO management committee. Member of KSČ.

ŠPLÍCHALOVÁ. Member of ÚRO Presidium. Member of NSS.

ŠRÁMEK. Leader of the Popular Party. Deputy Prime Minister 1945-8.

ŠROBÁR. Minister of Finance, 1945-6. Former Slovak Democrat, became Chairman of the new Slovak "Freedom Party" in 1946. Minister of Unification, 1948.

ŠVERMA. Member of KSČ Politburo from 1929. Died in November 1944 fighting with the partisans in Slovakia.

ŠVERMOVÁ. Head of KSČ Organisational Department. Member of Politburo.

UHLÍŘ. A National Socialist politician.

URSÍNY. A leading Slovak Democratic politician. Deputy Prime Minister, 1945-7.

VANDROVEC. Member of ÚRO management committee. Member of NSS.

VILÍM. Right-wing Social Democrat. General Secretary of SDS.

WÜNSCH. Member of ÚRO Presidium. Left-wing member of NSS.

ZÁPOTOCKÝ. Member of KSČ Politburo. Chairman of ROH.

ZENKL. Chairman NSS, 1945-8. Deputy Prime Minister, 1946-8.

ZUPKA. Chairman of Slovak Trade Union Council. Member of KSS.

Bibliography

Archives

Všeodborový archiv ÚRO ("All-trade union archives"), Prague.
ÚRO Plenum 1945-1948. ÚRO Plenary sessions 1945-1948, Minutes.
ÚRO Představenstvo 1945-1948. ÚRO Management committee meetings, Minutes.

Published Documentary Material

Beneš, E. *The Opening of the Prague Parliament*, Prague, 1946.
Cadogan, Sir A. *The Diaries of Sir Alexander Cadogan 1938-1945* (ed. D. Dilks,), London, 1971.
Decrees of the President of the Republic of 24 October 1945. *Nationalisation in Czechoslovakia*, Prague, 1946.
Degras, J. (ed.) *The Communist International 1919-1943, Documents*, 3 volumes, London, New York, Toronto, 1965.
Eisenhower, D. D. *The Papers of Dwight D. Eisenhower. The War Years*, 5 Vols, Baltimore and London, 1970.
Erban, E. *Zpráva o činnosti ÚRO a další úkoly ROH: Referát z II všeodborového sjezdu ROH* ("Report on ÚRO's activity and the further tasks of ROH: Report to the Second National ROH Congress"), Prague, 1949.
The First Czechoslovak Economic Plan. The Explanatory Memorandum on the Bill and the Text of the Two-Year Economic Plan Act, Prague, 1947.
Forrestal, J. V. *The Forrestal Diaries*, ed. W. Mills, London, 1952.
Gottwald, K. *Spisy* ("Works"), Volumes I-XV, Prague, 1953-61.
Kabinet dějin odborů. *Sjezd velkého rozhodování I celostátní sjezd delegátů závodních rad a skupin ROH* ("The Congress of Great Decision: First National Congress of Delegates of Works Councils and ROH Branches"), Prague, 1968.
Klimeš, M. et al. *Cesta ke květnu: Vznik lidové demokracie v Československu* ("On the Way to May: the Origin of People's Democracy in Czechoslovakia"), 2 volumes, Prague, 1965.
Koho volit? Programy k prvním svobodným volbám r 1946: Program politických stran ("Who to vote for? The programmes of the

Political Parties in the First Free Elections of 1946"), Prague 1946.

KSČ — *Protokol VII sjezdu komunistické strany Československa, 11-14 dubna 1936* ("Proceedings of the 7th Congress of the Communist Party of Czechoslovakia, 11-14 April 1936"), Prague, 1967.

— *Sněm budovatelů: Protokol VIII řádného sjezdu KSČ ve dnech 28-31 března 1946* ("An Assembly of Construction. Proceedings of the Eighth KSČ Congress from 28-31 March 1946"), Prague, 1946.

— *Protokol IX řádného sjezdu KSČ 25-29 květnu 1949* ("Proceedings of the Ninth KSČ Congress 25-29 May 1949"), Prague, 1949.

— *Zpráva o činnosti komunistické strany Československa od VIII do IX sjezdu* ("Report on the Activity of the KSČ from the Eighth to the Ninth Congress"), Prague, 1949.

— *Únor 1948: sborník dokumentů* ("February 1948: A Collection of Documents"), Prague, 1958.

— *Přehled o složení nejvyšších orgánů KSČ v letech 1920-1945* ("A Survey of the Composition of the Highest Organs of the KSČ between 1920 and 1945"), *Pkd KSČ* no. 5, 1965, pp. 757-84.

— *Přehled o složení nejvyšších orgánů KSČ v letech 1945-1966* ("A Survey of the Composition of the Highest Organs of the KSČ between 1945 and 1966"), *Pkd KSČ* no. 6, 1966, pp. 390-429.

— *The Action Programme of the Communist Party of Czechoslovakia, 5 April 1968*, Nottingham, 1970, Spokesman pamphlet, no. 8.

— *Rozhodující střetnutí* ("The Deciding Battles"), Prague, 1973.

Král, V. *Cestou k únoru: dokumenty* ("On the Way to February: Documents"), Prague, 1963.

Ministry of Justice. *Trial of the Leadership of the Anti-State Conspiracy Centre Headed by Rudolf Slánský*, Prague, 1953.

Peša, V. *Dokumenty: Brněnský ilegální časopis, "Boj o zítřek" březen-duben 1945* ("The Illegal Brno Journal Boj o zítřek March-April 1945"), in *Brno v minulosti a dnes*, vol. 5, 1963, pp. 197-228.

ROH — *Zpráva o činnosti ROH k I všeodborovému sjezdu 19-22 dubnu 1946* ("Report on the Activity of ROH up to its First All Trade Union Congress, 19-22 April 1946"), Prague, 1946.

— *Bojem a prací k vítězstvi socialismu. Zápis I celostátního všeodborového sjezdu ROH* ("By Struggle and Work to the Victory of Socialism. Record of the 1st All-State Trade Union Congress of ROH"), Prague, 1946.

— *Jdeme správnou cestou: Krajská konference zaměstnanců v kovoprůmyslu v Praze, 6 dubna 1947* ("We are Going Along the Correct Path: The District Conference of the Metalworkers'

Union in Prague, 6 April 1947"), Prague, 1947.
— *Výroční zpráva KOR v Ostravě za rok 1946* ("Annual Report of Ostrava KOR for 1946"), Ostrava, 1947.
— *Zpráva k první celostátní konferenci svazu zaměstnanců v průmyslu potravin a poživatin* ("Report of the First National Conference of the Union of Employees in the Foodstuffs Industry"), Prague, 1947.
— *Zpráva o činnosti svazu zaměstnanců v kovoprůmyslu* ("Report of the Activity of the Metalworkers' Union"), Prague, 1947.
— *Jednotou odborů k jednotě národa: Z plenárního zasedání ÚRO konaného ve dnech 7 a 8 dubna 1948 v Praze* ("By the Unity of the Unions to the Unity of the Nation. Extracts from the Plenary Session of ÚRO held on 7-8 April 1948 in Prague"), Prague, 1948.
Slánský, R. *Za vítězství socialismu: Stati a projevy* ("For the Victory of Socialism: Articles and Speeches"), 2 volumes, Prague, 1951.
Stalin, J. V. *War Speeches, 3 July 1941-22 June 1945*, London, 1946.
— *Works*, vol. 6, Moscow, 1953.
— *Stalin's Correspondence with Churchill, Attlee, Roosevelt and Truman 1941-1945*, London, 1958.
Statistical Bulletin of Czechoslovakia, vols. I-III, 1946-1948, Prague.
Šverma, J. *Vybrané spisy* ("Collected Works"), Prague, 1955.
Svoboda, L. *Výbor z projevů a článků 1942-1945* ("Selection of Speeches and Articles 1942-1945"), vol. 1, Prague, 1970.
United States Department of State. *Foreign Relations of the United States*.
— *1944. Vol. III*, Washington, 1965.
— *The Conferences at Malta and Yalta*, Washington, 1955.
— *1945. Vol. IV*, Washington, 1968.
— *1946. Eastern Europe; The Soviet Union. Vol. VI*, Washington, 1969.
— *1947. Vol. III*, Washington, 1972.
— *1947. Eastern Europe; The Soviet Union. Vol. IV*, Washington, 1972.
ÚRO — *Budování jednotných odborů 1944-1946: sborník dokumentů* ("The Construction of the United Trade Unions, 1944-1946: a Collection of Documents"), Prague, 1965.
— *Kupředu k socialismu. Zpráva o činnosti ROH od I-II všeodborového sjezdu* ("Forward to Socialism. Report of the Activity of ROH from the First to the Second All Trade Union Congress"), Prague, 1949.
Woodward, E. L. and Butler, R. *Documents on British Foreign Policy 1919-1939*, Third Series, vols. I, II, London, 1949.
Zápotocký, A. *Nová odborová politika* ("New Trade Union Politics"),

Prague, 1948.
— *Jednota odborů oporou bojů za socialisaci* ("Trade Union Unity — a Source of Strength in the Struggle for Socialisation"), Prague, 1951.
— *Revoluční odborové hnutí po únoru 1948* ("The Revolutionary Trade Union Movement after February 1948"), Prague, 1952.

Newspapers and Journals

Daily Herald, 1946.
Mladá fronta, 1945.
Práce, 1945-8.
Právo lidu, 1945-8.
Rudé právo, 1945-8.
Svobodné slovo, 1945-8.
The Times, 1946.
ÚRO, 1945-8.
Vestník ROH, 1947-8.
Vestník závodních rad, 1945-6.
Zprávy tiskové komise ÚRO, 1945.

Autobiographies, Memoirs and other Primary Material

Beneš, E. *My War Memoirs*, London, 1928.
— "Czechoslovakia Plans for Peace", in *Foreign Affairs*, vol. 23, October 1944, pp. 26-37.
— "Postwar Czechoslovakia", in *Foreign Affairs*, vol. 24, April 1946, pp. 397-410.
— *Memoirs: From Munich to New War and New Victory*, London, 1954.
Byrnes, J. F. *Speaking Frankly*, London, 1947.
Djilas, M. *Conversations with Stalin*, London, 1963.
Feierabend, L. K. *Ve Vládě v exilu* ("In the Government in Exile"). 2 Volumes, Washington, 1965.
de Gaulle, C. *War Memoirs: Salvation 1944-1946*, London, 1960.
Husák, G. *Svedectvo o Slovenskom národnom povstaní* ("Testimony about the Slovak National Uprising"), Bratislava, 1969.
Kolský, J. *Pod revolučním praporem* ("Under the Revolutionary Banner"), Prague, 1963.
Kopecký, V. *ČSR a KSČ* ("The Czechoslovak Republic and the KSČ"), Prague, 1960.
— *Několik dokumentárních svědectví k výtvoření první vlády osvobozené republiky a k 9 květnu 1945* ("Some Documentary

Testimony Concerning the Creation of the First Government of the Liberated Republic and Concerning 9 May 1945"), *Pkd KSČ*, no. 11, 1960, pp. 3-21.
Kozelka, B. *Vzpomínky* ("Recollections"), Prague, 1968.
Laštovička, B. V. *Londýně za války* ("During the War in London"), Prague, 1961.
Lettrich, J. *History of Modern Slovakia*, London, 1956.
Löbl, E. *Sentenced and Tried*, London, 1969.
London, A. *On Trial*, London, 1970.
Masaryk, T. G. *The Making of a State*, London, 1927.
Moran, Lord C. *Winston Churchill: the Struggle for Survival 1940-1965*, London, 1966.
Ripka, H. *Czechoslovakia Enslaved: The Story of the Communist Coup d'Etat*, London, 1950.
Slánská, J. *Report on My Husband*, London, 1969.
Šlingová, M. *Truth Will Prevail*, London, 1968.
Smrkovský, J. *Byl jsem při tom* ("I Was There"), in *Práce*, 23 and 24 February, 1965.
Stettinius, E. R. *Roosevelt and the Russians*, London, 1950.
Stimson, H. L. and McGeorge Bundy. *On Active Service in Peace and War*, New York, 1948.
Stránský, J. *East Wind Over Prague*, London, 1950.
Táborský, E. "Beneš and the Soviets", in *Foreign Affairs*, vol. 27, January 1949, pp. 302-14.
— "Beneš and Stalin — Moscow 1943 and 1945", in *Journal of Central European Affairs*, vol. 13, July 1953, pp. 154-81.
— "The Triumph and Disaster of Eduard Beneš", in *Foreign Affairs*, vol. 36, July 1958, pp. 669-84.
Truman, H. S. *Memoirs*, 2 volumes, New York, 1955, 1956.
Vítězný únor 1948: Vzpomínky ("Victorious February 1948. Reminiscences"), Prague, 1959.
Welles, S. "Two Roosevelt Decisions: One Debit, One Credit", in *Foreign Affairs*, vol. 29, 1951, pp. 182-204.

Books and Articles in Czech and Slovak

Bajger, L. "Znárodnění ostravsko-karvinských dolů ("The Nationalisation of the Ostrava-Karvina Mines"), in *Slezský sborník*, no. 63, 1965, pp. 145-67.
— *Ostravsko po druhé světové válce* ("Ostrava after the Second World War"), Ostrava, 1971.
Bartošek, K. *Pražské povstání 1945* ("The Prague Uprising 1945"), Prague, 1960.

— "Antifašistická revoluce v Československu 1944-1945" ("The anti-fascist revolution in Czechoslovakia 1944-1945"), in *Revue dějin socialismu*, no. 9, 1969, pp. 663-74.

Bednařík, L. "Z dějin brněnské Zbrojovky od osvobození do znárodnění: 26 dubna do 25 října 1945" ("From the History of the Brno Zbrojovka Enterprise from Liberation until Nationalisation: 26 April to 25 October 1945"), in *Brno v minulosti a dnes*, vol. 7, 1965, pp. 11-25.

Belda, J. et al. *Na rozhraní dvou epoch* ("On the Frontier of Two Epochs"), Prague, 1968.

— "K otázce účasti Československa na Marshallově plánu" ("On the Question of Czechoslovakia's Participation in the Marshall Plan"), in *Revue dějin socialismu*, no. 8, 1968, pp. 81-100.

Benčík, A. and Kural, V. eds. *Partyzánské hnutí v Československu za druhé světové války* ("The Partisan Movement in Czechoslovakia during World War II"), Prague, 1961.

Bouček, M. *Praha v únoru 1948* ("Prague in February 1948"), Prague, 1963.

Bouček, M. and Klimeš, M. "Únorové události roku 1948" ("The February Events of 1948"), in *ČsČH*, vol. 21, 1973, pp. 1-12.

Chmela, L. *Hospodářská okupace Československa; Její methody a důsledky* ("The Economic Occupation of Czechoslovakia; Its Methods and Consequences"), Prague, 1946.

Dedek, V. *Varnsdorfští šli v předních řadách* ("The People of Varnsdorf Enter the Front Ranks"), Liberec, 1962.

Deyl, Z. and Snítil, Z. "K některým problémům hospodářské politiky KSČ v letech 1945-1948" ("Concerning some Problems of KSČ Economic Policy from 1945-1948"), in *Pkd KSČ*, no. 5, 1965, pp. 691-706.

Doležal, J. "K otázce partyzánského hnutí v českých zemích" ("Concerning the Question of the Partisan Movement in the Czech Lands"), in *ČsČH*, vol. 8, 1960, pp. 273-91.

— ed. *Z bojů za svobodu* ("From the Struggles for Freedom"), Prague, 1963.

— *Jediná cesta: Cesta ozbrojeného boje v českých zemích* ("The Only Way: The Way of Armed Struggle in the Czech Lands"), Prague, 1966.

Erban, E. and Dvořák, A. *ÚRO v pražském povstání* ("ÚRO and the Prague Rising"), Prague, 1946.

Janáček, F. "K otázkám strategie a taktiky KSČ v národně osvobozeneckém boji proti fašistickým okupantům" ("Concerning Questions of KSČ Strategy and Tactics in the National Liberation Struggle against Fascist Occupying Forces"), in *ČsČH*, vol.

4, 1956, pp. 51-85.

Janaček, O. "Osvobozenecký boj československého lidu v letech 1938-1945 ve světle novověkých dějin" ("The Liberation Struggle of the Czechoslovak People between 1938-1945 in the Light of Recent History"), in *Pkd KSČ*, no. 2, 1962, pp. 643-684.

— "Dílo Antonia Gramscího jako metodologické vychodisko ke zkoumání našeho přístupu k socialistické revoluce, ke zkoumání dějin čs. odboje" ("The Work of Antonio Gramsci as a Methodological Viewpoint concerning an Examination of Our Approach to Socialist Revolution and to the History of the Czechoslovak Resistance"), in *Historie a vojenství*, no. 4, 1964, pp. 705-35.

— ed. *Odboj a revoluce, 1938-1945* ("Resistance and Revolution 1938-1945"), Prague, 1965.

Jarošová, V. and Jaroš, O. *Slovenské robotníctvo v boji o moc 1944-1948* ("Slovak Workers in the Struggle for Power 1944-1948"), Bratislava, 1965.

Jarošová, V. et al. *Odbory na ceste k februáru* ("Trade Unions on the Road to February"), Bratislava, 1967.

Jukl, E. "Z historie bojů o poválečnou obnovu a znárodnění plzeňské Škodovky" ("From the History of the Struggles for the Post-War Renewal and Nationalisation of the Škoda Works in Plzeň"), in *Pkd KSČ*, no. 2, 1962, pp. 531-51.

Kabinet dějin odborů — *Nástin dějin československého odborového hnutí* ("The History of Our Czechoslovak Trade Union Movement"), Prague, 1963.

— *ROH při výstavbě socialismu* ("ROH and the Construction of Socialism"), Prague, 1965.

— *Odbory a naše revoluce: sborník studií* ("Trade Unions and Our Revolution. A Collection of Studies"), Prague, 1968.

Kalinová, L. and Brabec, V. "K některým stránkám vývoje struktury a postavení čs. dělnické třídy v letech 1945-1948" ("Concerning Some Aspects of the Development of the Structure and Position of the Czechoslovak Working Class from 1945 to 1948"), in *Odbory a naše revoluce*, pp. 48-93.

Kaplan, K. "Poznámky ke znárodnění průmyslu v Československu 1945" ("Notes on the Nationalisation of Industry in Czechoslovakia in 1945"), in *Pkd KSČ*, no. 6, 1966, pp. 3-23.

— *Utváření generální linie výstavby socialismu v Československu* ("The Creation of the General Line for the Construction of Socialism in Czechoslovakia"), Prague, 1966.

— "Hospodářská demokracie v letech 1945-1948" ("Economic Democracy from 1945-1948"), in *ČsČH*, vol. 14, 1966, pp. 844-61.

— *Znárodnění a socialismus* ("Nationalisation and Socialism"),

Prague, 1968.
— "Odbory v mechanismu lidově demokratické moci v letech 1945-1948" ("Trade Unions in the Mechanism of Popular Democratic Power 1945-1948"), in *Odbory a naše revoluce*, pp. 94-128.
Kašpar, J. "Členská základna komunistické strany Československa v letech 1945-1949" ("The Membership Base of the KSČ from 1945-1949"), in *ČsČH*, vol. 19, 1971, pp. 1-25.
Kolár, F. J. *Zestátnění průmyslu a peněžnictví* ("The Nationalisation of Industry and Finance"), Prague, 1945.
KSČ Ústav dějin. *Příruční slovník k dějinám KSČ* ("A Pocket Dictionary of the History of the KSČ"), 2 volumes, Prague, 1964.
KSČ — *Padesat let práce, bojů a vítězství KSČ na severu Čech* ("Fifty Years of Work, Struggles and Victory for the KSČ in Northern Bohemia"), Ústí nad Labem, 1971.
Koucký, V. *Ilegální KSČ a pražské povstání* ("The Illegal KSČ and the Prague Rising"), Prague, 1946.
Kozák, J. "O hlavních problémech dějin KSČ v období 1945-1948" ("Concerning the Main Problems of KSČ History in the Period 1945-1948"), in *Pkd KSČ*, no. 2, 1962, pp. 747-54.
Král, V. *Otázky hospodářského a socialního vývoje v českých zemích v letech 1938-1945* ("Questions of Economic and Social Development in the Czech Lands from 1938-1945"), 3 volumes, Prague, 1957-9.
— ed. *Přehled československých dějin* ("Survey of Czechoslovak History"), Prague, 1960, volume 3.
Křen, J. "Dr Beneš za války" ("Dr Beneš during the War"), in *ČsČH*, vol. 13, 1965, pp. 797-826.
Kural, V. "K problémům českého partyzánského hnutí" ("Concerning Problems of the Czech Partisan Movement"), in *Z bojů za svobodu*, pp. 139-78.
Lehár, L. "Úloha revolučního odborového hnutí v únoru 1948" ("The Role of the Trade Union Movement in February 1948"), in *ROH při výstavbě socialismu*, Prague, 1965, pp. 98-134.
— "První všeodborový sjezd" (" The All Trade Union Congress of ROH"), in *Odbory a společnost*, no. 1, 1966, pp. 36-54.
— "Závodní milice v letech 1945-1948" ("The Works Militia from 1945-1948"), in *Odbory a naše revoluce*, pp. 249-75.
Matějka, J. *Gottwald*, Prague, 1971.
Mlýnský, J. "Upevňování a rozširování výsledků národní a demokratické revoluce v Brně" ("The Consolidation and Broadening of the Results of the National and Democratic Revolution in Brno"), in *Brno v minulosti a dnes*, vol. 5, 1963, pp. 11-31.
Moravec, J. "Nástup komunistů ostravského kraje za získání většiny

národa" ("The Drive by the Communists of the Ostrava District for the Gaining of the Majority of the Nation"), in *Slezský sborník*, no. 61, 1963, pp. 3-23.

Mrázek, dr. O. *Lidovláda v hospodářství* ("Popular government in the Economy"), Prague, 1945.

— *Patnáct let rozvoje znárodněného průmyslu ČSSR* ("Fifteen Years of the Development of Nationalised Industry in the ČSSR"), Prague, 1960.

Olšovský, R et al. *Přehled hospodářského vývoje Československa v letech 1918-1945* ("A Survey of the Economic Development of Czechoslovakia 1918-1945"), Prague, 1961.

Opat, J. *O novou demokracii 1945-1948* ("For a New Democracy"), Prague, 1966.

— "K metodě studia a výkladu některých problému v období 1945-1948" ("On the Methods and Explanation of Some Problems of the Period 1945-1948"), in *Pkd KSČ*, no. 5, 1965, pp. 65-84.

Pachman, V. "K problematice dějin odborového hnutí" ("On the Problems of the History of the Trade Union Movement"), in *Pkd KSČ*, November 1959, pp. 21-42.

— "Boj o odborovou jednotu v letech 1945-1948" ("The Struggle for Trade Union Unity 1945-1948"), in *ČsČH*, vol. 8, 1960, pp. 793-813.

Peša, V. "Ústavení a činnost národniho výboru v Brně v dubnu až květnu 1945" ("The Establishment and Activity of the Brno National Committee from April to May 1945"), in *Brno v minulosti a dnes*, vol. 2, 1960, pp. 23-44.

— "Zemské vedení KSČ na Moravě 1941-1945" ("Regional Leadership of the KSČ in Moravia, 1941-1945"), in *ČsČH*, vol. 19, pp. 311-32.

Peša, V. et al. *Z dějin komunistické strany Československa na Brněnsku, 1921-1945* ("From the History of the KSČ in the Brno Region, 1921-1945"), Brno, 1962.

Růžička, K. *ROH v boji o rozšíření moci dělnické třídy, 1945-1948* ("ROH in the Struggle for the Spreading of the Power of the Working Class, 1945-1948"), Prague, 1963.

Růžička, O. and S. Vobořil. *Pražský květen* ("The Prague May"), Prague, 1966.

Šedivý, J. "Jestě jednou k únoru 1948" ("Once Again on February 1948") in *Pkd KSČ*, no. 6, 1966, pp. 500-513.

Šmídmajer, J. *Závodní rady a odborové hnutí* ("Works Councils and the Trade Union Movement"), Prague, 1947.

Snítil, Z. "O dvouletce a jejím místě v politice KSČ v roce 1946" ("On the Two-Year Plan and its Place in KSČ Policy in 1946"), in *Pkd KSČ*, no. 7, 1967, pp. 669-98.

— "Úloha jednotných odboru při přípravě dvouletky a organizaci našého hospodářství" ("The Role of the United Trade Unions in the Preparation of the Two-Year Plan and the Organisation of Our Economy"), in *Odbory a naše revoluce*, pp. 169-206.

Špičák, M. and Lipták, J. "Únor 1948 a československé ozbrojené síly" ("February 1948 and the Czechoslovak Armed Forces"), in *ČsČH*, vol. 21, 1973, pp. 309-34.

Tvarůžek, B. (ed.) *Osvobození Československa rudou armádou, 1944-1945* ("The Liberation of Czechoslovakia by the Red Army, 1944-1945"), Prague, 1965.

Veltruský, J. *Byrokracie, demokracie a dělnická třída* ("Bureaucracy, Democracy and the Working Class"), Prague, 1946.

Veselý, J. *Kronika únorových dnů 1948* ("A Chronicle of the February Days 1948"), Prague, 1958.

Vrabec, V. "ROH a znárodnění 1945" ("ROH and Nationalisation in 1945"), in *Odbory a naše revoluce*, pp. 129-68.

Zámečník, S. "ÚRO a české květnové povstaní v roce 1945" ("ÚRO and the Czech May Rising in 1945"), in *Odbory a naše revoluce*, pp. 9-47.

Index

Agrarian Party, 28, 30, 45
Allied armies, 49-50
Allied Control Council, 62
Anti-fascist coalition, 17, 31, 39, 40, 110
Antonov, General A., 53-4
Austro-Hungarian Empire, 23, 50, 98
Austro-Hungarian Social Democratic Party, 24

Babulík, 100
Basťovansky, 186
Beer, 167
Belgium, 35
Beneš, President E., 17, 20, 23, 31, 33, 40-6, 55-6, 61-2, 68, 71-2, 76, 83, 86-8, 96, 115, 120, 146, 182, 199, 208, 214, 226, 229, 230
Beran government, 70
Bíla Horá (White Mountain), 47, 73
Bílek, 100
Bílý, 224
Bismarck, 177
Boček, General, 228
Bodrov, 182
Boj o zítřek, 63
Bolton, G., 118
Bratislava, 55-6, 83, 86, 192-3
Britain, 9, 17, 28, 31, 32, 35, 52-3, 61, 154, 177
Brno, 18, 50, 55, 63, 100, 105, 112, 217
Bruins, 152
Building workers' union, 100
Bulgaria, 23, 197
Bullitt, 179
Byrnes, 164

Cadogan, Sir Arthur, 53
České Budějovice, 184, 221
Československé listy, 92
Chamberlain, Neville, 9, 11, 28
Chemical workers' union, 100, 104, 171
Churchill, Sir Winston, 53, 146
Cigler, 203
Cipro, V., 34, 91, 94, 102, 140
ČKD factory, 160, 185, 218
Cold War, 177-83, 236
Cominform, 19, 186-7, 213, 236
Communist International, 17, 25-7, 121; class against class, 25, 27; 7th Congress, 17, 27, 48, 91, 103, 109, 180
Communist Party, of Belgium, 111; of France, 111, 137, 187, 198; of Italy, 111, 137, 187, 198; of Soviet Union, 20, 109, 119, 141
Council of Three, 33
Czech National Council, 18, 34-5, 50-52, 55
Czech-Slovak relations, 45-6, 59-61, 235
Czech Union Bank, 75
Czechoslovak Communist Party. *See* KSČ
Czechoslovak-French treaty, 182
Czechoslovakia: army, 65-6, 110, 189-90, 193, 228; First Republic, 9, 17, 23, 28-31, 98; road to socialism, 119-20, 183, 187, 232, 238-9

David, J., 23, 93, 149
David, V., 122
De Gaulle, General, 179
Deutsche Bank, 30

Dimitrov, G., 27
Doenitz, Admiral, 55
Dolanský, J., 121-2, 201, 226
Dresdner Bank, 30
Drtina, 23, 55, 78, 81, 182, 194, 201, 207-8
Durbrow, 189
Durčansky, 191
Ďuriš, 60, 122, 151
Dvořan, 146

Economic Plan, Two-Year, 18, 149, 153-63, 166, 195-8, 230, 237
Eden, Anthony, 53
Eichler factory, 167
Eisenhower, General D., 53-5
Erban, E., 34, 102, 127, 131, 140, 158
Euro-communism, 13, 238, 240

February 1948 (events), 137, 142, 172, 177, 207-30, 235-8
Feierabend, L., 43, 88, 146
Ferjenčík, General, 191
Fierlinger, Z., 19, 23, 60, 75, 78, 83, 99, 141, 199, 225
Firt, 208
Food employees' union, 100, 104
France, 9, 17, 19, 28, 61, 148, 154, 202
Franek, 208
Frank, J., 122
Frejka, L., 72

General election, May 1946, 18, 143-52
Germanisation, 30
Germans, 41, 45-7, 62, 67-8, 70, 111, 144, 165
Germany, 17, 28, 29, 31, 52, 177, 190
Gestapo, 32-3
Glassworkers' union, 100
Göring, 30
Gottwald, Klement, 17, 18, 23, 26-7, 41-2, 46-7, 69, 72, 73, 78, 88, 115, 117, 119-22, 124, 151, 153-5, 157, 182, 184, 187-8, 201, 205, 208, 213, 217, 223, 225-6, 229-32, 236
Gramsci, A., 41
Great Depression, 24
Greece, 35, 40, 52

Hacha, 41
Hála, 23, 42, 45-6, 82, 208
Hanč, 164
Harriman, Averell, 178, 190
Havelka, 100
Hitler, Adolf, 9, 17, 29
Hlinka party, 30, 191
Horn, 120
Hungarians, 45-7, 62, 67, 70, 165
Hungary, 197
Hus, J., 116

Italy, 17, 19, 28

Japan, 190
Janata, F., 104
Jihlava, 184, 194
Jungmann, F., 34, 70, 96, 102
Jura, J., 79, 97, 100, 202

Kapoun, 100
Kennan, George, 179
Khrushchev, Nikita, 20
Kladno, 83, 86, 105, 112, 184, 217, 218
Klapálek, General, 228
Kliment, G., 71, 98, 100, 104, 122, 132, 135, 161, 172
Kočvara, 208
Kohler, B., 26
Kolár, 79, 89
Kollar, 116
Kolský, J., 79, 97, 98, 100, 135, 212, 218, 221
Kopecký, J., 208
Kopecký, V., 23, 26, 42, 45, 55, 56, 60, 63, 82, 116, 120, 122, 228
Kopřiva, L., 122
Korbel, J., 118
Košice, 18, 46, 52, 69, 83, 117,

141, 151; programme, 46, 48, 59-68, 72, 77-8, 81-2, 93, 109, 131, 146-7, 154, 157, 189, 190, 239

Kozák, J., 109

Krajina, 208

Krček, 146

Křivánek, 100

Krosnář, J., 26, 122

KSČ (Communist Party of Czechoslovakia), 17, 19, 20, 25, 26, 32, 34, 40-43, 45-6, 49, 50, 59-61, 63-4, 66, 110-12, 124, 166, 173, 174, 183, 187, 189, 195, 201, 205, 206, 239-40; 5th Congress, 17, 26; 7th Congress, 17, 27, 41, 122; 8th Congress, 18, 63, 109, 115-23, 133-4; 9th Congress, 232; Action Programme 1968, 12, 232; and Economic Plan, 149, 152-5, 161, 184-6, 195-8, 209; and elections, 117, 143-5, 150-52; in February, 207-18, 221-9; internal democracy, 120-21; leadership, 10, 12, 38, 40, 42, 45, 50, 62, 64, 92, 110, 112; membership, 112-14, 205; and nationalisation, 70-90 *passim*; post-February policy, 231-3, 235-7; security, 193-5; and Slovak crisis, 191-3; and SDS, 198-200; and trade unions and works councils, 91-3, 95, 97, 99-100, 102, 105, 134-42, 169, 209

KSS (Slovak Communist Party), 32, 59-60, 122, 150, 186, 191-3

Kubát, J., 34, 203, 222

Kučera, 100

Labour Party, British, 119

Land reform, 18, 67, 228

Laštovička, B., 23

Laušman, B., 23, 42, 45, 70, 72-5, 78, 82, 199-200, 226

Lenin, V. I., 120, 141

Lichner, 208

Lidice, 62

Löbl, E., 182

LS (People's Party), 23, 45-6, 59, 65, 124, 165, 193, 200; and Economic Plan, 153-4; and elections, 145-6, 148-50, 152; and February, 207-8, 213, 215, 225, 228; membership, 113; and nationalisation, 71, 74, 76-7, 81, 87; and works councils, 169, 171

Macura, 85, 100, 104, 133

Majer, 23, 46, 78, 81-2, 173, 201, 208, 215, 225-6, 230

Malík, 79, 97, 100, 103, 201

Marshall Plan, 19, 179-83, 187-8, 197

Masaryk, J., 124, 181-2, 209

Masaryk, T. G., 23, 116, 147

Medvedev, Roy, 39

Metalworkers' union, 98, 101, 104, 135, 171

Minc, H., 182

Miners' union, 103, 171

Molotov, 180-82

Moscow, 18, 23, 25, 32, 38, 40, 42-7, 60-61, 147, 209, 237

Mrázek, O., 80, 89, 97

Munich, 9, 17, 23, 28, 29, 31, 61, 87, 112, 117, 144, 146, 151, 236

Murphy, 54

Národní souručenství, 30

National Assembly, 18, 41, 65, 70-71, 74, 76, 83, 143, 153-4, 215

National committees, 18, 41, 50, 64-5, 194

National Federation of Employees, 34, 104

National Front: 1945-6 government, 18, 41, 44, 46, 56, 59, 70-71, 79-80, 89, 93, 115, 120, 122, 134, 143, 157; 1946-8 government, 152, 153, 164-5,

202, 210, 213-14, 217, 225-6, 229, 231; action committees, 226-8, 233; and Marshall Plan, 181-3; post-February, 231-2; tensions within, 184-7, 196-7, 210
Nationalisation, 18, 42-3, 48, 68-90; decrees, 83-6; workers' agitation for, 71-2, 74-6, 78-9, 82-3, 85
Nazism, 29-32, 34, 35, 37, 49, 51, 53-5, 62
Nejedlý, Z., 122
Nepomucký, 120
Nosek, V., 23, 26, 60, 67, 110, 122, 141, 201, 207-8, 226, 230
Novák, 146
Novotný, A., 12

Occupation, Soviet and Warsaw Pact (1968), 13, 20
Olomouc, 86, 100, 194
Ostrava, 68-9, 71, 86, 100, 112-13, 184, 216, 221

Pacák, 23
Palacký, 116, 147
Paris aid conference (1947), 181-3
Paris peace conference (1946), 164
Partisans, 17, 34, 37, 49, 193
Passive revolution, 11, 231, 235-40
Peasants' Congress, 19, 210, 212, 215, 231
Pelikan works, 113
People's Militia, 20
People's Party. *See* LS
Peřina, 203
Perštýn, 215
Pešek, 197
Petr, 124
Pietor, 208
Plzeň, 71-2, 86, 112, 184, 217-18
Podbrezová, 37
Podmokly, 63
Poland, 23, 32, 35, 40, 111, 181, 182, 197
Poldina works, 30, 113
Popular Front strategy, 27, 28, 38, 42, 64, 79, 89-90, 109, 116-17, 122, 154, 180, 197, 237, 239-40
Population transfer, 59, 61-4
Potsdam, 39, 62-3, 111, 177
Práce, 63, 80, 96, 98, 131, 221
Prague Radio, 29
Prague Rising (1945), 18, 35, 50-52, 55
Prague Spring, 9, 12, 20
Právo lidu, 78, 81, 82, 214, 222
Předvoj, 32
Procházka, 76, 81, 208
Prokop Holý, 63
Protectorate of Bohemia and Moravia, 29, 31, 33-5, 54
Pückler, General, 51

Red Army, 18, 23, 31, 33, 38, 39, 49, 52, 55, 56, 61, 65-6, 190
Red International of Labour Unions, 135
Resistance movement, 32, 34, 49, 239
Rheims, 51, 55
Ribbentrop, 29
Ripka, H., 82, 87, 93, 147, 182, 191, 192, 207, 208, 210
ROH (Revolutionary Trade Union Movement), 18, 76-8, 100, 102-5, 120, 124-42, 167-8, 173, 198, 200, 202, 204-5, 237; 1st Congress, 124-5, 132-7, 158, 166, 169, 202; 2nd Congress, 127, 171; Action Programme, 36, 37; and Czech-Slovak relations, 129-31; internal democracy, 135-42, 203-4, 233-4; and wages, 161-3; and women, 157-9; and works councils, 168-73
Rostow, W., 178-9
Rudé právo, 63, 69, 72, 78, 79, 82, 88, 98, 185, 199
Rudý prapor/Rote Fahne, 63

Rumania, 197

SDS (Social Democratic Party), 19, 20, 23, 25, 44, 59, 124, 165, 198, 201, 232; and Congress, 199-200; and Economic Plan, 153, 186; and elections, 145, 149-51; and February, 207-9, 214-15, 219, 222-3, 225-6; membership, 113, and unions, 93, 140, 203; and works councils, 171-2
Sidor, 191
Škoda works, 30, 71, 83, 113, 172, 222
Slánský, R., 19, 23, 26, 42, 93, 120, 122, 149, 184, 186-7, 213, 235
Slovak Democratic Party (DS), 45, 59, 71, 74, 76-7, 81, 87, 146, 149, 150, 152, 169, 191-3, 200; and February, 207-9, 213, 215, 225
Slovak National Council, 34, 36, 45-6, 60, 61
Slovak Rising, 17, 34
Slovak Trades Union Council, 192
Slovakia: Catholics, 146; crisis, 191-3; separatists, 29
Smetana, 116
Smrkovský, J., 18, 51, 122, 227,
SNB (Corps of National Security), 193-4, 207, 227-8
Soviet Union, 9, 10-11, 17, 25, 31, 36, 40-41, 43-5, 48, 56, 66, 118, 148, 154, 190, 195, 197, 236-9; and Cold War, 177-83; and government, 33, 39, 40, 52, 177, 209; treaty with Czechoslovakia, 17, 32, 41, 43, 61; troops, 13
Stalin, J. V., 20, 25, 54, 61, 110, 119-20, 139, 178, 181-3, 188
Stalingrad, 23, 31, 39
Stalinism, 11-12, 120, 123, 234-5, 237-40
Steinhardt, 146-7, 149, 164, 187, 190-92, 199, 209

Stránský, J., 23, 45, 76, 81, 100, 141, 182, 207-8
Suchý, 146
Sudeten Germans, 24
Svoboda, L., 62, 124, 209, 228
Svobodné slovo, 81-3, 185, 194, 207-8, 214-15, 222

Široký, 26, 122
Šivera, 124
Šling, Otto, 235
Šmidke, 42
Šmídmajer, 170-72, 232
Šoltész, 124
Špic, J., 100, 104
Šplíchalová, 212, 223
Šrámek, 23, 208
Šrobár, 75
Šverma, J., 26, 42, 92, 102
Švermová, M., 26, 116, 120, 122

Teheran, 39, 52, 54, 179
Third Reich, 29, 30, 49
Thorez, M., 119
The Times, 119
Tiso, 191
Tito, Marshal, 38
Toussaint, General, 51
Trade unions. See ROH, ÚRO
Truman, H., 190
Truman Doctrine, 19, 179-81
Tvorba, 89
Tymeš, 230

Uhlíř, 23, 42
Ukrainian Front, 2nd, 50
United Nations Economic Commission for Europe, 181
United States of America, 35, 40, 54-5, 148, 154, 164, 190, 236; and Cold War, 177-81; and government, 17-18, 31, 39; troops, 53-4, 56
ÚRO (Central Trades Union Council), 35, 50, 69-74, 79, 83, 88, 91, 93, 101, 133-6, 185, 200, 203-4, 210, 232-3, 237; and February, 210-12, 218-19, 221-6; foundation, 94; journal, 166;

management committee, 125, 135, 155, 166, 167, 172-3, 200, 211, 212, 222, 233; National Economic Commission, 80, 85, 97, 196; organisation, 94-100, 102-5, 124-31; plenary sessions, 79, 96-8, 103, 105, 134, 166, 168, 172-3, 196, 201-2, 204; presidium, 77, 80, 97, 100, 125, 186, 211-12, 218; and production, 155, 163; and public employees, 200-202, 221-2

Valo, 42
Vandrovec, 172, 201, 222-4
Varnsdorf, 9, 167
Versailles Treaty, 23, 236
Veselý, 100
Věstník závodních rad, 96-7, 102
Vilim, 124, 226
Vítkovice works, 30, 172, 185, 216, 221-2
Vlasov army, 51
Vycpálek, 100
Vysočany, 217, 226, 227

Warsaw, 33, 50
Works councils, 18, 19, 43, 48, 68, 74-5, 78-9, 91-102, 105, 120, 234, 237; and Congress, 19, 207, 210-15, 218-25, 228, 231; decrees, 100-102; elections, 168-74; militia, 50, 66, 213, 227
Wünsch, 97, 149

Yalta, 39, 52, 111, 177, 179, 180, 190
Yost, 186
Yugoslavia, 33, 38, 53, 181, 197, 236-7

Zápotocký, A., 66, 69-72, 79-80, 97-100, 102, 122, 129, 131-6, 141, 155, 157, 161, 168, 170, 172-3, 201-3, 205, 211, 219, 223-4, 226, 230
Zátka mill, 167
Zbrojovka works, 30, 63, 83, 93, 113, 222, 227, 228
Zenkl, 81, 93, 182, 207-8
Zhdanov, 187
Zorin, 209
Zupka, F., 131, 172, 192

Živnostenská Bank, 75